Mellon vs. Churchill

Mellon

vs.

Churchill

THE UNTOLD STORY
OF TREASURY TITANS AT WAR

JILL EICHER

PEGASUS BOOKS

NEW YORK LONDON

MELLON VS. CHURCHILL

Pegasus Books, Ltd.
148 West 37th Street, 13th Floor
New York, NY 10018

First Pegasus Books cloth edition March 2025

Interior design by Maria Fernandez

Library of Congress Cataloging-in-Publication Data is available.

ISBN: 978-1-63936-642-2

10 9 8 7 6 5 4 3 2 1

Printed in the United States of America
Distributed by Simon & Schuster
www.pegasusbooks.com

For Gary

CONTENTS

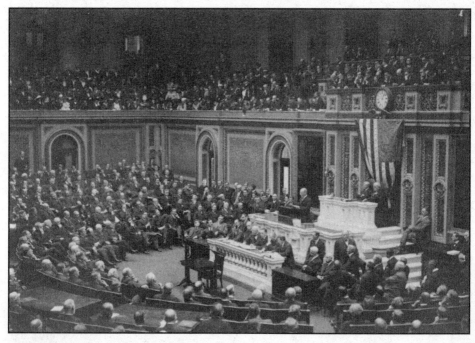

In asking Congress on April 2, 1917, to declare war against the German government, President Woodrow Wilson also called for the generous extension of financial credit to the Allied nations. *Courtesy of the Library of Congress, Washington, DC.*

INTRODUCTION

The Great War of 1914–1918 was indeed the First World War, waged by groups of nations on five continents, using long-range weapons, advanced technology, and faster communications than civilization had ever known. From it emerged a set of moral issues that had no precedent, nor answers to the questions they raised, which remain largely unresolved to this day. Above all, what do nations owe to one another, in terms of trust, honor, and fairness, in an interdependent world?

One of the great clashes of minds on this matter—one American and one British—was rooted in the wartime loans made by the United States to the European Allies, and in the demands made afterward by the Allies for reparations from Germany. The divergent views on this question of what postwar nations owed one another, emphatically articulated by Andrew Mellon of the United States and Winston Churchill of Great Britain, made newspaper headlines on both sides of the Atlantic and continued to do so long after the war had ended. Yet historians and biographers have neglected to discuss the two men as protagonists in those arguments and rarely mention that they ever met.

America made its first loan to the Allies on April 25, 1917, three weeks after President Woodrow Wilson asked Congress to declare war against Germany. Having served as banker to the Allies during three years of war, Britain had exhausted its international credit and hovered on the verge of insolvency. The reality was that only the U.S. government could provide the financing Britain and the Allies needed to continue to fight German aggression. Their cause now carried too much risk for commercial sources of financing. The cost of money had risen to 6 percent and even the J. P. Morgan banking consortium—which had backed Great Britain and France since 1915—found it impossible to raise funds, given that the Allies could no longer provide collateral, and that Britain was about to default on a Morgan loan of $400 million.[1]

Germany was winning the war, not in the trenches of Belgium and France where the slaughter had been ongoing since August 1914, but on the high seas. Its campaign of unrestricted submarine warfare—the practice of using submarines to sink merchant ships without warning—was succeeding in cutting off Britain's supplies and munitions. Four fifths of the island nation's food came by sea. The German naval strategy, tested in early 1916, and put into operation in 1917, was to sink enough tonnage to bring Britain to its knees in a matter of months. If the sinking continued at the same rate, Great Britain, still regarded as a great sea power, would be defeated by the end of the year. Its Admiralty "could see no means to avert disaster," and informed a US naval liaison that Germany would win the war if its submarine warfare "remained unchecked."[2]

Germany's submarine attacks, which included torpedoing neutral American vessels, breached the rules of war and maritime commerce. The United States responded by declaring war on Germany on April 6, 1917. President Woodrow Wilson had been an outspoken opponent of militarism, and his November 1916 reelection campaign had succeeded on a peace platform and the slogan "He Kept Us Out of War." Five months after the election, however, the president explained his change of position in a stirring speech to a joint session of Congress on April 2, 1917, asserting that "the menace to peace and freedom lies in the existence of autocratic government backed by organized force, which is controlled wholly by their will, not by the will of their people." He urged the legislative branch to authorize the United States to go to war to make the world "safe for Democracy," and to sanction "the most liberal financial credits" for the Allies, arguing, "They are

German Submarine Attacking British Merchant Ship, 1916, illustration by Willy Stöwer. Unrestricted submarine warfare overwhelmed the Royal Navy and transformed the conflict into an economic war. *Courtesy of the Library of Congress, Washington, DC.*

in the field and we should help them in every way to be effective there." Many critics agreed with him and had, for months, been urging US action to defend Europe.[3]

Wilson's call for Congress to extend credit to the Allies stemmed in part from his realization during his 1916 reelection campaign that the nation was in an exceptionally strong financial position. The United States had reached the tipping point at which it could lend more to other countries than it needed to borrow from them to carry out its business. America had become a creditor nation for the first time in its history. "Our business hereafter," he said in a speech to Detroit businessmen in July, "is . . . to lend, and . . . to finance the world in some important degree." In his final campaign speech in New Jersey, Wilson spoke of the strategic power of being a creditor nation: "We have become, not the debtors, but the creditors of the world, and the part that other nations used to play . . . we are playing. We can determine to a large extent who is to be financed and who is not to be." America's new economic power was a bitter political blow for Great Britain, which had mismanaged its international credit in waging war against Germany, and consequentially became dependent on the United States for financing.[4]

Both Andrew Mellon and Winston Churchill were involved in the war at this time, but in quite different ways.

While Mellon, one of America's wealthiest and most imperceptibly ambitious men of his era, had not yet considered public office, his commercial banks in Pittsburgh had played a significant role in lending to the Allies before the United States entered the war. They were part of the Morgan consortium organized to make loans to the warring European governments. Mellon's keen analytic mind propelled him beyond the risk/reward calculation of extending credit, and into the seed financing of business ventures in steel, aluminum, oil, and chemicals which manufactured needed war materials. One of his companies, Koppers, produced ingredients for making the explosive known as TNT, from the by-products yielded in the manufacture of steel. Mellon's enterprises were benefitting economically from the war, yet the sixty-two-year-old financier was concerned by the challenges emerging from widespread economic disruption and the soaring levels of the national debt caused by the war. An admirer of Alexander Hamilton, the first Treasury secretary of the United States, Mellon believed in the guiding principles Hamilton established as the financial policy of the American government—balanced budgets and disciplined debt reduction. As a son of a banker, Mellon understood the unprecedented opportunity and formidable challenge the United States faced by becoming a creditor nation. Few understood the authority and responsibilities of being a creditor better than he did. He had been lending money since he began working in his father's bank at the age of nineteen.[5]

The war advanced Churchill's career at first, but then almost destroyed it. Elected to Parliament in 1908, he had risen to the Cabinet position of First Lord of the Admiralty before the war began. His involvement in the disastrous 1915 Dardanelles naval attack discredited him among his colleagues and resulted in his removal from the Admiralty. Churchill had been the most forceful advocate of the strategy, believing it key to Britain's victory in the war. As his close friend Violet Bonham Carter observed, he had "staked his heart" on it both militarily and politically. Blamed for its defeat, Churchill then sought redemption during a six-month tour of duty as an army major in the trenches on the Western Front. Back from the war in May of 1916, he continued to represent Dundee as the Scottish city's member of Parliament, and to speak in the House of Commons. As a member of the Liberal Party, he championed free trade and government-led efforts to address social problems. While politics was Churchill's passion, he made his living as a writer and lecturer. Now forty-two, he was applying those talents to the goal of returning to a Cabinet position with ministerial authority. It was a bitter moment for him when his friend and ally, David Lloyd George, became prime minister in December 1916, yet failed to offer him a Cabinet seat. Churchill was still too great a political liability.[6]

Days after the United States entered the war, the Lloyd George government sent a twenty-five-member delegation to Washington, with the goal of securing American financing and naval support. Churchill was again left out. The mission, led by Arthur Balfour, the British secretary of state for foreign affairs, included Lord Cunliffe, the governor of the Bank of England, as well as other officials. During their weeklong crossing of the Atlantic, members of the mission anxiously read reports sent by wireless communication of ships sunk by German submarines.[7]

Wilson had not requested that the British make the trip. He feared they would attempt "to take charge of us as an assistant to Great Britain" and insisted that, if they came, no treaties were to be signed.[8]

The delegation arrived at Union Station in Washington on April 22, with Balfour, Cunliffe, and others in top hats and frock coats, looking every bit the way Americans pictured English diplomats. Two days after their arrival, Congress passed the legislation required to make loans to foreign governments and authorized up to $3 billion for that purpose. Not a single dissenting vote was cast in either the House or the Senate. This "Emergency Bond Issue" required that the money be loaned at the same cost of its borrowing. That meant that whatever it cost the US government to acquire the money, which it would do by selling Treasury bonds, it would lend that money to the Allies at the same interest rate. The US government promised the American people that each loan would "take care of itself" and not be a future burden to taxpayers.[9]

Once Congress had voted to enter the war, there was little opposition from the American public to loaning funds to the Allies. Some argued that the money would be a substitute for sending men. The fact that the financial assistance would be spent to buy American goods and munitions, and was to be paid back with interest, were reassuring factors. *The Sun*, a New York newspaper sold mainly on the street to the working classes at a penny a copy, noted in a sub-headline, UNITED STATES HOWEVER WILL GET EVERY DOLLAR BACK IN WAR PURCHASES. This set expectations that the Allies would repay every cent borrowed from America.[10]

In his office at the Treasury Building in Washington on April 25, 1917, William G. McAdoo, secretary of the Treasury, handed over a bank draft for $200 million to Lord Cunliffe of the Bank of England.

It was the largest financial transaction ever executed by the US government. In return, the British ambassador to the United States, Sir Cecil Spring-Rice, gave the US Treasury a promissory note for the money. "The evidence of the debt on the part of Great Britain," the *Commercial and Financial Chronicle* reported, "is in the form of a single note for the full amount" and bearing "a like rate of interest with the United States Treasury certificates." The *Washington Herald* put it in plainer language: "England is to pay three percent for the money and is to repay it in long-term bonds." This marked the restoration of British credit, and the beginning of its indebtedness to the United States government.[11]

Balfour did not attend the Treasury signing for the $200 million loan but delivered remarks that day to a group of American officials and members of the press. Advised of Wilson's thoughts, he dispelled rumors that the British intended to "inveigle the United States" and "entangle it in formal alliances." That was unnecessary, he said, arguing that there was a deeper relationship involved.[12]

"Our confidence in the assistance which we are going to get from this community," Balfour said, "is not based upon such shallow considerations as those which arise out of formal treaties." Rather, he stated, "No treaty could increase the undoubted confidence with which we look to the United States, who, having come into the war, are going to see the war through."[13]

This subject of trust in one another and honoring promises would become a theme in Anglo-American relations going forward. Three weeks after Wilson had called on Congress to declare war, the United States took over from Great Britain as banker to the Allies by extending credit to them for the vast amounts of munitions, food, and other war supplies needed to prosecute the war. The funding from the United States eliminated the Allies' financial and supply problems and greatly benefitted American industry. Mellon would later hail it as "the greatest credit operation in the history of the world."[14]

The British press noted the immediacy of the American funding on the day after the loan agreement was signed. "American financial aid for the Allies is now in actual operation," said one report, adding, "part of the American billions will soon reach the French, British, and Italian governments." Although so welcome at the time, the loans would become the subject of controversy and dispute over the coming decades.[15]

President Wilson, for his part, saw America's new economic influence as leverage to persuade the warring nations to adopt his administration's plan for the peace process.[16]

Treasury Secretary McAdoo, the official tasked with the duty of raising the money to be loaned, explained to Congress that the cost of the war—sending an army overseas and lending to the Allies—would be enormous. He proposed a funding plan to finance the war with a combination of one-third taxation, and two-thirds borrowing. The borrowing would take the form of bond issues that would be sold to the American people, banks, and businesses. They would be paid interest every six months for the use of their funds.

McAdoo envisioned this borrowing as "a great popular loan" to involve Americans emotionally and financially in the war effort, and he named the instruments Liberty Bonds. He organized a campaign—a mobilization of patriotism—to sell the bonds in partnership with the Federal Reserve System. It was met with widespread enthusiasm and little resistance despite the fact that most Americans had never owned a security. The first of four Liberty Loan drives began on May 14, 1917, and there would be a fifth Victory Loan after the war ended. All were oversubscribed. His decision to marshal patriotic pride rather than asking Americans to bear the real economic cost of the war—through heavy taxation or market-rate borrowing costs—would have profound political implications in the postwar years.[17]

Additional legislation adjusted the rates and conditions to make the bonds continually attractive. Boy Scouts, poster artists, movie stars, and opera singers all participated in the sales effort, which was called, quite early on, "the biggest publicity campaign . . . in world history," and perhaps it was. It raised over $21 billion. Of that, more than $10 billion was loaned primarily to thirteen foreign governments during and immediately after the war.[18]

One of the many large supporters of the Liberty Bond drive was Andrew Mellon, who personally purchased $1 million of bonds in the initial offering, and at least $60 million more through his banks by the end of the second drive; but he did so quietly. Mellon valued his privacy and rarely disclosed either his views or his actions, preferring to support political initiatives he endorsed discretely. His biographer concluded that Mellon's investments in the Liberty Bonds were made patriotically. It is also possible that Mellon bought the bonds because they were good investments, with an effective yield of more than 9 percent for those in the highest tax brackets.[19]

After the United States entered the war, the Allies used over $7 billion in credit provided by the American government to buy war materials. Almost two million American men crossed the Atlantic to fight alongside European troops during the next twenty months. The federal government, in partnership with American industry, produced thirty-six naval destroyers in record time to patrol supply routes in European waters and serve as convoy escorts. Due in part to US financing, the ground troops it sent, and the engagement of its navy to protect shipping, the war ended in an armistice on November 11, 1918.[20]

Peace talks began two months later, in Paris, where President Wilson presented his plan for a new world order based on principles of democratic freedom and self-determination. It was meant to transcend politics and emphasize collective security by establishing a league of nations. While Wilson was trying to win approval from the Allies for his plan, they were trying to engage him in a discussion of an all-around settlement of war debts and German reparations. Overtures from the British and French officials suggested that they expected the discussion to result in an agreement to cancel all financial obligations arising from the war.

In response to suggestions to liquidate war debts, Wilson reiterated his administration's policy—America intended to collect the debts and would settle with each debtor nation individually; reparations would be a separate matter for the Allies to resolve on their own.

Unlike the war debts—which were consensual agreements based on the trust, honor, and credit of the debtor—reparations were punitive indemnities imposed on Germany by the Allies. The total amount of reparations to be exacted proved impossible to set in the face of postwar European politics and competing national interests. The Allies left the sum to be determined by a reparations commission that would apply a "capacity to pay" methodology in assessing Germany's economic situation. This methodology would later be employed by the United States in negotiating the settlement of war debts with the Allies.

After word of Wilson's rebuff reached London, Churchill alerted his fellow ministers to its significance. He had been brought back into the Lloyd George Cabinet in 1917 and had recently been made the Secretary of State for War and Air. Churchill told his colleagues that their assumption that the United States would cancel wartime indebtedness was grossly mistaken. Should the United States hold Britain responsible for the debt, he warned, it would mark "a complete alteration of our financial position in relation to America." Churchill made clear the political reality of the moment—in its desperation for American credit to avoid losing the war, Britain had ceded its financial supremacy to the United States. He proposed that the British government should "make the Germans responsible for the discharge of their overseas debt." In his view, Britain should transfer responsibility for its American debt to Germany and leave the matters of collection to the United States. The British Cabinet did not act on Churchill's proposal, but the accuracy of his assessment would increasingly influence attitudes and policy in the years to come.[21]

The peace talks culminated in the Treaty of Versailles which ended the war and established the conditions for postwar reconciliation. The treaty required Germany to pay the equivalent of M20 billion (approximately $5 billion or £1 billion) "in gold, commodities, ships, securities, or otherwise," for "the restoration and economic life of the Allies, pending the full determination of their claims." It became known as the "guilt clause" of the treaty and it would have profound political ramifications in the years ahead.[22]

The US delegation that Wilson took with him to Paris did not include any members of Congress, a political mistake that would catch up with Wilson tragically. Even before this miscalculation, the legislative branch had expressed its resentment of the administration. For more than a year, the US Senate had attacked White House policies in response to "the historic growth of presidential power." Bipartisan Senate efforts "to wrest control of the war effort from the President," further estranged Wilson from Congress.[23]

Republican Senator Philander Knox of Pennsylvania, who was also the corporate lawyer for several of Mellon's businesses, argued that the treaty exposed the United States to the possibility of ceding its sovereign power by authorizing an international body to determine its participation in world affairs, "whether in men, armament or money." Many of his colleagues felt the same way. As a result, the Treaty of Versailles—which included the establishment of a League of Nations for which Wilson had advocated so fervently and had been approved at the Paris conference in June—would never be ratified by the United States Senate.[24]

Up to this point, the beliefs of Andrew Mellon and Winston Churchill were in accord on principal issues: the entry of the United States into the war and the loans to the Allies. On the League of Nations, however, they held opposing views. Not known at the time was Mellon's role in funding a group of senators, including Knox, who were opposed to the United States joining the League. Mellon was supportive of loaning money to Europe, but strongly opposed the idea of the Allied debtors having a consensus-driven forum to determine repayment to the United States, as set out in the League charter.

Dubbed the "Irreconcilables," the Senate group did not believe that the opposition of Henry Cabot Lodge, the Republican leader of the Senate and chairman of its Foreign Relations Committee, went far enough. Lodge wanted to derail membership in the League by imposing numerous reservations to the ratification of the Treaty of Versailles. The Irreconcilables—fourteen Republicans and two Democrats—did not want to ratify it at all.[25]

Knox was one of their influential leaders. He believed that the League violated the US Constitution and would lead to more wars. He argued that American independence would be lost when "our conduct is dictated by others, when our continued existence depends on the will of others, when we are no longer able to avail ourselves of our wanted means of defense." In a speech on August 29, 1919, Knox warned that by joining, the United States would be obligated "to go to war to protect the covenants of the League." He concluded by saying that "the only safe way for us to deal with it, is to decline to be a party to it."[26]

Mellon rarely discussed his political views publicly but was a strong supporter of the Republican Party. He socialized with Knox and their mutual Pittsburgh friend and business associate, Henry Clay Frick. At the urging of Knox, who had previously served as attorney general of the United States and as US secretary of state, Mellon and Frick quietly bankrolled a coast-to-coast publicity campaign organized by the Irreconcilables to prevent the United States from joining the League. This involved renting auditoriums, promoting speaking tours and rallies, and hiring an occasional brass band.[27]

Realizing that serious opposition to the League was building in the Senate, from both the Irreconcilables and Lodge's "Reservationists," President Wilson launched a national campaign of his own to build support for the ratification of the treaty and the League. The campaign would evolve into a fight over what American foreign policy would be, and whether it would be set by the executive branch or by Congress.

While on the Colorado leg of his tour, Wilson collapsed from exhaustion on September 25. He returned to Washington, where he then suffered a massive stroke. Despite being physically incapacitated, he sent instructions to the Senate Democrats to hold firm and not vote for Lodge's plan with reservations. Ironically, this resulted in the Senate voting against joining the League. In the first of two separate votes on November 19, 1919, the Democrats and Irreconcilables defeated ratification of the treaty with Lodge's reservations. In the second vote, for the treaty as written, the Reservationists and Irreconcilables defeated Wilson's Democrats.[28]

The tension on the Senate floor was startling, and the outcome staggering, even to reporters who regularly covered Congress. "The extreme bitterness which marked the closing hours of the debate has seldom been equaled," the *Baltimore Sun* reported. The correspondent for the

Washington Post called it "one of the most dramatic and spectacular sessions in the nation's history."[29]

Public reaction ran predictably along party lines, with Wilson's supporters branding the rejection of the treaty as "shameful" and "tragic." The *New York World*, a Democratic-leaning paper, editorialized sarcastically: "In Russia, Lenin and Trotsky shed tears of joy. Bolshevism took on a new lease of life." The *Washington Times* quoted a Republican-leaning authority on international law, praising it as "the final overthrow of the Wilsonian dictatorship."[30]

The news that the United States had rejected the treaty and would not join the League of Nations shocked the Allies. The *New York Times* headlined its story on the French reaction, PARIS RESENTFUL OVER SENATE ACTION, and reported, "All they can see in the situation is that America has gone back on the bargain she made." A British account viewed "those in opposition to President Wilson's great plan as betrayers of the interest of humanity."[31]

Winston Churchill, who shared the moral opinion that the United States had betrayed the rest of the world, now stepped forward as one of the harshest critics of American foreign policy. Despite his position in the Lloyd George Cabinet, he published an essay in London's *Illustrated Sunday Herald* on November 30, the title of which asked the question on many minds in Europe: "Will America Fail Us?"

Churchill charged that the United States had a binding obligation to Europe in the aftermath of the war. He argued that "the League of Nations was an American plan, pressed upon the powers at the Peace Conference with the influence and power of the United States," and underscored his point by asserting, "The whole shape and character of the peace settlement was determined by American influence." Churchill pointed to the promises made by President Wilson, in "his stately ideals expressed in language which appealed to every heart," and urged America not to "squander irretrievably the whole victory gained."

Churchill recognized that the United States would increasingly dominate the world stage. "It is impossible to exaggerate," he wrote, "the gravity of the consequences which would arise" from America abandoning Europe before peace was achieved. "To carry such a policy halfway and to carry it no further, to destroy the old organization without attempting to supply the new," he admonished, "would indeed be an act from which America should recoil and which posterity would certainly condemn."[32]

The US Senate took up the League once more in March 1920, and again voted against joining it. Wilson still did not believe the American people were opposed to his view and proposed that the November election be considered "a great and solemn referendum on the League." This too failed embarrassingly for Wilson and the Democratic Party.[33]

While many Americans believed Wilson when he proclaimed that the postwar peace would bring "greater opportunity and greater prosperity," they encountered a very different reality once the war economy ended. The consequence of his administration having financed the war by the creation of new money with the issuance of Liberty Bonds had led to widespread inflation, a severe recession, and unprecedented national debt. Millions of men returned to find businesses closed and unemployment rampant. This left a population disillusioned after having responded to the call to aid the Allies. As a result, public opinion turned against Wilson and his international entreaties.[34]

The Republican candidate for president, Warren Harding, emphasized that the Democratic administration was "forgetting our domestic difficulties in its engrossment with the chimera of world reconstruction." Harding won the presidential election in a landslide, taking over 60 percent of the popular vote and increasing Republican control of both the House and Senate. "Newspaper headlines grasped for superlatives," a Harding biographer recorded. While division over whether the United States should join the League dominated the political scene, the American economy was a more decisive factor. A large majority of voters had had enough of the financial hardship brought about by what was now regarded as "Europe's War."[35]

Britain and the other Allies would soon be dealing with a new, and unfamiliar cast of characters who held an opposing view of America's political role and responsibilities in postwar Europe, but who agreed with the established US policy on war debts and reparations. Andrew Mellon was virtually unknown to most Europeans—and Americans—when he was appointed secretary of the Treasury in Harding's cabinet. In a very short time, however, he would become the bill collector for the war debts, which would lead to a decade of antagonistic interactions with Great Britain that ultimately put Anglo-American relations in jeopardy. These hostilities would intensify with Churchill's rise to the position of chancellor of the Exchequer in the British cabinet, putting him in charge of *his* nation's Treasury.

Mellon and Churchill would not meet face-to-face until 1923, when Mellon interrupted his London vacation to attend a memorial service at Westminster Abbey celebrating Anglo-American friendship. They would meet again on four other occasions during the next ten years, including a top-secret dinner arranged as an intervention of sorts by high-level officials on both sides concerned about the impact the Mellon-Churchill antagonism was having on relations between the two countries. The plan for the dinner was to allow the two Treasury titans to find common ground and join forces against the economic issues poisoning postwar peace. These meetings have largely been left out of the history of the interwar years. The disputes between the two men, which were widely publicized at the time, have also been largely overlooked.

This account of the issues Mellon and Churchill debated, and how they affected the politics and Anglo-American relationship of their times, attempts not only to fill that void, but to suggest how these two great intellects—one a reserved and soft-spoken American, and the other, a bold and outspoken Briton—shaped moral questions that their respective countries would confront again, and that the world still faces today.

MR. MELLON GOES TO WASHINGTON

No one imagined that Andrew Mellon would be considered for the position of secretary of the Treasury in the Harding administration. Newspaper speculation about the cabinet began on the day after the 1920 election, and within weeks, two different candidates had been suggested as sure bets.[1]

Mellon was virtually unknown outside his hometown of Pittsburgh. The only person from Pennsylvania being considered for the cabinet was Senator Philander Knox, a prominent Republican who had served in the Taft, McKinley, and Roosevelt administrations. A reporter traveling with Harding on his post-election trip to Panama wrote from the cruise ship on November 21 that "Knox stands first" among the likely picks for secretary of state.[2]

The idea of a Mellon appointment to Treasury began taking shape, however, on the evening of November 29, at the reclusive banker's home in the East End of Pittsburgh, when Knox arrived from Washington for a two-night stay as a houseguest.[3]

It was quite a house. The Tudor-revival estate in Squirrel Hill towered above twenty-eight wooded acres. Asymmetrical in design, with peaked gables, elaborate chimneys, and a storybook-like, half-timbered wing, it evoked an English manor, complete with formal gardens, tennis courts,

Andrew Mellon, secretary of the Treasury, walking from the East Wing of the White House in 1921 to his office in the Treasury Building. He would take this route to and from cabinet meetings for the next eleven years, serving under three US presidents. *Credit: The Everett Collection.*

and room for ten automobiles in the carriage house. Nine live-in servants tended to the house and family of three. The interior—made up of no fewer than forty rooms—was richly decorated with Chinese porcelain and eighteenth-century French furniture, all of which provided a fitting setting for Mellon's growing collection of Old Master paintings.[4]

Knox knew Mellon well. For almost forty years, he had provided counsel to his friend on many of his personal and business transactions. They had long played in a weekly game of poker and they both liked to relax over a glass of whiskey. The two of them could talk comfortably in any one of the first-floor rooms, several of which were decorated with carved-wood paneling, marble fireplaces, and impressive artwork. Knox had not yet seen some of Mellon's newly acquired paintings, including portraits by Rembrandt and Hals, and landscapes by Constable and Turner. On that cool November evening, they had much to discuss and could sit by a fire and drink.

Given the speculation about Harding's cabinet appointments, there were various scenarios to consider, but two in particular. The first involved Knox as secretary of state. The second imagined Mellon as secretary of the Treasury.[5]

Knox would not refuse an appointment. Foreign policy was his focus, but he did not believe the State department post would be offered to him, nor did he want it. He would be more effective by remaining in the Senate, where that policy was set—as President Wilson had learned the hard way in his battle to persuade the Senate to ratify the Treaty of Versailles.

It was the second scenario, involving Mellon, that Knox had come to discuss. Never was the need greater for someone who could put the nation's finances in order and restore conditions for business to prosper. Knox had made the trip, perhaps on an inkling, to find out whether Mellon would accept the Treasury post in Harding's cabinet if it were offered.

Mellon would later remember having told Knox that he "had no wish to enter public life" or "to disengage from all his business activities."[6]

Perhaps, though, Mellon's memory was not entirely accurate. He was more involved in the Republican Party and wielded more influence than ever before. He had attended a Republican convention for the first time in June 1920 and increased his financial contributions significantly during the Harding campaign. One of Mellon's banks had also made a large loan to the Republican National Committee. The most telling indicator of Mellon's deepening engagement and elevated stature involved the party's chairman, Will Hays. On several occasions during the busy days of the fall campaign, Hays had left the committee's New York City headquarters to meet with Mellon on Long Island to discuss the political and financial situation. Whether intentionally or by circumstance, Mellon had become a player in American politics.[7]

During Knox's stay at Mellon's Woodland Road home, they no doubt reminisced over drinks and cigars and contemplated the future. At the age of sixty-eight, Knox had no desire to embark on another difficult job. He had made his fortune years ago in his law practice before entering public service. The senator sensed, however, that his still-ambitious friend, even at sixty-five, might be open to a new challenge.

By the time Knox left, he understood that Mellon would not refuse the job of Treasury secretary. He also knew, without having to ask, that Mellon would never campaign for the job. Harding would have to ask him to take it.

∽

Knox immediately began formulating a plan to convince the president-elect that Mellon should be Treasury secretary.

To help him make his cabinet selections and inform his policy decisions, Harding announced that he would invite "the ablest and most experienced minds" to his home in Marion, Ohio.[8]

Within days, Knox was ready. He launched his plan by paying a call on Will Hays, the chairman of the Republican National Committee who had also managed Harding's post-convention campaign. Hays himself was assured of a cabinet post and he found the idea of Mellon for secretary of the Treasury bold and appealing. He agreed to join Knox in inveigling an invitation to Marion to make the case to Harding for a Mellon candidacy. Hays had remained in Washington, as he was not involved in the cabinet selection process, but Knox knew that Hays held considerable sway with Harding.[9]

Time was short. Knox feared that Harding might offer the job to another candidate at any moment. Knox and Hays got to work at once.

Knox got himself elected chairman of the Congressional Committee on Inauguration on December 9. Seven days later, Hays, as party chair, appointed Ned McLean, an important supporter of Harding and the owner of the *Washington Post*, to the prestigious position of chair of the civilian Inaugural Committee. This came as something of a surprise—although a welcome one—to McLean and his wife, Evalyn. In short order, Hays then secured an invitation for the inauguration officials—which now included McLean and Knox—to meet with Harding in Marion.[10]

Knox and Hays had one other obstacle to overcome. This was Harry Daugherty, an Ohio friend of Harding who had managed his preconvention campaign and remained the president-elect's closest political advisor. Daugherty, who was also assured of being in the Cabinet, was supporting another candidate for the Treasury post. Through some skillful communications exchanges, Daugherty agreed to join Knox and Hays on their visit to Marion. The trip would provide an opportunity for them to bring Daugherty around to their plan.

Shortly before 4:00 P.M. on December 29, Knox arrived at Washington's Union Station and made his way to the *Berwick*, Ned McLean's private railway car. Built for comfort and conviviality it was the length of a standard Pullman car with four staterooms, berths for servants, and an elegant dining area with a pedestal table and fashionable mahogany chairs. Against the car's rear wall, a built-in buffet housed the dishes and cutlery. A china cabinet with leaded-glass windows stored the barware and tea service.[11]

Knox knew Mellon better than anyone. He was prepared to argue to Harding that if he truly wanted to bring the best and most capable men into his cabinet, Mellon was the right man for Treasury. He had witnessed, firsthand, Mellon's ability to transform good potential into great accomplishments, time and time again. He believed Mellon was one of the few cases in which wealth was an accurate measure of ability. Knox had told a reporter that he regarded Mellon as "the greatest constructive economist of his generation."[12]

He and Hays now had the entire evening, and five hundred miles of track, to bring Daugherty around in the comfort of the *Berwick*.

∽

By the time they arrived in Marion for a 7:30 breakfast with Harding, Daugherty was sold on Mellon. Knox and Hays then won over the president-elect with little difficulty, despite Harding telling them that "he had gone rather far" with another candidate. Like Hays, Harding found the Mellon suggestion appealing and Knox's presentation persuasive.[13]

The next morning, McLean's paper, the *Washington Post*, ran a front-page story about the Knox visit with Harding, including a brief mention, in the sixth paragraph, of a new candidate for Treasury secretary, Andrew Mellon. In Pittsburgh, the new candidate was the headline: A. W. MELLON, LOCAL BANKER, CONSIDERED FOR CABINET.[14]

Mellon was home that day with his children, hosting a luncheon for his relatives and planning to go to a New Year's Eve dinner later. A message from Knox reached Mellon during the family gathering, corroborating the morning's news that the president-elect was "favorably considering" him for the Treasury post. Mellon's nephew, William Larimer Mellon, observed that in contrast to the tone of elation in the message from Knox, Mellon appeared flattered, but almost downcast. Mellon noted his apprehensions about the difficult job the new Treasury secretary would confront in his diary that evening. The following day, Mellon wired Knox with the directive that "nothing further be done to encourage the president in this matter."[15]

Knox received some help from his fellow Pennsylvania senator, Boies Penrose, who now joined the public campaign for Mellon. He and Knox were an odd pair. Penrose was a huge man, six feet four inches tall and weighing over three hundred pounds, with a full head of hair and a bushy mustache. Knox stood at just under five feet, five inches, and was clean-shaven and bald. Both though were equally influential. Penrose told the *Pittsburgh Post* that Mellon's appointment would have his "hearty approval," and that "there is no one better qualified for it," but that it would be difficult to get him to accept it. [16]

Knowing how tenaciously he regarded his privacy, Mellon's relatives thought it "unthinkable" that he would be interested in the position. His nineteen-year-old daughter, Ailsa, however, was delighted with the idea, despite still bearing scars from the humiliating publicity of her parents' divorce ten years earlier. Mellon had married late in life, when he was forty-five, to an English beauty less than half his age. His wife, Nora, began an extramarital affair before their second anniversary, and the relationship continued over several years. Ultimately, she decided to seek a divorce. Mellon launched a very public battle for custody of nine-year-old Ailsa and her three-year-old brother, Paul. It laid bare Mellon's ruthless determination to win at any cost, even if it meant sacrificing his privacy. The struggle over the children went on for two years, as did the sensational and embarrassing headlines. [17]

The details of Mellon's wife's infidelity were widely reported, occasionally with photographs of the children, which only she or her lawyers could have provided to the press. According to papers filed by Mellon's lawyers, his wife had been "indiscreet" with a con artist masquerading as a British army officer in many locations, including Pittsburgh, New York, and Paris, aboard a German ocean liner, and at the Hotel Savoy in London. A writer for the *Washington Herald* quipped that the bill of particulars in the divorce case read like "an abridged world atlas." [18]

Despite Nora's efforts to turn Ailsa and Paul against him, Mellon never said an ill word about her. Paul would later write that he only learned of his mother's infidelity after his father's death. Paul also recalled that the "evil rumors" about their mother, and the "dark and frightening days of the divorce," were more disturbing to Ailsa than anyone had imagined. [19]

At the time of Mellon's potential appointment to the cabinet, Ailsa had completed finishing school and busied herself with balls, cotillions, fundraisers, and other social and charitable events. She had recently made her debut and was expected to soon find a suitable match and marry. Paul had come home for the holidays from the Choate School in Connecticut. Much of the new house had been expanded with them in mind. Their mother had never lived with them there, and the move to the house on Woodland Road was perhaps Mellon's attempt to create a happier life for all of them. Now, at the age of sixty-five, did Mellon really want to become a public person and expose himself, and his teenage children, to more publicity?

Still undecided, Mellon accepted Harding's January 2 invitation to meet in Marion, where he told the president-elect that he was not seeking the appointment and would prefer that another candidate be found. Knox, however, continued to believe that Mellon would not refuse the job if offered it and continued to keep Mellon's candidacy on course. For the next month, there was much discussion of Mellon's business conflicts, which Knox assured him could be resolved. Taking the job would require Mellon to resign as a director from more than sixty corporations, including some twenty-eight banks and financial institutions. Knox prevailed and when all seemed settled, he telephoned on the first of February to inform Mellon that he was Harding's choice. Mellon noted in his diary the following day that he had told Ailsa he was accepting the job in Washington "on her account."[20]

While the matter was not yet settled officially, Mellon went to Washington on February 28, four days before Inauguration Day, to look for an apartment. Whether Ailsa believed he took the job entirely for her benefit, or because of her urging, she was happy to go.

∽

Shortly after his arrival in Washington, DC, Andrew Mellon stood in the public line outside the Treasury Building to pay a courtesy call on the man he would be replacing. News reporters who happened to be inside 1500 Pennsylvania Avenue that morning discovered Mellon lost in the corridors and showed him the way to the office of the Treasury secretary.

"I just came down to look around," Mellon told them quietly. He did not have an appointment with the outgoing secretary, David Houston, who—as Assistant Secretary S. Parker Gilbert had to inform the unexpected visitor—was in New York that day. Mellon and Gilbert spoke in the office suite for two hours. The press concluded that Mellon was Harding's choice and that he was taking the job, despite his statement that there was "no significance" to his visit. Understatement was a Mellon trait. [21]

Washington did not quite know what to make of him. Observers were usually underwhelmed by their first impression of Mellon. Once he assumed office, one reporter stated the obvious and undeniable facts: "The oldest man in the Cabinet, and the richest, is the shyest." Many described him as shy—or reserved, or diffident, or of a retiring disposition. They often noted that he disliked public speaking, avoided publicity, and shunned the spotlight. Some even commented that he looked "frightened" or "scared to death" when attention focused on him in public. All agreed, though, that Mellon was polite to the point of timidity. [22]

He was typically well dressed, in suits tailored in London, and neatly groomed, with a cropped gray mustache and a full head of well-trimmed, silver-toned hair, parted off-center. Thin and seemingly frail, with bushy eyebrows that made his eyes appear even more deep set, he wore pointed collars and modern neckties. One description of him would stick: "He looks like a tired double-entry bookkeeper who is afraid of losing his job." Mellon never seemed to make any attempt to alter the bland impression he usually left. It was one of the qualities that made him so effective in business and at the poker table. He had capitalized on being reticent and inscrutable all his life. [23]

As a public official, however, Mellon now had to talk with the press. He would answer their questions courteously, but usually told them little of substance. On one rare occasion though, he explained why he took the job.

"When I was asked to become Secretary of the Treasury, I at first thought it would be impossible for me to do so," Mellon explained. "I could not see how I could quit what I was doing. I had realized, however, that I would have to retire from active life some time and I was sixty-six years old. This post in Washington afforded me a place to light. I decided that I would take it, would discharge its duties, and when the work was done, I would be free to settle down, either to a quiet life or otherwise as I might feel inclined." The revealing statement seemed to be a candid one.[24]

But Mellon knew the work would not be easy, nor finished anytime soon. In the aftermath of the war, widespread economic disruption across the country had left millions unemployed after factories closed, banks failed, and businesses shut down. Social unrest spread as the American economy remained mired in an industrial depression. Compounding the devastation, the national debt stood at $24 billion, more than four times prewar levels, bloated by over $10 billion in foreign loans. The grim state of the American economy, however, paled in comparison to that of the rest of the world. The war had plunged Europe into a punitive recession, destroyed industries, paralyzed trade, and destabilized currencies. The postwar slowdown ensnared Japan in a deflationary panic crippling its economy. Russia's repudiation of both its monarchy, as well as its wartime indebtedness to the United States and Great Britain, underscored the dire state of its finances. The world was in shambles, but Mellon believed he "might be able to accomplish something to the good."[25]

∽

April 1, 1921, was a pivotal day for American foreign policy. The Harding cabinet had been meeting for four weeks by then, concentrating mostly on domestic issues, but the visit of René Viviani, the former premier of France, had shifted the attention of the administration back to Europe. The stated purpose of Viviani's trip was to convey France's respect to the new American president. The real agenda had to do with reparations.

Because the United States had not ratified the Treaty of Versailles, it was still technically at war with Germany. The French feared that if the new US administration made a separate peace with Germany, it would undercut the treaty's provisions requiring Germany to pay reparations to France and the other Allies. Germany had already stopped making payments in March, claiming it was impossible, and war-torn France was desperate for money and credit. Viviani had come to solicit the United States to pressure Germany to pay reparations.[26]

The cabinet had reached its policy decision on the reparation issue at its previous meeting and it would be good news for France, but it had not yet been made public. At this meeting, the cabinet would focus on the issue of war debts owed to the United States by France and the other Allies. Mellon was ready with the facts and figures.

The ten cabinet officers, by tradition, were seated according to the seniority of their departments, all of them in new, matching armchairs, to which silver plaques with their names would soon be attached. Charles Evans Hughes, secretary of state, sat closest to the president, on his right. Mellon sat on the president's left. The heads of the most recently established departments sat five chairs back on either side. This put Secretary of Commerce Herbert Hoover at the far end of the room near the fireplace. Harding's only break with his predecessors' protocol was to include his vice president in the meetings. Calvin Coolidge sat at the foot of the long mahogany table, with the president at its head, in a chair with a higher back than the others. According to Harding's unwritten rules, nothing that was discussed in the cabinet room was to be revealed to the press unless the president chose to do so himself.[27]

On the matter of war debts, Mellon's figures showed that more than $10 billion were owed, principally by thirteen countries. This represented almost half the national debt. It was the largest liability ever recorded on the federal balance sheet. Most of the loaned money had been raised from the American people during the Liberty and Victory Bond campaigns. One-third of the bonds, $7.5 billion, were now coming due, and it was Mellon's job to craft an immediate plan to refinance them. If the war debts were not repaid by the Allies, or if they were canceled by Congress and stricken from the asset side of the Treasury's ledger, the debt would be borne by US taxpayers. It was a simple, but irrefutable, matter of accounting.

A banker all his life, Mellon had extensive experience with debtors who could not repay and managing nonperforming loans. Some had to be written off, others could be forgiven either out of sympathy or generosity, but in most cases, he preferred to "keep the debt alive" by restructuring it. That gave the debtor another chance to repay the lender and the lender another chance to avoid realizing a loss. To Mellon, the creditor's job was to find a way for the debtor to repay as much of the debt as possible.[28]

Harding asked around the table whether anyone saw a reason for wiping the debts off the books, either as noncollectible, or as straight donations to the debtor nations. The unanimous opinion was that the debt was still a "live asset" that someday would be repaid. Hughes, Mellon, and Hoover—considered the cabinet's "big three" by the press—were in complete agreement.[29]

Washington reporters found Harding to be a breath of fresh air, particularly after the final years of the Wilson administration. Due to security concerns and his illness, President Wilson had not held meetings with reporters since the submarine warfare days of 1916. A former publisher who could set type, Harding had reinstated the tradition of press conferences, announcing that one would be held after each of the two weekly cabinet meetings. Following the April 1 meeting, he was scheduled to meet with "Washington correspondents" at 4:00 P.M.[30]

The first news he gave them was on paper. It was a memorandum from Secretary Hughes that had been sent earlier in the week to the foreign minister of Germany through an American commissioner in Berlin. Dated March 29, it stated, "This Government stands with the Governments of the Allies in holding Germany responsible for the war and therefore morally bound to make reparations so far as may be possible." The statement made clear US support for the Allies and dashed German hopes of forging a separate peace with America. Harding told reporters that the idea that the United States would take a policy favoring Germany over the Allies was "absurd." This message was exactly what France and Viviani had hoped to hear.[31]

Harding's second announcement concerned war debts. The *Baltimore Sun* reported that the president had "let it be known that the Cabinet has discussed the whole question of the Allied debt to the United States today and had agreed without dissent that the debt was 'a valued asset' of this Government." The *New York Times* added that there was "unanimous agreement" that "the money lent should be returned." The *New York Herald* put it more simply reporting that the cabinet had decided that "there will be no cancellation of the loans by this Government."[32]

The policy of the United States on reparations and war debts was now clear as far as the president and his cabinet were concerned.

⁂

It now fell to Mellon to collect the debts. In a formal request to the president on June 20, 1921, Mellon asked for the authority to act autonomously, without congressional approval, in refunding "the debt of foreign governments to the United States arising out of the European War." The amount was detailed to the penny: $10,141,267,585.68. Treasury lawyers had advised Mellon that the department needed congressional authority to determine "the form and terms of the settlements," and particularly, "the rate, or rates of interest, the maturity dates, and the right to extend the time for payment of interest on the indebtedness to be refunded." This undoubtedly pleased Mellon, who preferred having a free hand to set the terms himself.[33]

In addition to negotiating the terms of repayment, Mellon wanted to deal with each debtor nation individually, in keeping with the Wilson administration's policy. This would prevent borrowers from banding together to pressure the United States into a potentially disadvantageous negotiating position.

While Mellon believed that the United States should insist on the settlement of war debts, his attitude was both pragmatic and sympathetic.

He explained in his letter to Harding that, for some of the debtor nations, "it is impossible for them to make payment on their obligations as they now mature," or even on the "maturing interest." Arguing for latitude, he wrote, "To insist on payment might be disastrous to the peoples of such countries." Without the requested broad powers, Mellon said, it would be "impossible to deal fairly with the debtor countries and at the same time protect the interests of this country." Mellon asserted that the terms for the debt settlements would need to be set "within the ability" of each country "to carry out." The job was to find a workable solution between creditor and debtor.[34]

Mellon was informing the president that he would use his own best judgment to strike the most equitable deal for all. To him, it was essentially a matter of fairness and good business.

Harding sent Mellon's petition with a cover letter to the House and Senate with proposed legislation. In the Senate, it fell under the jurisdiction of the Finance Committee, which Boies Penrose chaired. Penrose was among those who jealously guarded the Senate's role in making foreign policy. He could not have been happy with the executive branch asking Congress to cede so much authority, even to Mellon. Penrose himself did not criticize the petition, but other senators were pleased to do so. Newspapers described the powers the administration requested as "broad and almost unlimited."[35]

Senator Kenneth McKellar of Tennessee, a Democrat, issued a rebuke: "If a Congress is so subservient as to give power like this to the Secretary of the Treasury, such a Congress would be servile enough to approve whatever action the Secretary might take."[36]

Senator Reed Smoot, a Republican from Utah, made it a bipartisan snub, stating, "Frankly, I think this bill gives the Secretary of the Treasury too much power."[37]

A hearing on the administration's petition began on June 29, on the third floor of the Senate Office Building. Mellon brought a briefcase full of documents and a new assistant secretary with him. He had purposefully chosen Eliot Wadsworth, a Harvard-educated electrical engineer, who could handle questions intelligently, but could not speak from experience about Treasury matters because he had only recently been appointed. A wise judge of talent, Mellon delegated freely to those he believed right for a job. Wadsworth was his man for this one.

Mellon had Wadsworth read the opening statement. Following it, the hearing became a tedious series of pokes and prods, mostly by Senator James A. Reed, a Democrat from Missouri, and Senator Robert La Follette, a Republican populist from Wisconsin. Everyone seemed to make news before the monthlong hearing was over, except for Mellon, the taciturn star witness, who viewed the war debts as an accounting matter, not a political issue. The six Democrats on the sixteen-member committee could not win the vote, but they would stretch the hearing out over seven increasingly contentious sessions, through late July, in Washington's oppressive heat.

Due in part to Mellon's expression of sympathy for the plight of the European debtors in his petition, several senators feared that he might therefore be inclined to use the power he sought to forgive the foreign debts. While news reports speculated that Viviani of France had originally planned to suggest debt forgiveness, Great Britain had, in fact, made such a request. It had been big news in February, even to members of Congress, when Austen Chamberlain, the British chancellor of the exchequer, had disclosed publicly that his government had suggested to the Wilson administration that "the whole of the debts of the Allied and Associated Powers should be wiped out."[38]

La Follette wanted the British request for cancellation to be included in the official record of Congress and drew it out of Wadsworth that Chamberlain had sent a note on February 9, 1920, to Russell Leffingwell, an assistant secretary at the US Treasury, stating, "We should welcome a general cancellation of intergovernmental war debts." The initiator of the request was Basil Blackett, the controller of finance at the British Treasury, who had spent time in Washington during the war, and had met with the Wilson administration's representatives at the 1919 peace talks in Paris. While the suggestion of cancellation had never been made formally, Chamberlain's letter to Leffingwell served that purpose. To Chairman Penrose, however, it seemed to fall a bit short of that mark, and he noted that it appeared to be more like "a social correspondence."

Undeterred, La Follette followed up, asking, "Mr. Wadsworth, have you another communication bearing on the same subject?" This time he hit pay dirt. Mellon knew what was coming and nodded to Wadsworth to read the August 5, 1920, letter from David Lloyd George, the British prime minister, to President Wilson. It proposed "the reduction or cancellation of inter-Allied indebtedness." There it was, in print—a letter from the British prime minister to the president of the United States, proposing cancellation of all indebtedness related to the war. La Follette not only succeeded in recording the request but also in rekindling fears about the debts.[39]

Senator Henry Cabot Lodge, chairman of the Foreign Relations Committee, also had something he wanted recorded in the *Congressional Record*. On July 18, in the Senate chamber, Lodge read the previously unpublished response from President Wilson to Lloyd George's letter requesting cancellation. In it, Wilson strongly rejected the suggestion, stating that cancellation "would require Congressional authority." He made America's position clear that "it is highly improbable that either the Congress or popular opinion in this country will ever permit cancellation of any part of the debt of the British government to the United States."[40]

This made news in Europe as well. Wire services and transatlantic cables now made it possible for a story that took place on the Senate floor in Washington on Monday to be read in British and French newspapers on Tuesday morning. Although Lodge's information claimed that the Wilson letter was written in October 1920, it was actually dated November 3, 1920, the day after the election of Warren Harding. The US position at the end of the Wilson administration was clear: the debts were not going to be canceled. Mellon and the Harding administration intended to continue that policy. Several members of the Senate Finance Committee believed otherwise.[41]

The hearing sessions dragged on, and so did the summer heat. La Follette introduced a new line of attack, questioning why the interest on foreign loans was being deferred. It reflected either an innocent or intentional oversight on his part, as it was a policy that had been established by the Wilson administration and approved by Congress. Wilson's second Treasury secretary, Carter Glass, had explained the deferment in a December 18, 1919, letter to Congress, stating that Europe's recovery had not gotten to the point where its governments could pay even the interest on the debts. Glass informed Congress that Treasury was therefore implementing a moratorium "during the next two or three years." Glass argued that demanding immediate payment would therefore "retard the economic restoration of those countries" and prevent them from purchasing American goods.[42]

Missouri's Senator Reed wanted to know if there was anything that would keep the United States from collecting the interest right away. "What I want to get at," he said, "is there any understanding, express or implied, which in any way obligates us to extend this interest, or which would embarrass us in any way by insisting upon the payment of the interest?"

Mellon replied, "I think there was an understanding in these negotiations, so far as they proceeded, that for two or three years this interest would not be insisted upon but would be deferred and extended."[43]

When Reed then pressed the point the following day by asking whether Mellon felt morally bound by agreements made by his predecessors, the Treasury secretary answered that, yes, he felt the United States should honor the current policy. Mellon reasoned that it had been agreed to by Congress, understood by the debtor governments, and been in place for the last two and a half years.

Mellon had understood, from the very first day of the hearing, that no evidence or argument would result in Reed or La Follette voting to give him full authority. It was also clear that several other senators believed the Wilson administration's failure to report the British overtures regarding debt cancellation to Congress had subverted the Senate's role in setting foreign policy. It was determined to reclaim its power from wartime presidential appropriation. As Penrose had said before the new administration took office, "It makes no difference who is Secretary of State, the Senate will make the foreign policy." His committee was putting the Harding administration on notice that the Senate would not allow the secretary of the Treasury to act on foreign policy matters without its approval.[44]

Penrose nonetheless gave Mellon a chance to allay concerns by asking him, "There is no intention on the part of the present administration to cancel or forgive any part of this indebtedness of foreign nations, is there?"

"No," Mellon replied flatly.

"That has been bruited about," Penrose added, then asked, "though so far as conditions are at present, it is absolutely without foundation?"

Mellon stated categorically that the Treasury had held a consistent position that the debts "are obligations owing to their country, and valid obligations that must be eventually paid."[45]

On July 28, after more than ten hours of testimony over the course of a month, the hearing ended. The following day, newspapers reported that the Republican-majority Senate Finance Committee had voted nine to five to recommend that the Treasury secretary be granted "a free hand" to negotiate the terms for the collection of Allied war debts. La Follette, as expected, voted with the Democratic minority.[46]

But it wasn't as final as that, and Mellon's hand would not be as free as he hoped it might be.

2

CHURCHILL IN THE HIGHLANDS

O n the day that President Harding announced that he intended to continue efforts to collect the war debts, Winston Churchill was serving in the British cabinet as secretary of state for the colonies. He was not, however, in his office in Whitehall or at his home in London's Sussex Square. Rather, he was at sea on the Mediterranean, aboard the Italian luxury liner *Esperia*, traveling first class with his wife, Clementine. They were returning from Egypt, a journey that would bring them back to London by way of Sicily, Naples, and Genoa, and then by train from the South of France.[1]

Although Winston had been on official Colonial Office business, Clemmie had asked to go along, mainly for the diversion and recreation. "The sea voyage in the warmth would do me good," she had explained in making her case, "and I should love it." Her husband, who had now become an avid landscape painter, had readily agreed, and had taken along his easel and brushes.

It had been an adventure for both of them. Winston had chaired a conference in Cairo, attended by more than forty delegates, to discuss how his new Middle Eastern department would handle the mandates of Mesopotamia and Palestine that had been assigned to Great Britain in the League of Nations Covenant. He had recruited T. E. Lawrence, the archeologist, army officer, and author—known as Lawrence of Arabia—as his chief advisor to help develop a plan to install Arab emirs as rulers of territories in the region, and "to make the Middle East an area which would be cheap to administer and free from political unrest." Gertrude Bell, a respected, Oxford-educated archeologist and Mideast expert in her own right, joined them as added insurance to achieve the goals of economy and stability in Britain's new mandates. "Gerty," as Lawrence called the Baghdad-based senior British government official and former intelligence officer, rivaled him in rank and shared his devotion to the Arab people.

Before he left for Egypt, Churchill had boasted to Britain's Chancellor of the Exchequer Austen Chamberlain, the guardian of the nation's finances, "I am determined to save you millions." This revealed his ambition for the conference he had so carefully choreographed, to demonstrate his ability to manage government spending effectively to the man whose job he coveted. The goal of the conference was to build support among local leaders for the adoption of a new organization of the region. The negotiations and outcomes of the conference would then be detailed in a report for the cabinet, to be presented to the House of Commons in June.[2]

Because the conference proceedings were not open to the press, most of the coverage reflected the romantic and exotic aspects of the trip. This included Churchill's painting excursions. One to the pyramids resulted in a widely published photograph of a group of the conferees in front of the Great Sphinx of Giza mounted on camels. On the day it was taken, Winston had fallen off his. Accounts differed, but all generally agreed that Churchill had been thrown by his mount. Seeing that he wasn't hurt, Clemmie lightened the moment, quipping, "How easy the mighty are fallen!" While Winston's bodyguard found the camels "misanthropic and egocentric," it seems that the accident was caused more by a loose saddle girth than a toss by a recalcitrant beast. Bell, who spoke Arabic fluently and rode camels with ease, recorded in her personal papers, that as the camel rose from its knees, the colonial secretary resembled "a mass of sliding gelatin." She also noted that Churchill was offered a horse instead but refused. "I started on a camel," he growled as he remounted, "and I shall finish on a camel."[3]

Winston Churchill, *Cairo from the Pyramids with the Artist Painting*, 1921. Churchill kept this painting, with the small image of himself at the easel, in his personal collection. It remains at Chartwell. *Credit: The National Trust, Chartwell.*

The group set off for Sakkara, a ride of nearly three hours, south through the desert. While the others toured the ancient ruins and recent excavations, Churchill planned to paint. This required "a special camel loaded with Mr. Churchill's canvases, easel, and paints." From a spot in the shade of the stepped Pyramid of Djoser, he painted a view of the Cairo skyline aglow in the yellow and chartreuse hues of the afternoon sun, across an expanse of muted desert sand straddling the green Nile valley. The shadows, reflections, and contrasts were inspired by what he later described as the "fierce and brilliant" light of Egypt.[4]

That afternoon, the others in the party had had enough of camels and decided to motor back. Lawrence dismissed the colonial secretary's camel-weary bodyguard who returned to Giza with the others. That left Churchill and Lawrence alone to make the long ride back together. The romance of the scene was imaginatively captured by a modern scholar, with the two of them making "their own way back, riding their camels through the desert at full trot all the way as if warriors together flush with victory." That was no doubt the way Churchill wanted to be seen—and the way that Lawrence wanted his Arab followers to see his British friend and ally.[5]

While they were in Egypt, news arrived from London that the post of chancellor of the exchequer had become open due to the resignation of Andrew Bonar Law, leader of the House of Commons, and the subsequent election of Austen Chamberlain to that office. This, to Churchill, was more than just an opportunity—it was a matter of right and destiny. His father had been chancellor but had risen no higher in government before his death at the age of forty-five. Winston still had his father's ceremonial robes and many knew of his ambition to be chancellor of the exchequer as a crucial step to becoming prime minister, the brass ring his father had also hoped to attain.

The British political press had fun with the pickle in which Churchill now found himself, being on another continent when the job he coveted suddenly became available on Downing Street. "There is much amusing comment at the moment," wrote the Glasgow *Daily Record*, "over the fact that while all the political excitement is astir at home, Mr. Churchill should be away, 'painting the pyramids.'" Similar reports placed him "out of the limelight" and "missing the bus."[6]

As thrilling as it had been in Egypt, seeing its majestic sites and landscapes, and riding through the desert with Lawrence, Churchill realized that his position as colonial secretary was too narrow and confining. Even before he had reached the first port of call on the return trip aboard the *Esperia*, he lamented having been out of the loop in London. On his second day at sea, April 2, the London papers reported that Lloyd George had appointed Robert Horne, not Winston Churchill, to the post of chancellor of the exchequer. It was not the ending to the Cairo conference he had imagined.

As important as the chancellorship was in Churchill's ambition, participation in the British government's relations with the United States figured even more prominently in his plans. In addition to the devastating news of the Horne appointment, he would also learn what had happened at the Harding cabinet meeting on April 1. The decision to seek repayment of the loans made to the Allies, coupled with the policy to abstain from the settlement of reparations, proved to Churchill that the United States intended to withdraw from a collective approach to the reconstruction of Europe. This made the limitations of his present job even more frustrating, not only because it restricted his influence in British political circles, but it prevented him from having a leading voice in the international dialogue on world affairs.

While Churchill was crossing the Mediterranean, the Washington correspondent for *The Times* observed that "on the one hand, America is giving notice to the world that she stands with the Allies for the consummation of the victory gained as the result of common action, but on the other she allows the Allies to understand the manner of her cooperation 'for the good of the world' must be conditioned upon the interests of her own citizens to a greater degree than is believed to have been thought desirable by Mr. Wilson."[7]

❧

Back in London, Churchill brooded. He felt "cheated" of the chance to become chancellor of the exchequer by his fickle ally, David Lloyd George. It simply was not fair.[8]

For two weeks, he had listened to the heady arguments of Bell and Lawrence about what Britain owed to the Arabs and Palestinians. Now home, the news from Washington confirmed that not only had the Harding administration taken the position that Europe owed it billions of dollars, but that there was no longer any hope of the United States joining the League of Nations.

By June, he was speaking out on subjects that were clearly not in the portfolio of the colonial secretary. In a speech in Manchester, some two hundred miles north of London, he revived the theme of his 1919 article, "Will America Fail Us?" He was now thoroughly convinced that it would.

"As long as these colossal debts hang over the world," he warned, "all its financial arrangements will be disorganized, and its trade will be gravely and grievously restricted." This marked the beginning of his growing conviction that the United States was shirking its moral obligation to cancel, rather than collect, the war debts. He would appoint himself to take up that cause. First though, he needed to claim the mantel of statesman and did so when he told the Manchester audience: "It is no good trusting in a paper League of Nations," suggesting that it should now be "the part of Britain" to lead France and Germany "to set Europe on her feet again."[9]

Lord Curzon, the foreign secretary, promptly complained that Churchill was exceeding his authority and speaking in a way that led the press to assume his statements were "invested with special Cabinet authority," which they were not.[10]

This did not deter Churchill. He knew he had something the others lacked, and that was the ability to get his name, and more importantly, his ideas, into newspapers. In what was becoming a more connected world with faster communications, he could make news when he painted pyramids or posed on a camel. Readers and editors in world capitals saw him not just as a politician, but as an engaging personality and irresistible character. His plan was to resurrect his political career by speaking—and writing—as a leading thinker on prominent issues, not as an obedient member of a stodgy British cabinet.

An opportunity soon came about with the news that the United States planned to have a "conference on the limitation of armament" in Washington. Prime Minister Lloyd George received the invitation on July 10 and announced the following day that he was accepting it. After months of tensions between the United States, Great Britain, and Japan over their respective plans to achieve naval supremacy, this pleased the British government and particularly, Winston Churchill. He wanted to be involved and immediately started drafting a cabinet memorandum. He could see the linkage between sea power, the global economy, and war debts; and cautioned that the conference "may possibly end in the United States having decisively the strongest navy in the world."

Germany had turned over its important naval ships to be dismantled or sunk, and many of its commercial ships as reparations, leaving Great Britain, the United States, and Japan as the three major military powers at sea. If Britain were to reduce her fleet in a disarmament agreement, the United States might take over the rule of the seas that the Royal Navy had long commanded. "If they choose to put up the money," Churchill argued, the United States had "a good chance of becoming the strongest Naval Power in the world and thus obtaining the complete mastery of the Pacific."

War debts, as far as Churchill was concerned, belonged on the conference agenda. In his four-page memo, he suggested that "some arrangement in regard to international debt" should be discussed. He warned, "The American jingo forces who will be pushing their naval programme will also press for the strictest execution in payments of debt and interest on the debt."[11]

This was an accurate projection. In late July, on the floor of the US Senate, William Borah, a Republican from Idaho and a fierce opponent of military spending, suggested that the United States use the war debts as a lever to compel France and Great Britain to disarm. "Should some of the deliberating nations show a reluctance to enter wholeheartedly into the discussions," he argued, "this government would feel justified on insisting on a prompt payment of its debts." He added that Great Britain was spending $2 billion yearly on her army and navy, while France, "the most militaristic nation on earth, was maintaining an army of eight hundred thousand men." Meanwhile, they were not paying even the interest due on their loans to the United States.[12]

DISARM OR PAY UP, BORAH TELLS EUROPE was a headline in the *New York Times*, and the idea took hold in Congress, which announced pointedly that Mellon's bill for "unlimited authority" to collect the Allied war debts would not move forward until after the November disarmament conference was held.[13]

In London, the American idea of leveraging the Allied indebtedness was reported as using the war debts "as a club to force disarmament." On August 3, Churchill injected himself publicly into the matter in the House of Commons, speaking in favor of a bill to spend millions of pounds on the British naval program, which included four new "capital ships." This term was used for warships of the first rank in size and armament, each equipped with sixteen-inch guns, and comparable to—or better than—the ships planned by the United States and Japan, which had been detailed in an American study of comparative naval strength published in January by news organizations on both sides of the Atlantic. Without superior capital ships, Churchill argued, Britain risked sinking to the position of a third-rate naval power, echoing the British Admiralty's earlier warning to the cabinet in response to the American report. He supported the admiralty's position that the Royal Navy should again rule the seas, and that the British Empire required the largest fleet in the world.[14]

"We must rely at sea on our own strength," Churchill told the Commons, and stressed that there should never be a need to supplement the island nation's sea power with that of other governments.

"Only in that way," he said, "would we be able at the Washington conference to play the part of a real peacemaker; only in that way to be able to walk hand in hand with the United States, not as a supplicant for protection, but as an equal partner in a common victory and an equal partner in the fair future of the world."[15]

It was a moving speech. His audience loved it, and cheered. The *Westminster Gazette* noted with a left-handed compliment that "his gestures and voice had an agreeableness and dignity which they do not always have." The new American ambassador in London, George Harvey, sent a telegram to the US secretary of state, quoting from Churchill's speech and reporting that an amendment to kill the spending bill was "defeated by 346 votes to 34." Churchill's speech, and the fact that *The Times* of London came out against it, appeared in hundreds of American newspapers, and launched several editorials about naval disarmament. In Paris, *Le Matin* noted that the British vote to build the "quatre superdreadnoughts" made a curious preface to a disarmament conference.[16]

Churchill understood, however, that if you were going to negotiate disarmament, it would help to be armed to the teeth when you arrived.

Churchill's hope to discuss war debts at the Washington conference was dashed when Treasury Secretary Andrew Mellon announced on August 16 that no "international conference on finance" would be held "simultaneous with the disarmament conference," which was planned for November 11, the third anniversary of the Armistice. Churchill and Mellon had not yet met, but now there was a name connected to the US policy of collecting the war debts.[17]

☙

Like several of his colleagues in the British cabinet, Churchill had planned to spend his summer holiday in Scotland. The moors and glens of the Highlands offered a respite from his disappointments and the mounting public displeasure with the Lloyd George government over spiraling unemployment and growing tensions with Ireland. His plan also made his annual visit to his constituency in Dundee on the eastern coast of Scotland more convenient. Despite living almost five hundred miles away in London,

Churchill had represented the working-class city in Parliament since 1908, when Sir George Ritchie, a local political leader, determined that "we must get that brilliant young man to represent the city and put Dundee on the map." They became devoted friends and allies over the years; Ritchie kept Churchill informed on local matters and organized his infrequent visits while Churchill focused on national issues in London.[18]

Earlier that summer, Ritchie had alerted Churchill to the growing despair in Dundee as the Lloyd George government sought more austerity in social benefit programs, particularly in unemployment assistance. More than 20 percent of the population of Churchill's district were unemployed, and many were without adequate food or shelter. As misery turned into devastation, accusations that Churchill was not serving his electorate were taking root. The strife had reached the point, Ritchie warned, that jeopardized Churchill's seat in Parliament. He would have an opportunity to win back voters on September 24, when he was scheduled to give a speech in Dundee. But what could he say to his local constituency when the national government he also represented was failing to alleviate their suffering?[19]

While many in London society would be heading north in late summer to shoot grouse and catch salmon, Churchill was not intending to go there to hunt or fish. He needed the time to think and reflect so that he could write a speech that would save his seat in the Commons.

Before Churchill could get away from London on holiday, a family tragedy occurred. His beloved two-year-old daughter, Marigold, died suddenly from blood poisoning on August 23. It had already been a wrenching year of personal losses—his mother to a gangrene infection, and his brother-in-law to suicide—but this bereavement left Churchill and his wife, Clementine, "stupefied by grief."[20]

They had not expected Marigold's death from what seemed at first a routine childhood illness. While Winston and Clemmie had stayed behind to attend to their ill daughter in Kent, they sent their other three children on to Lochmore, a lodge eighty miles northwest of Inverness, high in the Scottish Highlands. The visit had been planned for some months. Sadly,

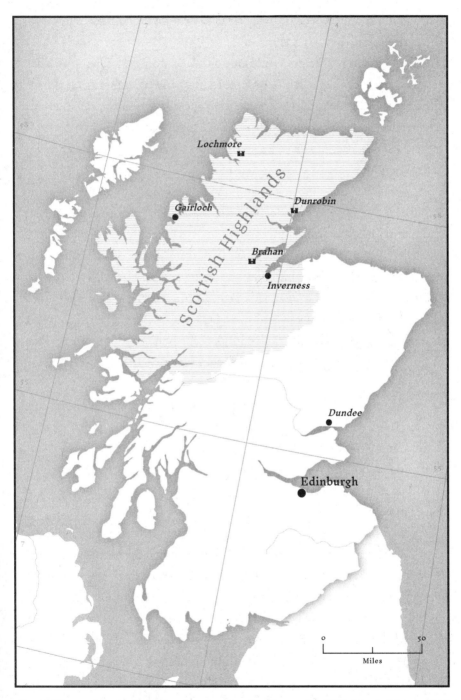

Churchill's travels in Scotland from late August to late September 1921. *Map by Morgan Kraft.*

Marigold did not recover and what was to be a joyful holiday reunion for the entire family never came to be.

After burying Marigold in London, Winston and Clemmie then rejoined their children at Lochmore. It was only by chance that during the time they needed most to grieve, they were in one of the most remote and beautiful places on the British island, staying with perhaps Winston's closest friend, Hugh Grosvenor, the Duke of Westminster, whom many called Bendor.[21]

It was a place they knew well and remembered for its good fishing and remarkably vivid sunsets reflected off a high stone hill in shades of lilac and plum. The Churchill family spent ten days there. Winston had known Benny, as he called his friend, since they were young officers during in the Boer War. They had shared many adventures and holidays, but what connected them most during this visit was that Bendor had also lost a child, his four-year-old son and only male heir, who had died in 1909. The recent tragedy was "a bitter reminder" for Bendor and his wife Violet of their loss, and they "did everything they could do to console" Winston and Clemmie.[22]

During the first week of September, Clemmie took charge of settling the children in school back in London, while Winston's sense of duty drove him to press on through his grief, even though it meant leaving her. She understood this and supported him. As their daughter Mary Soames would later explain, Clemmie "sustained him by her love and her belief in his destiny."[23]

As previously planned, Winston made a sixty-mile trip east to Dunrobin Castle, the home of another family friend. Located on the northeast coast of Scotland, overlooking the Moray Firth inlet from the North Sea, Dunrobin was built in the Scots baronial style—a romantic blend of French chateau and Scottish fort—with narrow turrets capped with conical spires and a few battlements for effect. A private train, the *Dunrobin*, ferried royal visitors and special friends like Churchill in an observation car that enabled travelers to view the Highland scenery with their backs to the engine as they made their way to Dunrobin's own rail station.[24]

An eastern view of Dunrobin Castle in Sutherland County of the Scottish Highlands. *From a 1908 postcard.*

The aristocratic amenities of the 189-room castle offered comfort and refuge. Owned by the Duke of Sutherland, whom Churchill knew as Geordie, Dunrobin was built on a cliff above the sea, with parterres and fountains between it and a stretch of beach. To the west were thousands of acres of craggy woodlands, where stags with magnificent antlers could be stalked and shot for sport. It was the natural beauty of the place, however, that Churchill now sought. He wrote to Clemmie that he was setting "off to the river" with paints and canvas "to catch pictures—much better fun than salmon." All the while though, he wrote of "feeling the hurt" of the loss of "the Duckadilly," his pet name for Marigold.[25]

Geordie was also mourning a family loss. His younger brother Alistair, a decorated war veteran, had recently died at the age of thirty-one. While serving as a captain in the Royal Horse Guards, he had been severely wounded in action and left for dead by the Germans in a trench. For his gallantry in battle, he had been awarded the Military Cross. Geordie had not only lost his brother, but also his only heir. Winston noted, in his letter to Clemmie, that he had first visited Dunrobin more than twenty years ago, when Geordie and Alistair were "little boys," lamenting that "now Alistair is buried near his father's grave overlooking the bay."[26]

The other guests at Dunrobin were mostly in their late twenties and early thirties, and included the Prince of Wales and his brother, the Duke of York, both of whom Churchill knew, owing to his own aristocratic bloodline. While the future kings and Geordie went stalking for deer, Winston told Clemmie he preferred to go out to "my stream," where he painted "a beautiful river in the afternoon light with crimson and golden hills in the background."[27]

Geordie and his wife were modern in outlook. They were film fans known for treating guests to evening cinema parties featuring the latest American movies, many starring their friends Mary Pickford and Douglas Fairbanks. Churchill described the enormous party as a lively set, who played constant lawn tennis and had many pleasant things to do, yet the heartbroken visitor found them "extremely young." At forty-six, Winston confessed to Clemmie that "the reflections of middle age are mellow."[28]

Despite being distraught over his family loss and Clemmie's grief, his constituency speech was never far from his mind. In writing to Clemmie of painting outdoors in his newfound spot, he also told her that he had been "thinking out the headings" of the address to his constituency and hoped he would be "given a quiet and patient hearing as I intend to make a very careful and thoughtful speech."[29]

Churchill was not the only one thinking about the political situation. On the same day he wrote Clemmie, a newspaper in Northern Ireland noted that "Mr. Churchill's appearance at Dundee next Saturday is being anticipated as an event of importance in the political world." It would be "the first big platform opportunity for stating the Cabinet's point of view on Ireland and unemployment."[30]

Churchill's time for reflection and speechwriting had already been interrupted once during his holiday in the Highlands by the call of duty. Lloyd George, who was vacationing a hundred miles to the west, near the seacoast town of Gairloch, had summoned his cabinet to an urgent meeting in Inverness, the capital of the Scottish Highlands, to discuss several alarming political developments. Demands from the Sinn Féin party for Ireland's independence were provoking more deadly violence and threats of civil war. Demonstrations, brought on by spiraling unemployment, were turning more destructive, too, as an anguished British populace saw little economic relief in sight. In addition, a strategy was needed for the upcoming disarmament conference in Washington.

In acknowledging Inverness city leaders for arranging the "momentous" cabinet meeting on short notice, Lloyd George told reporters that the "historic precedent" for holding a "Cabinet Council" meeting in Inverness went back all the way to Mary, Queen of Scots. For the ministers already on holiday in Scotland, it was a drive of an hour or two, but for the unfortunate few in London, it was a ten-hour, 560-mile train trip. For Churchill, the meeting took valuable time away from his speechwriting. The "historic occasion" also involved him in two motoring accidents on the way there and back, and a two-night stay at Brahan Castle, which Lord Seaforth had made available to accommodate Lloyd George and his cabinet.[31]

Between the Inverness meeting and Churchill's return to Dunrobin, riots broke out in major cities across the United Kingdom, including Dundee, where thousands of unemployed took to the streets in the dark of night. By daylight, blocks of broken storefront windows marked their rampage. On September 9, thirty-two people appeared in Dundee police court on charges of mobbing, rioting, and "shop-breaking." One woman was arrested for the theft of two tins of condensed milk and a roast mutton. A laborer was charged with stealing "a flannelette sheet" from a draper's shop. Three other men were apprehended after breaking into a public house and making off with three gallons of brandy. Government support was coming to an end for many of the unemployed and there was scant political will in Parliament to change the law to extend benefits. [32]

Knowing he was in the untenable position of having to defend government policies that exacerbated the miseries of his constituency, Churchill asked Ritchie to arrange a meeting for him with the Dundee Town Council on September 23, the day before his widely anticipated constituency address. With so much riding on the speech, Churchill calculated that it was better to let his critics express their hostilities before the local Town Council than at a packed hall of constituents that was certain to be covered by the national press. Just a week earlier, Churchill confided his apprehensions to a fellow cabinet member: "What on earth I am to say I cannot yet conceive." [33]

Churchill missed his first planned event in Dundee—a conference on the women's vote sponsored by the Dundee's Women's Liberal Association—scheduled for Thursday evening, September 22. His departure from the Highlands had been delayed due to Lloyd George summoning his ministers to a second conference in Gairloch the night before, to discuss developments in Ireland and the growing unrest caused by unemployment. Churchill had to motor west from Dunrobin, a seventy-mile journey over rugged, but beautiful, country. A reporter who made the trip from Inverness to Gairloch—in a motor coach with eight Labour Party mayors from London who wanted to speak to the prime minister about unemployment—described the route as going "through the wildest and grandest of Highland scenery, by rocky defiles and over mountain oases, where we watched the wild deer and the glorious tumbling of mountain torrents." Their trip took six and a half hours. Another of their sightings was Churchill's car passing them on the way.[34]

The Gairloch meeting began on Wednesday evening and reconvened Thursday morning, ending just before noon. Churchill then motored to Inverness, arriving barely in time to catch the 4:20 P.M. train to Dundee, a five-hour trip, which would not get him to Dundee in time to attend the women's conference. Ritchie stood in for him, but they both knew that it was a significant missed opportunity for Churchill, as women represented almost half of Dundee's eighty-thousand voters.[35]

While few knew of his change of plans, the police still closed the public entrances and exits at Dundee's train station in response to threats made to disrupt Churchill's visit. Reporters were stationed outside while a small group of local dignitaries, including Ritchie, waited inside for the train's 9:25 P.M. arrival. Moments after it steamed into the station, Churchill stepped onto the platform. Clad in a dark overcoat, with a Homburg on his head and a walking stick in hand, he made his way out of the station to an awaiting car, surrounded by an entourage of well-wishers. Despite the friendly welcome, police took no chances and stood on the running boards of the car as it motored to the Royal Hotel, where he would stay during his visit.[36]

Continued threats kept authorities on high alert the following day. Shadowed again by his loyal bodyguard, Churchill and Ritchie walked to the Town Council's morning meeting to discuss the government's unemployment policies and allow the town folk to vent their frustrations. There, outraged residents accused the government, and Churchill personally, of not taking action to alleviate the suffering caused by unemployment. Dundee's MP tried to diffuse hostilities by offering hope for future enhancements to unemployment assistance. While highly contentious, the meeting achieved

Churchill's objectives. Angry Dundonians had had their say, and their response was covered mainly by the local papers.[37]

Churchill's constituency address the following afternoon, September 24, was held at Caird Hall, Dundee's newly completed concert facility. A local philanthropist had made the eponymous gift to lead the transformation of the depressed section of the city and spur the building trades. Police officers patrolled the streets on both foot and horseback. Jobless demonstrators carrying banners assembled near the hall, some wedging themselves into the crowd. At one point, police diverted a gang seemingly intent on storming the hall.

To encourage Churchill supporters and deter demonstrators, Ritchie organized the event as admission by ticket only. A queue of ticketholders, some four abreast, stretched along the front side of the building. Hundreds of requests for tickets had been refused. After discovering that counterfeits had been distributed, Ritchie stationed officials at the entrance doors behind the massive columns of the front façade to check tickets for authenticity.[38]

As threatening as the atmosphere was outside the hall, the audience inside took their seats as quietly as if they were in church. More than three thousand people gave Churchill a largely cordial welcome when he stood up from his chair at the center of the raised platform, flanked by local leaders. Mostly bald, of stout heart and body, and brimming with vitality, Dundee's member of Parliament pushed back his finely tailored morning coat, putting his left hand on his hip. With the double chain of his pocket watch fixed to his waistcoat and the text of his speech in the other hand, he was ready to begin his address.

Beginning with an acknowledgment of the harshness of the postwar years still shaping the present day, Churchill struck a rapport with his audience. He called on their patriotism in reaffirming the government's position on Ireland, further drawing them into his sway.

His *séjour* at Dunrobin had given him time to see a path forward. He would argue that unemployment was not entirely the fault of the British government, but a consequence of America's reluctance to take responsibility for its obligations to Europe, and, most particularly, for its shortsightedness on war debts.[39]

Churchill charged that the United States was blind to the fact that the war debts could never be repaid. "Monstrous debts of hundreds and even thousands of millions of pounds," he asserted, "have been scored up by one great country against another. These debts and indemnities far exceed the means and methods of payment." This assessment had been made previously by other economists and financial leaders, but Churchill made the charge his own, striking an emotional chord in describing the madness of it all.

He continued, reasoning that there was no practical way for countries to repay either in goods or gold without damaging the market economies of creditor and debtor nations alike. "The countries who are to receive the payment," he insisted, "can only receive a limited quantity of foreign goods dumped as a result of a war debt or a war indemnity in any one year without gravely affecting their own industrial system and taking the bread out of the mouths of their own working people." This was particularly true in the wake of new tariffs erected by the Harding administration and those in place across Europe. Policymakers were using tariffs to effectively increase prices of imported goods to make them less attractive to domestic buyers.

The consequence of the American government's myopia, Churchill argued, was the collapse of world trade—and the resulting unemployment—under the weight of the billions of dollars in loan obligations to America hanging over the world. This echoed his Manchester speech from three months earlier. To bring home his argument to Dundonians, he pointed to the crowds of their unemployed neighbors demonstrating in the streets just outside the hall as proof. Many inside could hear them singing songs that championed the working poor and the socialist movement.

Churchill went on to tell his audience that they would be paying high taxes for years to come because Great Britain could not "repudiate the interest" on the debt to the United States, which cost the nation approximately £350 million a year. The bottom line, he claimed, was that America's determination to collect the debts compelled European leaders to divert their attention from the needs of their people. He beseeched his listeners to envision the "curious spectacle—if, indeed, it were not so pathetic—the great nations of the world present at this moment!" Churchill urged them to see the folly: "The great gifted nations in the civilized world—America, England, France, Italy—all hoping to get enormous sums of money out of each other or out of Germany . . . you may say that debt collecting has become a principal industry and takes first place in the minds of many politicians and Parliaments and even peoples."

Churchill had a remedy. He proposed settling war debts by moving them off the world's balance sheet into an alchemy of paper losses. "It would, in my opinion," he posited, "be for the benefit of the world if all international obligations arriving out of the war were reconsidered, were reduced to practical dimensions, and placed in a category by themselves." Churchill did not originate the idea of pooling or consolidating the war debts. While he was drafting his constituency speech at Dunrobin, a Belgian delegate at a meeting of the League of Nations in Geneva had suggested it, and newspapers had featured the idea in headlines. Cheers erupted as Churchill sold the borrowed idea to his primed audience.

Using humor to his advantage, Churchill invoked an image of the "mountains of gold in her vaults"—meaning those in the United States. "Many of those bright sovereigns we used to see in by-gone days all safely packed away," he jabbed sarcastically and so expressively that it was understood what he meant—now, over there, in America! This brought laughter from the crowd as they visualized their money stacked in the vaults of New York bankers.

Turning to the upcoming conference in Washington on disarmament, he said he had "high hopes." Churchill noted that the conference marked "the effective reentry of the United States into the responsibilities and difficulties of world politics." Knowing that his remarks would reach a larger audience, Churchill proposed that Washington consider adding economic issues to the conference agenda, specifically the matter of "normal exchanges"—reiterating once again his point about the disruption caused by war debts to global trade—which would be "more valuable" and "even more urgent" than a discussion on disarmament.

He tempered his optimism for the reengagement of the United States, however, by reminding his listeners that America had abandoned Europe by not ratifying the Treaty of Versailles or joining the League of Nations. Churchill urged them to see that, since the illness of President Wilson, there had been a "void" in American leadership. "For nearly two years," he asserted, "some of the greatest questions, involving the life and death of peoples, had to remain unanswered, and even untouched" while Britain and France waited "to learn what part, if any, the United States would play."

He closed, seemingly intending to praise America, saying "I rejoice, therefore, to see that mighty power, with all its influence, with all its ideals, with all its undoubtedly good intentions," but then finished his thought by shaming the United States for the long delay in assuming "the position which is at once her duty and her due."[40]

In one hour and ten minutes, Churchill had deftly shifted part of the blame for Europe's ills to the United States. He received thirty bursts of cheers during his speech, a standing ovation, and loud applause at the finish. Nevertheless, police officers whisked him out the back door while the audience was still on its feet and escorted him back to his hotel and, shortly thereafter, to the train that would take him home to Clemmie and his family in London.[41]

Churchill won plaudits and praise in Britain for the Caird Hall speech, especially for the idea to "wipe the slate clean of international indebtedness . . . in the true interest of all parties," by pooling war debts. An Irish reporter observed, "it looks then as if Mr. Churchill, in his Dundee speech, was giving Washington a lead."[42]

Across the Atlantic, the New York Times reported that Churchill's remarks were viewed by Washington observers as "significant." They related, though, that his suggestion to discuss war debts at the upcoming conference in Washington had not made "a favorable impression." The article relayed the official US position on the matter, stating that, "The American delegation in the conference will be in no position to discuss the pooling of the allied war debts until Congress enacts the pending bill giving authority to the Secretary of the Treasury for the refunding of foreign debt."[43]

With the death of his daughter casting its shadow, Churchill's month-long holiday in Scotland began in sorrow, but his time there gave rise to an unanticipated opportunity to be at the center of cabinet activities. In the three most pressing political issues of the moment—peace with Ireland, unemployment, and the Washington disarmament conference—he had been included as a valued conferee and voice. His appointment as one of the eight ministers empowered to deal with Irish negotiations on an emergency basis boosted his standing. The New York papers reported that he was likely to be one of the four delegates from Britain appointed to attend the disarmament talks, citing his experience as first lord of the admiralty and other cabinet posts which "could be of great service in Washington."[44]

His travels to Inverness and Gairloch and the meaningful time spent with the prime minister had also enhanced his standing as a statesman. Choosing to attend the last-minute meeting in Gairloch instead of the women's event in Dundee, however, offended female voters in his home district. That decision would hurt Churchill in the election the following year, especially as he was already perceived as an opponent of women's suffrage. Nonetheless, the net effect of his summer holiday elevated both his national and international reputation.[45]

In a confidential memorandum to the Lloyd George cabinet, titled "The Unemployment Situation" and dated four days after delivering his Dundee speech, Churchill proposed how Britain should handle its indebtedness to the United States. He asserted that while "we are not free agents, nor have we the power to decide," there was "no doubt in which direction we should strive to go." He was referring to the position both the prime minister and the chancellor of the exchequer had taken by publicly calling into question the fairness of requiring the repayment of debts incurred in the common cause of war. Churchill advised, "We only have the power to discover and declare a policy and to labor through every channel of diplomacy, finance, and trade to secure the concurrence of other powers in that policy."[46]

In other words, Churchill believed that public opinion in Europe and America needed to change. He was arguing for Britain to launch a campaign to compel the United States to cancel war debts based on moral principle. It was unstated, but understood, that he intended to play a leading role in it.

3

THE BALFOUR NOTE

B y the winter of 1922, Ailsa and "A. W.," as Mellon was called by his family, had settled into their Washington apartment at 1785 Massachusetts Avenue, one block east of Dupont Circle and less than a mile from the Treasury Building. The twenty-room suite spanned the entire top floor of the Beaux-Arts building. It had been designed to be one of the most luxurious residences in the city and was described as one that would be perfectly at home in the eighth arrondissement of Paris.[1]

Almost two dozen French windows and a balcony wrapped around Mellon's quarters, distinguishing it from the other apartments below. Conceived for elegant living and entertaining made easy by modern convenience, it offered multiple telephone extensions, a walk-in refrigerator, cedar closets, a silver safe, service elevator, and a servants' wing with bedrooms for five maids. The dining room measured over eight hundred square feet and could accommodate large dinner-and-dance parties, which were popular at the time.

The apartment provided the perfect setting for Mellon's growing art collection, which now included Turner's *Mortlake Terrace* and Rembrandt's *Lucretia*. An oval reception hall, opulent living room, and grand salon, all with fourteen-foot ceilings, offered an ideal space for guests to appreciate the fine paintings and choice appointments. A friend pointed out that the annual rent for the apartment's eleven thousand square feet would be more than double the Treasury secretary's salary. The affectionate dig elicited a faint smile from Mellon, who replied, "Every little bit helps."[2]

For the first time in either of their lives, the diffident A. W., and the similarly aloof Ailsa, engaged in the whirl of social events and official functions that came with public life in Washington. During the month of January, they hosted dinners in their apartment for President and Mrs. Harding as well as for the vice president and Mrs. Coolidge. In the week between those dinners, they held another for Secretary of State Charles Evans Hughes and his wife and included Mrs. Cornelius Vanderbilt, the celebrated socialite, as a special guest. While A. W. attended formal functions and state receptions all month, including a dinner in honor of the former British prime minister, Arthur Balfour, Ailsa sometimes filled in for her father at events, as she did at a White House reception for the Diplomatic Corps.[3]

A Washington newspaper wrote that Mellon was rather averse to having his twenty-year-old daughter assume the heavy burdens of a cabinet hostess, which the reporter noted were "very heavy indeed," adding that "her youth always seems particularly striking when she stands beside the wives of other political officeholders, or accompanies her father to official functions, where most of the guests are twice her age." There was nothing girlish or unsophisticated about Ailsa, though. Habitually dressed in haute couture, with her pale auburn hair coiffed in a smart bob, Ailsa understood the privilege and responsibility her father's wealth had bestowed on her. It was the contrast between her age and the seasoned indifference she projected that truly set her apart. The effect acted as a shield around her tall, lithe frame as she "assumed her place as a cabinet hostess."[4]

Ailsa's love of dancing enabled her to overcome her awkward shyness and to enjoy social life in those early months in Washington. During the December holiday season of 1921, she had hosted a dinner-and-dance soirée in the apartment for over a hundred guests, whom the press reported as mostly "of the younger set." A. W. was not fond of dancing, but he was happy to follow his daughter's lead.[5]

While Mellon was adjusting to the social demands and ceremonial obligations of his position as Treasury secretary, he was also adapting to other unfamiliar pressures. Having never answered to higher authority during his business career, Mellon now found himself at retirement age, subject to government oversight, political forces, and public opinion.

On January 31, 1922, the Senate passed legislation that implicitly denied the request he had made to the Senate Finance Committee in the summer of 1921, for complete autonomy and broad powers to settle the outstanding war debts. Instead, Congress established a five-member World War Foreign Debt Commission devised expressly to limit Mellon's authority, although allowing him to chair it as Treasury secretary. The other four members were appointed by the president but required the consent of the Senate. They included Secretary of State Charles Evans Hughes, Secretary of Commerce Herbert Hoover, Senator Reed Smoot of Utah, and Representative Theodore Burton of Ohio. All were Republicans.

Resentment of the executive branch, and fear that Mellon would be inclined to cancel the war debts, further provoked Congress to impose strict terms for settlement, setting a minimum interest rate of 4.25 percent with a maximum repayment period of twenty-five years. To make congressional power over US policy on war debts absolute, the legislation expressly forbade any cancellation of foreign indebtedness.[6]

Although it had little opposition from either party, it was an ill-conceived piece of legislation and would create problems rather than solve them. It sent the whole matter of settling the war debts on a politically charged track and began a moralistic debate that would embroil the American and British Treasuries for years to come.

⁂

In the wake of the debt commission legislation, a highly credible critic—perhaps the most credible—emerged. Russell Leffingwell, the assistant Treasury secretary during the Wilson administration who oversaw wartime lending to the Allies, believed that the United States should take a different approach than that set by Congress.

Leffingwell had worked with the British architect of the international credit operation designed to finance the war—John Maynard Keynes—in 1917. The British Treasury had sent Keynes along on a mission to bring the US Treasury into Britain's credit operation. The reality of the circumstances, as Leffingwell put it, was that "the credit of the government of the United States was the last financial resource of the Allies."[7]

Keynes attitude toward Leffingwell and the other American government officials was described by his British colleague, Basil Blackett, as "rude, dogmatic, and disobliging," and not surprisingly, he made a "terrible impression" on them. While Blackett objected to Keynes's impolitic behavior, he agreed with the economist's feeling of superiority toward American Treasury officials, from a policy and intellectual perspective. In reality, the US Treasury leadership was as inexperienced as creditors as the British were as debtors. After the war, Keynes masterminded—to great acclaim—a movement to incinerate the "paper shackles" of wartime indebtedness in a "general bonfire," to effectively terminate the credit operation he had created. The suggested incineration, however, depended on the United States and its willingness to torch over $10 billion that had been lent to the Allies.[8]

Shortly thereafter, in February 1920, Leffingwell had fielded the request from Austen Chamberlain for a general cancellation of war debts and advised Carter Glass, Wilson's second Treasury secretary, in drafting its refusal.[9]

Many thought Leffingwell would succeed Glass when the former congressman was appointed to fill a vacancy in the Senate in 1920. Distinguished by his intellectual curiosity, penetrating gaze, and prematurely white hair, Leffingwell projected a commanding presence that inspired respect, a characteristic which perhaps goaded Keynes. Leffingwell certainly knew the job and had the qualifications. A graduate of Yale University and Columbia Law School, he had formulated much of the administration's foreign economic policy and overseen the Liberty Bond campaign, in addition to managing the Allied lending program. To the surprise of many, he was passed over by the stroke-impaired Wilson, who instead appointed his close friend, the secretary of agriculture, David Houston, to lead the Treasury Department.

In August 1920, when a second request for debt cancellation was made by Prime Minister Lloyd George directly to President Wilson, Leffingwell had already resigned from the Treasury department and returned to the New York law firm he had left to serve in government. Knowing that he took with him the reasoning behind US war debt policy, he continued to advise the Treasury Department and to be kept well-informed by Assistant Treasury Secretary Parker Gilbert, whom he had recruited from his firm to succeed him. This provided a conduit for institutional knowledge concerning war debt policy to pass from Leffingwell through Gilbert to Mellon.

With the creation of the debt commission in 1922 by Congress, Leffingwell believed that the British government would once again press for cancellation. Given that Congress had expressly forbidden the commission from doing so, this would leave little leeway for negotiation by Mellon and the commissioners. While Leffingwell had been opposed to Britain's calls for outright cancellation of all war indebtedness, his thinking had evolved to one of practical consideration. He believed Congress, in its legislation, was being not only unreasonable, but acting contrary to American economic interests, and "utterly stupid" politically.

In May 1922, Leffingwell gave a speech to the American Academy of Political and Social Science, with the intention to warn of the economic consequences of the short-sighted congressional legislation. He argued that the commission should have "adequate power to consider the problem of inter-Allied indebtedness, not with its hands tied and eyes blindfolded" as he believed this one was. He asserted that some concessions to the European Allies were not only necessary but wise. "The international war debts do not represent wealth created, but wealth destroyed," he reasoned. "In this respect, they differ from private international debts created in the ordinary course of business." This was not an unfamiliar view to the audience as it built on an essential point he had made in an article published earlier in the academy's journal. In that article, he had written: "We were engaged in war, not conducting a commercial operation. Indeed, there was no rate of interest which would float several billion dollars of Liberty Bonds or Notes as a commercial operation." Leffingwell had tried to lay bare the deceit he believed to be at the core of congressional thinking on war debts that the indebtedness of the Allies to the United States represented political debts, not commercial loans.[10]

Leffingwell's comments were clearly directed to Congress, but its members were not in the audience. Moreover, Leffingwell was no longer a government official, which further limited his influence.

"It is childish," he admonished, "to continue to assert that all the debts must be paid when everyone knows that some of them can't and won't be."[11] Leffingwell argued for Congress to allow the commission to approach the debts realistically, more as political debts, given the economic reality of the Allies' circumstances. His argument for forbearance, however, went against not only current thinking in Congress, but American public opinion as well.

A few months later, Leffingwell tried once again to persuade Congress to see the advantages of taking a more benevolent stance, this time writing in the *Yale Review*, "The future of civilization, we know, depends so largely upon Anglo-Saxon cooperation and good will that it is of extreme importance that the British debt to the United States be so dealt with as not to leave a sense of injustice either in America or in England." He argued that, "the maintenance of the debts as valid obligations impairs the credit of the debtors; is a grave handicap to their economic recovery; and, therefore, is a grave obstacle to the world's trade and to our own welfare." Thus, he concluded, restoring credit to the European Allies was essential. "The debtors are not only debtors but customers," he wrote. "We could not afford to hold the debts over them if there were no likelihood of their being paid. A good customer is better than an insolvent debtor."[12]

That was an argument that resonated with Andrew Mellon, and one that he, as Treasury secretary, would make going forward. For the time being, however, Mellon and the debt commission had no choice but to proceed on the course set by Congress.

∽

On the morning of April 18, 1922, Mellon convened the first meeting of the World War Foreign Debt Commission at the Treasury Building on Pennsylvania Avenue in a conference room in his suite of offices on the third floor. It would become the commission's office until its term concluded. Press photographers were brought in to commemorate the event, with the five commission members—Mellon, Hughes, Hoover, Smoot, and Burton—seated around an oval wooden table under an oil portrait of a previous treasury secretary whose likeness appeared as solemn as theirs.[13]

Eliot Wadsworth, the assistant Treasury secretary, whom Mellon had chosen to accompany him to the Senate Finance Committee hearings, was the only other Treasury employee present. The commission voted first to make Wadsworth its secretary with responsibility for taking the minutes. After granting themselves a $20,000 budget for expenses, the commissioners then passed a resolution that reiterated the United States policy on war debts. Each of the debtor nations would be asked to submit a proposal for how it planned to settle its debts. The resolution directed Hughes, as secretary of state, to inform them that the commission "desires to receive any proposals or representations which said Government may wish to make for the settlement or refunding of its obligations."[14]

Hughes did so via telegrams to the American ambassadors, including the message: "It may be that your government will desire to send financial representatives to Washington," and if so, he added, Washington would like to be informed of the personnel who were coming and when they were "likely to arrive." There was no doubt left. The United States expected each of its borrowers to settle their debts promptly.[15]

∽

The polite but firm request from the American debt commission was no doubt unwelcome to each of its recipients. It was met with what would be described as "a deafening silence from Britain," the only solvent debtor among the Allies and the one that owed the largest amount to the United States.[16]

The British government had been wrestling with the issue of its American war debt for quite some time, but always with the idea of cancellation rather than repayment. Since the end of the war, it had assumed that the United States would join with Britain, as the war's other principal creditor, in taking cooperative action by forgiving all indebtedness incurred by the conflict. This idea of a coordinated gesture of an all-around cancellation was first proposed officially by Basil Blackett, the controller of finance of the British Treasury. A civil servant and not a politician, Blackett had become Britain's foremost expert on financial matters since Keynes's departure from His Majesty's Treasury.[17]

In a February 1920 memorandum to Austen Chamberlain, Blackett wrote, "The statesmanlike thing to be done was for the United Kingdom and the United States of America to make a 'beau geste' by offering to wipe out the whole of such indebtedness by a stroke of the pen."[18]

He added, however, that the US Treasury "has, from the first, been horrified with even the mention of such a plan," owing to congressional intransience on the issue. Blackett had observed that firsthand during the three years that he was posted in Washington.

Upon his return to London later that month, his thinking had evolved, and he recommended that Britain act alone in what he called "a dignified and independent action" to forgive all its debtors unilaterally. Blackett advised that the British Empire could afford both to forgive its debtors and to repay the US. He argued that the financial burden, "although very heavy, would not be an impossible one, and might bring some important compensations." Bearing such a burden would make Britain's example even more noble and might serve to inspire the United States to follow its example.[19]

Among those who applauded this approach was Lord Curzon, then the British foreign secretary. "We obtain the moral leadership of the world at a stroke," he enthused, "and we obtain it when it is a practical necessity for Europe to have it." He went even further than Blackett and projected that there "might well be similar action on the American side before the year was out."[20]

Winston Churchill, then secretary of state for war, had a markedly different view. Since the United States had refused for several years to even discuss Britain's rationale for a joint cancellation of all obligations originating from the war, Churchill recommended a more chastening gesture. In a memorandum dated April 23, 1920, he wrote that Curzon's support of Blackett's plan was "altogether unjustifiable," because it would weaken the British position in securing cancellation of its debt to the United States. Instead, Churchill proposed an alternate strategy: "We should declare publicly that we are perfectly ready to wipe out every European debt owing to us *if* the United States will accord us a similar release from the fifty per cent smaller sums we owe them." From this conditional and nuanced position, he said, "we should not budge." The United States, Churchill argued, "has already pillaged us of twelve hundred millions of our securities, to continue to exact from us payment to the uttermost farthing of a debt contracted for a common cause," he believed, might "call forth a violent outbreak of anger in this country."[21]

Cabinet Secretary Maurice Hankey understood that Churchill's intent was to shame the United States into cancellation. He explained in a memo addressed only to prime minister David Lloyd George: "On today's minutes you will find a mention of the subject of inter-Allied indebtedness. This was brought up without warning by Churchill." He added: "Churchill's view is that we should make it quite clear that we should like to see Germany remitted some of her debt by France; that we should be glad, in order to secure this, to remit some of France's debt to us, but only on the condition that America would make a corresponding remission of her debts. His idea is to mobilize the whole sequence of debts in this order, so as to put America in an invidious position before the world."[22]

That concept and its intention, introduced by Churchill in 1920, became the framework in 1922 for the British response to the request by Mellon and the debt commission. Rather than answering the US request for proposals to settle the debts, Churchill would persuade the British cabinet to make a proposal of its own to the Allies: if America insisted on repayment by its debtors, Britain would only collect from hers what she owed to the United States. This would become known as the Balfour Note.[23]

⚬⚭⚬

The discussions that led to the British cabinet's decision to issue the Balfour Note began only after Robert Horne, now the chancellor of the exchequer, reminded its members that Washington was still waiting for their reply some six weeks after the request arrived from the American debt commission.

On June 16, 1922, the British cabinet met in Austen Chamberlain's room in the House of Commons, a space provided for him in his new position as its leader. This would be the room in which, during three additional meetings, they would debate how to respond to America. Fourteen ministers attended the first of these sessions, and from the very beginning, it became apparent that there was a stark divide in the cabinet.

The minutes of the first meeting reflected the two opposing factions that quickly developed, but they did not always reveal the identity of the individual speakers.

One faction though, was clearly led by Horne, who was in favor of a straightforward repayment of Britain's debt to the United States. He argued that "however unconscionable we thought the attitude of the United States Government to be . . . it would be incompatible with our national honour to refuse to pay . . . and inconceivable that Great Britain would ever place herself in the humiliating position of being in fact a defaulter to America." Chamberlain, Horne's predecessor as chancellor, agreed.

The other side was led by Churchill, now serving as colonial secretary, and supported by David Lloyd George, the prime minister, who chaired the meeting. They were not only opposed to settling the debt with America, but in favor of making a proposal of their own to the Allies—all of whom were also debtors to the United States—that they should stick together and "present to America a united front" in adopting "the British view that the policy of the United States Government in the matter was a wrong policy."

The minutes recorded that the discussion revolved around several points that certain members felt needed to be communicated to the Allies. One of them was "that public opinion in the United States had little or no opportunity of learning the strength of the British case . . . it was most important that the United States should realize that by insisting on the payment of debt she would be making herself in effect the tax-gatherer and rent-collector of the civilized world."[24]

The other point involved turning the Allies against the "unreasonable and inequitable" request by America. This required that the message—which was termed a "despatch"—"emphasize the fact that, much as Great Britain regretted having to demand payment from her Allies, no other course was open to her, having regard to the action of her American creditor."

This attitude was largely along the lines of Churchill's 1920 memo about the debts and his proposal to castigate the United States for its selfish attitude. It also reflected his view that public opinion in America and Europe could be changed, "so long as we do what is just and right." Such a message, the cabinet agreed, would have to be "very carefully worded." The task of drafting it was assigned to Arthur Balfour, Britain's best-known statesman to Americans.[25]

Two weeks later, when Balfour read the first draft of the "despatch" to the cabinet, the members agreed to include two additional points. Both, however, bore disingenuous elements and reflected the considerable resentment toward the United States. The first was "a statement to the effect that Great Britain's debt to the United States was incurred for the sole purpose of financing her other Allies." This point, which had been central to Keynes's argument for all-around cancellation of war debts by bonfire, belied his own admission years earlier that "Britain had only one ally, France, and the rest were mercenaries."[26]

The second point articulated "the willingness of the British Government to forego Great Britain's reparation claims as part of a general scheme for liquidating inter-Allied debts." This was less generous than it seemed on its face. Under the Treaty of Versailles, Britain had already received a great number of Germany's merchant ships as reparations for those lost or damaged owing to the war, on a "ton for ton" basis. Germany also gave up control of its overseas colonies. Of these, South West Africa, German East Africa, New Guinea, and parts of others in Africa and Oceania came under control of the British Empire. The British "mandate" of Mesopotamia also presented an opportunity to profit from the vast oil reserves believed to exist there.[27]

Before the cabinet met again to discuss the Balfour draft, several of its members heard directly from the American ambassador in London that Washington was growing impatient to hear from them. George Harvey, whom President Harding had appointed to the prestigious diplomatic post, had been instructed by Secretary of State Hughes to take "the first opportunity to express informally" that a British representative should be sent without delay as the American debt commission desired "to begin discussions with the British Government at the earliest possible date."[28]

Harvey was a colorful character, a millionaire who had made his fortune in newspapers, street railways, and magazines. Politics, however, was his true love, and at fifty-eight, he was at the top of his game. He had worked on Woodrow Wilson's successful nomination as the Democratic Party's candidate for president in 1912, but he broke with Wilson to help defeat Wilson's pet project, the League of Nations, in 1919.

If there really was a smoke-filled room in which Warren Harding was chosen as the Republican Party nominee for president in 1920, George Harvey was in it. The zip he had added to Harding's campaign speeches played a large role in his being rewarded with the job of ambassador extraordinary and plenipotentiary of the United States to the Court of St. James's.[29]

Like Winston Churchill, Harvey understood the value of publicity and knew how to get his name and his picture in newspapers. His large, horn-rimmed "American glasses" were one of the distinctive touches in the look he had created for himself. The London papers referred to them as "his goggles." His impeccable wardrobe and tailoring, however, were entirely British.[30]

When Harvey received instructions from Hughes to remind the British cabinet that they had not responded on the debt matter, he was involved in a very different undertaking. Harvey had arranged a busy, three-week schedule for an important American visitor, William Howard Taft, who was not only a former president of the United States but the current chief justice of the Supreme Court. Like Harvey, Taft was a Harding appointee. While the Supreme Court was in its summer recess, Taft would be visiting Great Britain purportedly to study the efficiency of its lower court system, but it was also the beginning of the London social season—the annual interval of hobnobbing by British politicians and social elites in a whirl of garden parties, balls, and charity events—and Mrs. Taft would be traveling with him.

Their first event was a welcome at the Pilgrims Society dinner on June 19, which, unknown to Harvey or anyone else outside the British cabinet, took place just three days after it had decided to draft the Balfour Note. The society's purpose was to foster Anglo-American friendship. Ironically, Balfour was not only present at the dinner, but gave the welcoming toast in the ballroom of the Victoria Hotel. "The fundamental duty of the Pilgrims," he said, "whether they sit in New York or London, is to draw in ever closer the bonds which unite our two countries." Before raising his glass, he added, "Our friendship is based on solid grounds and its roots are deep."[31]

Taft replied by saluting Balfour's "high ideals of international relations," and then touched, in part, on the importance of Anglo-American unity. "We had suffered from the war," he said, "but less than our European allies. While that increases our competitive powers, it also increases our responsibility. Our people know this." He added, "They know, therefore, that it is of the utmost importance that friendly relations between the two great countries . . . should be made closer not only for the benefit of both but for the welfare of the world."[32]

The irony of the moment was undoubtedly not lost on Balfour, who had already drafted the note to the Allies expressly because neither he, nor his fellow cabinet members, believed that the American people recognized their responsibility in the aftermath of the war.

Taft and his wife had planned to stay at a London hotel, but Harvey convinced them that it would be more convenient if they stayed with him at his ambassadorial residence in Belgravia. On Saturday evening, June 24, the white stucco, four-story townhouse on Chesham Place where the ambassador resided was surrounded by hundreds of London police and agents of Scotland Yard as well as by crowds of Londoners who had gathered to watch the arrival of King George V and Queen Mary for what would be called "a glittering spectacle," reminiscent of mid-Victorian days.[33]

Forty guests had been invited by ambassador and Mrs. Harvey for a dinner in honor of Chief Justice Taft. As they arrived, the crowd outside was not disappointed. Clad in Court dress, Prime Minister Lloyd George, as well as cabinet members Lord Balfour and Lord Birkenhead, carried jeweled swords and wore "Napoleonic cocked hats." With the exception of Taft, who wore his judicial robes, the men, including Ambassador Harvey, were garbed in knee breeches and stockings. Resplendent in shimmering gowns, the women flitted about like fireflies with the sparkle of their diamond tiaras and opalescent pearls reflecting off the circling silver trays and grand mirrors. The rooms were decorated in the queen's favorite colors, pink and mauve, and the two round dining tables were topped with roses and cattleya orchids. The king took Mrs. Harvey into dinner on his arm and Ambassador Harvey escorted the queen. It may have been the high point of Harvey's social life.[34]

Remarkably, war debts came up in the conversation between King George and Chief Justice Taft, who recalled later: "He said that if we insisted on collecting the debt from Great Britain, Great Britain would have to collect her debt from France, and that would be very hard." Taft believed that the king was "evidently hoping that we would give up the debt," but he disabused him of that notion by explaining that it would be quite unpopular for the American Congress "to propose such a waiver."[35]

Despite the high-level exchange of opinions, this was not a political evening, but instead, a festive one. As the orchestra played on and American singers performed, the king and queen mingled freely, staying past midnight, which was quite unusual for them. According to a news report,

Harvey was "warmly congratulated and thanked for one of the finest evenings of the London season."[36]

Taft and Harvey seemed to have London in the palm of their hands, with luncheons, dinners, speeches, more mingling with royalty, honorary degrees for Taft, all building up to the first grand event—an outdoor Fourth of July celebration with a crowd of more than two thousand at Lansdowne House, a large estate in Berkeley Square, lent by its owner—followed that evening by a gathering of the American Society at the Savoy Hotel. "It is of the utmost importance," Taft said there, "that Britain and America should stand together." This principle that he had been advocating during his visit, that the future of the world rested on British-American cooperation, was delivered in an engaging way and was met with outward enthusiasm.[37]

Taft's status as a former president and Harvey's ambitious personality made a good combination. By this time, they had spoken together often enough to be comfortable teasing one another in front of audiences, "jollying," as a British columnist put it, and it made for good entertainment while delivering their serious message of Anglo-American friendship.[38]

British and American relations appeared to be at a high point: "More American tourists were in England today than on any Fourth of July since before the war," papers reported. American flags flew over London hotels and "head waiters asserted that not so much champagne has been sold since the Armistice."[39]

Harvey's reputation got a boost from both the British and American press, both of which noted a change in the ambassador's manner and method. Those who had regarded him as "pyramidically portentous" in the past, now saw him differently. An American correspondent who covered the Fourth of July dinner at the Savoy enthused: "There is a sparkle, a zest, a vibrancy, not only to what he says but in the way he says it, that were wholly lacking before. The American ambassador was the star of the night."[40]

⁊

Harvey's mission from Washington, however, was not only to be charming and entertaining, but to remind the British government that it had not replied to the American debt commission. This he did the following day, July 5, at 10 Downing Street, where the prime minister was hosting a small, private luncheon in honor of Taft. Afterward, the prime minister invited Harvey and Taft to remain for a discussion with cabinet members Lord Birkenhead, Winston Churchill, and Andrew Bonar Law, who had resigned from the government due to ill health but was still an influential figure in British politics.

Harvey began by explaining that the invitation to Britain to send a delegation over before the other countries "had not been accidental." Washington wanted to clear away the debt between them, so that Great Britain and the United States could "stand together as the only creditor powers in dealing with the rest." The two countries, "with their immense joint influence, would be standing on the same platform and able to adopt a common policy toward all the nations in need of help."

Harvey's message from the Harding administration about settling Britain's debt as a prerequisite to joining forces in "common policy" was not what Lloyd George and Churchill wanted to hear. They had long been advocating for the United States to agree to an all-around cancellation of the debts only to have them rebuffed. Perhaps out of frustration, they had come to the conclusion that the Balfour Note was the only course left for Britain to pursue.

Harvey had no way of knowing that and continued to deliver his message. Not sending a delegation, Harvey told them, would be "a disastrous blunder," if he might say so, "and that a great opportunity was being lost."

At times, there were two conversations going on simultaneously around the table. One of these was between Harvey and Bonar Law. Harvey planted the idea that once the British debt was funded—"at say, four and a half percent,"—the United States government could then make opportunistic bond offerings in the public markets. Because these new bond issues would have the implied backing of American credit, he argued, they would likely appreciate in value and thus "the real interest charged upon this country would fall to anything from two to two-and-a-half percent."

This, it would turn out, had not been well understood, as Bonar Law later claimed that Harvey had told him that the United States might settle the British debts at 2 to 2.5 percent interest.

While Harvey was having this conversation with Bonar Law, Lloyd George was at the other end of the table, where Taft was explaining to him that it would be best to send a delegation before a new Congress was seated in March.

A question, perhaps from Churchill, was posed. Since "the funding legislation was in any case fixed"—as it was, at no less than 4.25 percent—was there any point in sending a delegation?

Harvey replied that, yes, there was. New legislation could be pursued. The commission could report that "funding was not practicable without some amendment of the law passed last session, and the Administration might then be able to then bring in further legislation on the funding question before March." Taft concurred and argued strongly that the present opportunity should not be lost.

Harvey explained that he was speaking frankly and informally, but stressed that it was "really a crucial moment in Anglo-American relations, and he could not see why a British delegation was not sent at once." Indeed, it was a turning point, but Harvey did not realize that the prime minister's lunch would turn out to have been the last opportunity to dissuade the British government from sending a plea to cancel the debts rather than sending a delegation to the United States to settle them. [41]

Edward Grigg, Lloyd George's private secretary, who was tasked with making a record of the luncheon table conversation, had developed a deepening concern about how the cabinet was proceeding on the debt issue and in drafting the Balfour Note. Knowing that the cabinet would be meeting again on July 7, Grigg took it upon himself the night before to write a private memo of his own to the prime minister, advising him that he felt strongly that it would be a mistake to send the proposed note drafted by Balfour to the Allies. A graduate of Oxford and a former journalist, Grigg had distinguished himself during the war and had served afterward as a military attaché to the prince of Wales before taking the post of personal secretary to the prime minister.

Grigg wrote, "I feel that not to fund and pay it would be a blow to British credit and a slur on British character." Grigg's note mentioned that "the City"—London's financial center—was wholly in favor of repaying the debt. He noted that he had been influenced by Basil Blackett, the author of the "beau geste" strategy, and added, "Blackett tells me that the whole City would rather pay every penny of our debt than face the loss of our credit by trying to manoeuvre ourselves out of it." Grigg, who was aware of Churchill's efforts in framing the Balfour Note, then added, "That Winston is the protagonist of the bargaining policy deepens, if anything could, my suspicion of it." Rather than "demean ourselves," Grigg advised that Britain should instead present "a great moral example."[42]

When the cabinet met and discussed Balfour's note the next day, July 7, Lloyd George made no reference to Grigg's plea. Nor was there much effect on the cabinet by the previous week's Fourth of July rhetorical professions of Anglo-American friendship. The prime minister informed the others that he and some of his colleagues had met with Harvey and Taft and recounted what had been discussed. Principally, the American statesmen had urged them to send a delegation to Washington and to send it before March, when the current Congress would end. Lloyd George also reported that Harvey had been understood to say that "once the debt was funded . . . the real interest" might be reduced to "two to two and a half percent" in an issue of bonds backed by American credit, thus codifying the misunderstanding.

Also present at this cabinet meeting was Auckland Geddes, the British ambassador to the United States, who had returned to London after speaking with the American secretary of state, Charles Evans Hughes, ten days earlier. Geddes relayed that Hughes believed the war debts would likely have to be canceled in the long term, but that cancellation in the near term was not possible. Geddes added that Hughes had told him that Treasury Secretary Mellon shared his opinion.

"At the moment, however," Geddes stressed, it is "out of the question for any American Administration to come forward with the proposals for cancelling the debt or any substantial part of it." Geddes added that, in the United States, "public opinion regarded the debt as money actually lent by America to other countries on a commercial basis." Leffingwell's argument on this point obviously had not changed American hearts or minds.

This new information—whether from Taft, Harvey, or Geddes—did not dissuade the cabinet from the idea of dispatching Balfour's note. The ministers did agree to send a delegation to the United States in September, which they communicated to Harvey. They also made a concession to Geddes's recommendation that the note be written so as not to offend in any way "the susceptibilities of the American people."

The cabinet directed Balfour, Geddes, and Horne to review the note and to use their discretion to "soften any passages which might . . . reflect on the attitude of the American people—but—while keeping to the general scheme and tone of the draft."[43]

It was just that scheme and tone that Edward Grigg found particularly alarming. When Balfour expressed an interest in his "argument," Grigg sent him a copy of the memo he had written to Lloyd George, as well as a cover letter that further explained his concerns. Grigg wrote, "It is my almost fanatical conviction that we are taking a wrong turn."

Grigg reminded Balfour that Ambassador Geddes had told the cabinet that America might forgive the debt sometime in the future, but only if, he recounted, "by funding now and avoiding any semblance of putting pressure upon American public opinion or holding it up to obloquy." Grigg argued that the Balfour draft did exactly that, and that "its whole argument and purport . . . is to hold the American people up to international contempt." This was a blunt criticism, but Grigg went even further, asking: "Can it ever be right or wise to weaken our moral authority vis-à-vis the U.S.A.? It is our greatest asset."

He ended with a polite apology for his presumptuous letter: "Please forgive this outburst. It is indefensible to have written all this to you, who have a thousand times more knowledge and experience."[44]

Before the cabinet would meet again, Basil Blackett, who, in his official capacity as the chancellor of the exchequer's principal advisor on
financial policy, had advised his first chancellor, Austen Chamberlain, to
take the high road in 1920, now argued to his second, Robert Horne, that
the Balfour draft should not be issued. It seemed to him, Blackett wrote
in an official memorandum, "to be so fraught with evil consequences, that
I venture to appeal to you for its reconsideration before it is too late."[45]

At that time, few civil servants commanded as much influence at the
British Treasury as Blackett did. Educated at Oxford in the classics,
Blackett joined Treasury in 1904 after placing first on the civil service exam.
Fit, charming, and usually well-tailored in dark suits set off by starched-
white rounded Edwardian collars, his lampshade mustache capped an ever-
present friendly expression. He was described by a colleague as "a cheerful
cherub with the methods of a steamroller." He had quickly distinguished
himself by his work ethic and financial acumen. In 1914 and 1915, he was
sent to the United States on financial missions, and then served as HM
Treasury's representative in Washington from 1917 to 1919. He knew
the history and the facts of the war debts minutely and he expressed his
concern to Horne about the inaccuracies and the inflammatory nature of
Balfour's note.[46]

"I call this an insincere policy," Blackett wrote, "because I believe it is
impossible of execution." Citing the figures of the debt owed to America
in contrast to the Allies' capacity to repay Britain, he concluded, "The idea
that we can really collect from Europe what we owe America is, I submit,
entirely erroneous."

Blackett, who had been knighted for his service in 1921, could not stand
by when the honor of the British Treasury was being put at risk by a disingenuous economic policy based on numbers that did not add up. As the
first civil servant to be appointed to the position of controller of finance at
Treasury, which had been created to provide the chancellor with wise and
informed counsel, he was not about to remain silent.

He laid out the choice to his superior: "A sincere policy of funding our
debt . . . designed to rescue Europe from chaos might well bring the U.S.A.

The Cabinet Room at No. 10 Downing Street, where the final debate on the Balfour Note took place. *From* Survey of London, *London County Council, 1931.*

in to our help. An insincere policy will have the reverse effect." Blackett closed his argument to Horne with two questions, the first being, "Is it really possible to pretend in face of these figures that we are sincere in our professed policy of paying the U.S.A. and making Europe pay us the equivalent?" In the second, he asked, "And if we really mean to try and save Europe and are merely venting our preliminary grumble before doing so, is it worthwhile to begin by pillorying American selfishness?"[47]

When the cabinet met again on July 25, this meeting, unlike the previous three on this topic, was held at 10 Downing Street in the cabinet room, with the prime minister "in the chair" and the seventeen ministers seated around the long table covered with green baize. Before them was Balfour's revised draft.

Written to be read as a magnanimous offer, the 1,500-word note, in nine paragraphs, articulated the British government's proposition to renounce all debts owed to Britain by its Allies, as well as its share of any further reparations from Germany. Its generosity and elegant language disguised a reproach directed at the American government. By officially linking war debts and reparations, the British government was knowingly putting its policy in direct opposition to that of the United States.

Moreover, the British offer was based on a condition. The United States would have to agree to write off, "through one great transaction, the whole body of inter-Allied indebtedness," pari passu. This was the controversial condition first proposed by Churchill two years earlier and reasserted by him at the first of the four recent cabinet meetings. Should America refuse to accept that condition, Britain would "regretfully" be forced to seek repayment from its debtors in order to repay the Americans. That was the stance Churchill had insisted on back in 1920, when he said that the British government should not budge from it.

Although the principle of common cause had not been discussed by the cabinet, it provided the moral foundation for the Balfour Note, just as Churchill's memorandum had. Balfour stressed that the debts had been incurred in a joint military effort "for the great purpose common to them all." This would now be Britain's rationale to show that the American approach to collecting war debts was wrong. "It cannot be right," the note stated, "that one partner in the common enterprise should recover all that she has lent, and that another while receiving nothing should be required to pay all that she has borrowed."

The Balfour Note also took direct aim at another US position which held that Britain's borrowing of money was contractual, with signed documents and set terms, just like standard bank loans. The note reasoned that "To generous minds it can never be agreeable . . . to regard the monetary aspect of this great event as a thing apart, to be torn from its historical setting and treated as no more than an ordinary commercial dealing between traders who borrow and capitalists who lend." The note continued in its altruistic posture, stating that "Great Britain is owed more than it owes," and that "we do not in any event desire to make a profit." It further asserted that "In no circumstance do we propose to ask more from our debtors than is necessary to pay our creditors."

To underscore the British government's generosity as a creditor, the note pointed out: "It should not be forgotten, though it sometimes is, that our liabilities were incurred for others, not for ourselves." This was based on the communiqué's charge that the United States would not lend to the other allies without Britain's guarantee, or as the note put it, "it was only on our security that they were prepared to lend it." This last assertion would be, to the US Treasury, the most inflammatory statement made in the note, and the most erroneous, although it would not say so immediately.[48]

The former and current chancellors were present at the meeting to discuss Balfour's revised draft that Tuesday morning in the cabinet room. Grigg's influence did not appear to have had an impact on either Lloyd George or Balfour, but Blackett's arguments did have one on Horne and Chamberlain. Neither had been vocal previously, but both would now voice their opposition to Balfour's note.

When Balfour opened the discussion by reminding the cabinet that in earlier versions of the note the policy embodied in it "had met with unanimous approval, Horne immediately disagreed, stating that he himself had never been in favor of it. In no uncertain terms, the chancellor charged that its policy was "profoundly wrong." Horne argued that the note "held up the United States as a Shylock" and that the consequence of its issue might be that the United States would demand repayment according to the existing terms set in the loan agreements—interest at 4.25 percent over a term of twenty-five years—which would be a "grievous burden" for Britain to bear. Worse, America could then issue bonds on the public market "in such a way to ruin our credit." By agreeing to settlement talks with the Americans, Horne asserted that there was a good possibility of securing better terms, perhaps, "a lower rate of interest and an extension of the funding period."

Horne reiterated that "he could not too strongly emphasize his conviction that the policy embodied in the note would make the position infinitely worse." This reflected the argument made by Blackett in his memorandum.

Churchill disagreed. "Our attitude was not," he said, "and should not be, one of quivering fear before the United States." He thought the Balfour draft, as it existed now, would be well received in Europe, and that "it would result in our Allies gathering themselves under the shield of England." Churchill had long lobbied for working to change public opinion in America to bring the United States around to an all-around cancellation of the debt. He believed the language of the note would not be resented there "after the first momentary irritation had passed away." Rather, the Americans, he predicted, "would be driven to search their consciences and ask themselves if they were in the right." Always colorful, Churchill sniffed at the chancellor's idea that America might give them a better deal if the note to the Allies was withheld. That, he said, "was but a pious, illusionary and vain hope, based on no reasonable foundation." Then he added, "On the other hand, it was equally imaginary that the United States would put the pincers in the fire and begin to tease and torture us."

Chamberlain spoke next, disagreeing with Churchill and siding with Horne. He argued that the note would add to the problem, not solve it. "We would be regarded as gibbeting the United States before the world," he said. In his view, "it was incompatible with our dignity and our primacy as a world power to ask again, and as a favor, what had been refused to us when advanced in the interests of world peace." While he, too, felt that Balfour's language was eloquent, the policy in it was so wrong that he was "afraid that the more brilliant and conclusive the character of the despatch, the more ruinous would be its effect."

Balfour, in response, pointed out that the note did not suggest that Britain would not pay the United States what it was entitled to ask for. Reading directly from the draft, he said, "These demands, which had been put forward with the most perfect courtesy, are within the undoubted right of the American Government."[49]

This may have been when Stanley Baldwin, the president of the Board of Trade, voiced his summation of the policy: "We will pay you if we must, but you will be cads if you ask us to do so."[50]

The prime minister wrapped up the discussion, conceding that, while the note "would make France and Italy a little angry with us," it was time "that we asserted ourselves and made clear that this whole trouble ought not to be settled at our expense." Lloyd George also stated that he was fully in favor of sending the note as written, that he "had not altered his view in the least." He disagreed with toning down the language in any way. "Why should we be apologetic to the United States?" he asked. "They had done their best to wrest our naval supremacy from us . . . and today, they are trying to wrest our financial and commercial supremacy." He supported Churchill's view that the purpose of the note was not to please Americans but to change their minds. "The publication of this document," he said, "and the controversy to which it would give rise, would have important educational results on American opinion."[51]

Whatever effect the note would have on the American public, it failed to win over everyone in the British cabinet. Horne and Chamberlain—the current and former chancellors of the exchequer—made the unusual request of asking to have their dissents recorded. They were noted, but confidentially, as the minutes of this meeting—like the others regarding the Balfour Note—were marked SECRET.

Six days later, on August 1, the Balfour Note was issued. It was sent to the diplomatic representatives of the six countries still considered as current debtors to Britain: France, Italy, Yugoslavia, Rumania, Portugal, and Greece. It was not directly addressed to the United States, but a copy was sent to the American embassy.

Until the eve of its issuance, the Balfour Note had been a well-kept cabinet secret. *The Times* of London learned of it first, on July 31, but the paper did not appear to have had an advance copy of the note itself. The wire services reported worldwide that it was forthcoming but specified only that it would put forward "at some length the official view that the debts owed to Great Britain by the European countries are practically and morally inseparable from the British war debt to the United States."[52]

The official release of the Balfour Note prompted a flurry of international comment.

The note blindsided officials in Paris, who were expecting a partial or complete cancellation of the French debt by Britain. Lloyd George had proposed exactly that in recent discussions, in return for France easing its demands on Germany. A conference to formalize such an agreement was just a week away. The realization in France that it may now have to pay up in full, was "instantaneously to cause general depression and dismay," according to an American newspaper report from Paris.[53]

France was in no mood to be dunned. The destruction of much of her eastern territory by German artillery and trench warfare during the war continued to retard her economic recovery. France believed it simply could not recover, nor pay her debts, without reparations from Germany. Making matters worse, the United States and Britain were now attempting to have France accept reduced reparation payments while, at the same time, reneging on their pledges to act cooperatively to protect France from further German aggression. "Who can expect anything but irritation from France," the French newspaper *Le Figaro* asked, "placed as she is between a Germany surfeited with gold and her own Allies gently placing a knife at her throat."[54]

The British reaction to the Balfour Note was not much better. The Associated Press report from London called the bulk of it "adverse." *The Times* of London reported that Balfour's note "was adopted against the view of the British Treasury," and feared "that the prospect of settlement is not improved by the note." The *Morning Post* editorialized: "We deeply deplore the note. We ought to have expressed to America our unconditional readiness to repay the debt." Much of the reporting by the press—with headlines like AMERICA RESENTS THE BALFOUR NOTE—focused on how America was reacting and how it might affect the outcome of the settlement of the debt. The "Londoner's Diary" column in the *Evening Standard* found the message in the Balfour Note tone deaf, commenting that "anybody who thinks that the massed millions of American people favor cancellation are strangely ignorant of popular American sentiment."[55]

The British views about American opinion were not an understatement. An editorial in the *Philadelphia Inquirer* opined—in something of a verbal political cartoon—that in the Balfour Note, "Uncle Sam is portrayed as a ruthless, relentless, hard-hearted Shylock," while "John Bull is depicted as the liberal, magnanimous and sympathetic creditor whose heart bleeds for his debtors' sufferings." A columnist syndicated by the *Chicago Tribune* called it a "stinging, red-hot note . . . all thickly sugar-coated," in which the United States was making it necessary for Great Britain "to put the screws on the Allies." Perhaps the most astute editorial comment about the message of the note and its disarming prose was: "Lord Balfour seems to think he can call us sheep thieves in language so elegant that we shall not understand it."[56]

Additional perspective came from the Paris correspondent of the *New York Herald*, who wrote, "In semi-official quarters the note is regarded as a trial balloon, with the intent to place the responsibility for a solution of the debt question squarely upon the shoulders of the United States." Another declared that the publication of the British dispatch would require the matter of the Allied debts to be studied in the light of the new developments "of which the principal will be the reception given to the Balfour Note by America."[57]

The Balfour Note's official reception in Washington ranged from unmistakably negative to aggressively hostile. Senator Porter McCumber, a Republican from North Dakota and chairman of the Senate Finance

Committee, called out its disingenuous nature. He charged that the American people would never approve of the cancellation of the debt and that the US Senate would never suggest such a thing. "Britain, in contrast to her creditors," he said, "is entirely solvent. She is offering to cancel claims against debtors on the verge of bankruptcy, from whom she cannot collect. We can collect from Britain."[58]

Across the aisle, Senator Thomas Watson, a Democrat from Georgia, and also a member of the Finance Committee, supported McCumber's statement, saying, "Any proposition to cancel our claims against England would not get of out the Finance Committee of the Senate in a hundred years."[59]

While the Balfour Note made headlines in France, England, and the United States for several days, Andrew Mellon said nothing publicly. His position, however, was made known promptly. Mellon, the press was told, believed that the "American Debt Commission must continue negotiations for funding the obligations owed to the United States without regard to the disposition which is shown by Great Britain to cancel war-time indebtedness." Furthermore, the Treasury statement included the not-so-subtle message that the Balfour Note would otherwise be ignored, explaining that since it was not addressed to the United States, "no official cognizance of its transmission should be taken."[60]

Privately, Mellon was enraged and offended. Like many others, he deeply resented the characterization of the United States as a greedy creditor, as well as Britain's ingratitude to America for having come to her aid. His staff at Treasury was also furious. The most disturbing part of the Balfour Note was the statement that Britain had only incurred its debt because the United States had refused to accept the credit of her Allies without a British guarantee. The inference behind this notion had originated with Keynes and it had long rankled Leffingwell. How the British government could continue to assert the false statement astounded Leffingwell, especially after Austen Chamberlain, when chancellor, had set the record straight during a 1921 speech in the House of Commons. Then Chamberlain had acknowledged that "an entirely erroneous impression" had evolved related to British borrowing from America. He stated, categorically, that "no loans made by the United States were ever guaranteed by us."[61]

Leffingwell had taken pains to close the issue once and for all by later echoing Chamberlain in both a speech and a published article, stating, "An impression has been created that the United States required Great Britain in some sense to guarantee or make herself responsible for loans to others of the Allies after the United States entered into the War. That impression is entirely erroneous."[62]

Parker Gilbert, Leffingwell's chosen successor, also seethed. Now Mellon's undersecretary—a post the Treasury secretary had persuaded Congress to create specifically to retain him—he railed to Mellon that the British insistence that our loans to them "were made in order to help their allies is about as irritating a piece of nonsense as has been pulled in the whole discussion about inter-governmental debts."[63]

The Balfour Note was the first communication from the British government about its indebtedness to be received by Andrew Mellon. Although reluctant to comment publicly, to his family, he deemed it simply "a lie."[64]

∽

By the afternoon of Thursday, August 3, when the House of Commons met in its final session before it adjourned for the summer, many in Westminster believed that the Balfour Note—launched like a missile by the Lloyd George government—had backfired.

Robert Horne, who had opposed the Balfour Note's purpose and tone, and had dissented from the cabinet's decision to issue it, gave it a respectable burial in his remarks on the floor. As chancellor of the exchequer, he put the best face on it by clarifying concerns that the British government was not trying to wriggle out of its agreement with the American government. "I wish to make it clear beyond all possibility of misapprehension," he said from the Treasury bench, "that we realize and recognize to the full, our obligation to pay our debt to the United States of America." This elicited a response of "Hear, hear!"—the common expression of approval in the House. Horne continued: "We do not mean in any shape or form to evade that obligation." He also affirmed that a delegation would be sent to America, "this autumn, for the express purpose of discussing the arrangements."[65]

His statement that Britain would pay was not challenged, nor contradicted, perhaps owing to the regret he expressed that an easier solution for the British taxpayer had not been found. "Whatever our wishes in other circumstances might have been," he stated, "we have got to face facts and adjust ourselves to realities." Seizing the moment, he closed his speech with a vision of a high road not taken: "We must turn our backs upon things which perhaps all the world was waiting for . . . that if only it had been possible that nations who fought in the war side by side . . . had been willing to regard their subscriptions to the cost of the war as contributions to our common success . . . we might have been able to rid the world of many occasions of irritation and plant in the heart of humanity a new and inspiring hope." This elicited cheers in the House and praise from the press.[66]

Excerpts from Horne's speech, including his closing statement, were telegraphed to the US State Department by Ambassador Harvey.[67]

Parliament adjourned the next day, not to reconvene until November 21. Horne's assertion that the British would pay, coupled with the US Treasury's statement that the Americans would not budge, deflated Britain's trial balloon and the Balfour Note sunk below the political horizon as the members of Parliament left for their summer holidays.

On the night of August 5, the coalition government of Lloyd George, after nearly six years in office, began its descent, although not all of its members realized it at the time. The Conservative members in his government, and the general public, had many reasons to want a change in the leadership, most notably, crippling trade issues, a souring economy, widespread unemployment, and the increasing tensions with Ireland. Also disturbing was the fact that France was threatening to take over the industrial Ruhr basin of Germany, should the impasse over Germany's default on reparation payments to France not be resolved. With its coal mines, factories, and blast furnaces, the Ruhr was vital to Germany. It was also vital to France, which needed its coal to make steel. French consumption of coal "far exceeded her production" and before the war, "the German output of coal had been about six times that of France." French Prime Minister Raymond Poincaré was adamant that one way or another, Germany must pay. If it did not, he threatened to use military force to seize control of the Ruhr, which could begin another war.[68]

Horne was on holiday in Scotland when Andrew Mellon issued a statement on August 24 in response to the Balfour Note, in which he diplomatically referred to the British government's claim—that England had borrowed funds on behalf of the Allies because the United States had required a guarantee—"as a misapprehension." This was perhaps a parody of Horne's statement to the House of Commons when he had said that he wanted to "make clear beyond all possibility of misapprehension" that Britain would pay its debt.[69]

Horne made no reply to the Mellon statement. There was no point to doing so. He was planning to lead the British delegation to the United States the following month, as previously announced. Horne was in fact hoping to use the first few days of the Washington trip to educate the Americans—no doubt to the delight of the British cabinet. He believed, as Montagu Norman of the Bank of England explained to his friend, Benjamin Strong, governor of the New York Federal Reserve Bank, that if Horne was "to address a few suitable audiences, he would do something to convert the American public to his way of thinking on the Debt and other questions and would so obtain the sympathy of your public and the goodwill of the Funding Commission."[70]

Horne was due to sail to America at the end of September, and to meet Mellon in person.

4

THE MELLON-BALDWIN AGREEMENT

O n October 8, 1922, the *Evening Standard* reported that Robert Horne's debt-refunding mission to the United States, due to depart in ten days, was likely to be postponed.[1]

Discontent with the Lloyd George coalition government, which included Horne and Churchill, had reached a point that put its viability at risk. The increasing likelihood that the government would not be able to survive a vote of confidence at the upcoming conference of the Conservative Party threatened the coalition Lloyd George had formed between it and his Liberal Party. Speculation that the Conservatives would vote to stand for election as a party and to end Lloyd George's control of government was mounting.

At a meeting on October 10, a dozen Conservative Party members— including cabinet ministers Austen Chamberlain, Lord Birkenhead, Arthur Balfour, and Stanley Baldwin—discussed the question of whether to keep the coalition together. Chamberlain, the leader of the party, spoke in favor of doing so. Birkenhead joined him in speaking "passionately for the need to retain Lloyd George's leadership." Balfour concurred. The only person who objected was Baldwin, who declared, quite boldly, "Lloyd George is the albatross round our neck, and we ought to get rid of him."[2]

Stanley Baldwin, as president of the Board of Trade, had been a minister in the Lloyd George government for little more than a year. He had been present at each of the cabinet meetings at which the Balfour Note had been discussed and debated, but had said nothing that was recorded in the minutes. Unlike his fellow Conservative ministers, Horne and Chamberlain, he had not dissented from the note's issuance.

Baldwin was not a prominent person in Whitehall. At the age of fifty-five, he was still considered a "junior member" of the cabinet, and remained "obscure" in the opinion of one observer, and "an insignificant figure" to another. Baldwin wanted to serve in Parliament, like his father had, but he seemed to have no ambition for higher office.[3]

He could afford to live the life he wanted. He and his father had built their iron and steel mills into giants in British industry, and they were well-liked in their Worcestershire constituency, where they had established a reputation as benevolent employers and patriarchs of the district. Baldwin and his wife, Lucy, owned a country estate there, which allowed them to enjoy a quiet life of gardening, book collecting, and spa vacations in France.

After he had called for doing away with Lloyd George at the Conservative Party meeting, Baldwin told Lucy that he was resigning from the cabinet and would likely not hold office again. He explained that he could not go along with the others and run for reelection as a Coalitionist: "I arose and spoke and told them that I for one could not and would not do it. I must be free and stand as a Conservative: I could not serve under Lloyd George again. The rest of the Unionist Ministers were aghast, and they were all apparently against me."[4]

By week's end, however, Baldwin had gained the support of at least four other minor members of the cabinet. Having had a change of heart on his plan to retire, Baldwin, instead, "devoted his energies to his new vocation of full-time revolutionary."[5]

He recognized that he was not viewed as a leader and that someone with more experience and standing was needed.

Baldwin, like many others, wanted Andrew Bonar Law—despite being in questionable health due to a throat ailment—to lead the party and take the reins of the government. The Canadian-born businessman had made his money as an iron merchant in Glasgow before entering Parliament.

He had previously served in Herbert H. Asquith's coalition cabinet, and in the Lloyd George government until his resignation in March 1921 on the advice of his doctor.

Baldwin knew him well. Bonar Law had brought him into the sphere of the cabinet by appointing him as his parliamentary secretary in December 1916, while Bonar Law was chancellor. He subsequently supported Baldwin's promotion to financial secretary of the Treasury in June 1917.

Notwithstanding his failing health, Bonar Law had recently indicated a renewed interest in politics by writing a letter to the editor of *The Times* that criticized the foreign policy of the government. "We cannot be the policeman of the world," he wrote memorably.[6]

His letter quickly led to speculation that he might step forward. The editor of *The Times* encouraged him with a lead article stating that "though Mr. Bonar Law no longer holds office, his influence is probably as great as that of any member of the Government."[7]

On the thirteenth of October, three days after the Conservative Party meeting, Baldwin went to see Bonar Law to express his support for his leadership. Bonar Law told him that he did not want to lead an uprising against his colleagues, nor did he believe he was well enough to do so. That seemed to put an end to it.[8]

Chamberlain, meanwhile, was angry with the "malcontents," as he called the rebellious Conservatives who were in favor of breaking the coalition. At a dinner on October 15 at Churchill's house in Sussex Square—attended by the pro-Coalitionists—Chamberlain decided to go on the offensive. He announced to the others that a vote needed to be taken promptly and that he was scheduling a meeting at the Carlton Club on October 19. This gave the rebels—the anti-Coalitionists—only three days to react and organize.[9]

On the morning of the vote, Lucy Baldwin picked up a friend, and the two of them went in her car to sit outside the grand Venetian-style building where the Carlton Club was meeting "so that we should hear the verdict as soon as possible." She did so, however, without telling her husband. "Such a crowd outside," she remembered. "Photographers, cinema men, policemen among others." Acquaintances came out from the meeting periodically and joined them in their car to give them updates on the proceedings. Lucy noted that "we were the only occupants of a car, all the other cars were waiting for their owners . . . we were off our heads with excitement."[10]

The *Evening Standard* framed the decision to be made at the meeting: "It must be a clear-cut issue between Coalitionists and anti-Coalitionists, between those who won't have Mr. Lloyd George as Prime Minister at any price and those who regard Mr. Lloyd George as the only practicable Prime Minister at the present time."[11]

When it came time for Baldwin to speak, he made the decision even clearer: "Take Mr. Chamberlain and myself," he said, "we stand here today, he prepared to go into the wilderness if he should be compelled to forsake the Prime Minister, and I prepared to go into the wilderness if I should be compelled to stay with him."[12]

The cheers and reception Baldwin received affirmed that the disaffected members had a majority. Immediately afterward, a motion was made and seconded that "the meeting declares its opinion that the Conservative Party . . . fights the election as an independent party, with its own leader and its own programme."[13]

More cheers followed for Bonar Law, whose voice was so weak that people had to strain to hear him. He made it clear, however, that he supported the motion, and announced that he would vote "in favor of our going into the election as a party fighting to win."[14]

When the ballots were tallied shortly before noon, it was Lloyd George who was being sent into the wilderness. "The collapse of the coalition government followed the dramatic result of the Conservative meeting at the Carlton Club," reported the *Evening Standard*. The newspaper also reported that the king, "whose sudden return to town this afternoon is an indication of the urgency of the crisis," had arrived back at Buckingham Palace from Sandringham before three o'clock. The ousted prime minister left 10 Downing Street an hour later to tender his resignation to the king, the paper reported, "following a day of political drama."[15]

Bonar Law approached Stanley Baldwin to be the first member of the new cabinet, and to serve as chancellor of the exchequer. According to Lucy, her husband "did not want to make anything out of the bouleversement," and had demurred, suggesting instead Reginald McKenna, who had served in that office before, and was well regarded by the City.[16]

On Sunday evening, October 22, Bonar Law arrived at Baldwin's home at 93 Eaton Square to let him know that McKenna had declined but would support the new government. When his visitor left, Baldwin went upstairs and, with tongue in cheek, told Lucy, "Treat me with respect, I am the chancellor of the exchequer."[17]

In the general election that followed on November 15, the Conservative Party won with a majority over the other four parties.[18]

But, reported the *Daily Telegraph*, "perhaps the greatest sensation in the whole election," was the defeat in Dundee of Winston Churchill, who had represented that industrial constituency for the last fourteen years. He had been ill and had undergone an appendectomy that kept him from campaigning. He finished a poor fourth in a field of six. "Although it was generally expected that his chances were none too good, no one dreamed for a moment that a defeat so absolutely overwhelming was in store for him." Churchill suddenly found himself out of government again.[19]

⚬

Having been chancellor of the exchequer for only two months, Stanley Baldwin left London on Wednesday morning, December 27, 1922, headed to Washington at the head of a delegation to negotiate the repayment of Britain's war debt to the United States. A small press contingent caught up with him at Waterloo Station, where he spoke briefly before boarding the 9:45 A.M. "boat train" to the port of Southampton, about seventy miles east.

"My mission concerns our I.O.U.s held by the United States," he told them, "and it is a delicate one. We are in the position of debtors, and we must tread lightly."[20]

Baldwin, having been a member of Parliament for nineteen years, was an experienced public speaker, although one who rarely made news. He understood, however, the importance of the moment. "We hope to fund this debt and get the burden of interest eased," he commented to those gathered around him with notebooks and news cameras, "but of course, the last word is with America."[21]

As for specifics, he said only that the mission's plan was "to come to permanent settlement on the terms of our debt to America," which totaled more than $4 billion. His delegation, however, would explain its proposals to the US Treasury Department only upon arrival. Nothing had been sent ahead, he stated. "At present, they know nothing," he added, "beyond the fact that we are coming."[22]

The other high-ranking member of the delegation, Montagu Norman, the governor of the Bank of England, was not present with the others, but waited out of sight in one of the railway carriages. He was in an early stage of developing his reputation for traveling incognito. The correspondent from the *Evening Standard* observed that "Mr. Norman kept well away from the interviewers and was with difficulty persuaded by Mr. Baldwin to pose to for photographers."[23]

They seemed an unlikely pair. Baldwin, a square-jawed, clean-shaven man of fifty-five, and married with six children, looked the part of the British official he was, in a three-piece suit with a Gladstone collar and his short, sand-colored hair parted neatly in the center.

Norman was four years younger, still a bachelor, and sported a wide mustache and goatee. A natty, but always well-tailored dresser, he had a fondness for wearing large scarves and Borsalino hats, one of which he had brought with him. He was often mistaken for an artist or musician, which he took no pains to correct. Once lured out of his carriage, however, "he had nothing to say."[24]

By contrast, Baldwin was reported to be "in a jolly frame of mind and chatted and joked with those around him," despite the massive debt issue to be faced with American strangers, as well as marine weather reports of rough seas ahead.[25]

The British contingent—nine in number—might have been smaller had any other White Star liner been departing for America on that date, but the opportunity to sail on the RMS *Majestic*, the newest, largest, and most

QUADRUPLE-SCREW R·M·S "MAJESTIC" 56,621 TONS
THE WORLD'S LARGEST LINER
WHITE STAR LINE

The *Majestic* became the preferred ship of British and American diplomats for trans-atlantic crossings. *From a publicity poster of the period.*

luxurious ocean liner in the world, inspired Baldwin to bring along his wife and his youngest daughter, who was sixth months shy of her twentieth birthday. The chancellor's principal private secretary, P. J. Grigg, also took along his wife, recording carefully later that she had paid her own passage.[26]

The *Majestic* was itself a reparation of the war, one of the many ships turned over to Britain by Germany according to the terms of the Treaty of Versailles, which required Germany to pay both monetary and in-kind reparations to the Allies, including the replacement of "merchant ships and fishing boats lost or damaged owing to the war."[27]

Under the principle of class-for-class and ship-for-ship reparations, the White Star Line was allowed to acquire it as compensation for the loss of its liner, *Britannic*, which had been destroyed by a German mine in 1916 while in service as a British hospital ship.[28]

The *Majestic* had made its maiden voyage from Southampton to New York on May 10, 1922, with great fanfare and publicity. Newspapers enthusiastically filled their pages with statistics, photographs, and descriptions of the remarkably well-equipped and spacious ship that boasted accommodations for five thousand people, eight kitchens, 190,000 pieces of linen, three wireless stations, storage for 2,500 bottles of champagne, and measured 965 feet in length.[29]

The crossing with Baldwin and his entourage would be the *Majestic*'s first New Year's Eve at sea. The five-day voyage promised to be an opportune holiday for all of them. Despite high winds on the English Channel that afternoon, the great ship departed from Southampton on schedule. It was due in New York on the second day of the new year—January 2, 1923.[30]

The weather only worsened as the *Majestic* crossed the English Channel to pick up additional passengers at the French port of Cherbourg. About sixty of those boarding there were members of the famous Moscow Art Theatre, which would be opening an eight-week engagement in New York in January.[31]

The *Majestic* sent a wireless message on its second day out that it was in a "whole gale" and in "very high seas" about five hundred sea miles west of the Lizard peninsula in Cornwall, the southernmost part of the British mainland.[32]

Many of the passengers became seasick, including P. J. Grigg and his wife Gertrude, and Baldwin's daughter Betty. Another wireless message from the *Majestic* on December 30, its fourth day at sea, reported that it had reduced its speed to sixteen knots "owing to mountainous seas and a gale which attained a velocity of one hundred miles an hour." The captain said "the storm was the worst of his career, and he believed the *Majestic* would now be two days late in reaching New York."[33]

Grigg later wrote that while he was "utterly prostrate," Baldwin was unaffected and "even paid a visit to the engine room during the storm!" Montagu Norman was equally resistant to the rough weather and wrote to his mother from the ship that "many people have been on the sick list." Baldwin's daughter, he told her, had been *quite* invisible for four days. Baldwin and Norman seemed to be the only members of the delegation who were not afflicted.[34]

Norman had only a slight acquaintance with Baldwin. He had written to his friend, the American central banker Banjamin Strong before he left, that "Baldwin is a level-headed, somewhat blunt man with a certain amount of charm and with a capacity for getting on with his fellow men." He added that "even if he is not clever, he has plenty of common sense."[35]

The two principals got to know one another better as the four-day gale eventually abated and was followed by a fog that forced the ship to reduce its speed even further to a cautious five knots. The extended trip allowed Norman to discover that the country gentleman in a tweed suit was also well-educated.

On the day of the ship's departure, *The Times* had run one-column sketches of each of them. Baldwin was described as "that almost extinct individual, the cultured politician," who, in his speeches, "will sometimes repeat the more obscure epigrams of antiquity, and he will repeat them correctly." While Baldwin had studied Greek and Latin at Cambridge, the writer pointed out that "he knows French only to read it," and was like a man from another century, who might be found "in a volume of the *Spectator* or in a novel of Jane Austen." The Americans were not going to meet the typical "John Bull" stereotype—"an uninteresting combination of beef-steak and boastfulness"—but rather "a very typical Englishman, quite simple in his tastes, direct in his address, possessed of a broad scintillating wit, and very charming."[36]

Baldwin had not been to the United States in over thirty years, when he visited his father's clients in the iron business there and in Canada. He had seen a lot of North America by railroad and horse-drawn vehicles, traveling with a college friend to Quebec, Montreal, Boston, New York, and as far west as Chicago. At the end of the business part of their trip, the two young men had gone south to see New Orleans. But that was before automobiles had transformed the country and before buildings in New York began to scrape the sky. He particularly wanted his wife and daughter to see Manhattan and its skyline.

Norman, on the other hand, had been to the United States only a few months earlier, quietly visiting New York and Washington, without making any news. The subsequent discovery that he had been there was reported in an exclusive story by *The Times* while the *Majestic* was en route. It also revealed that Norman had met with President Harding during an April visit and had engaged in discussions with three members of the debt commission—Hughes, Hoover, and Mellon. The report also stated that Norman had "attempted to convince them that Europe's position was hopeless unless the United States intervened."[37]

In its sketch of Norman, *The Times* noted his disdain for the press, adding that "many of those who come into contact with him feel there is an indefinable touch of mystery about him." The sketch included other insights: "In appearance, he recalls the early Victorian statesman," noting also that he was "a lover of music, poetry, and books" who also had "a collection of rare and beautiful woods." Norman's most distinguishing characteristic, however, was his aversion to publicity and the press. The writer attested that "the American newspaper man has no terrors for him."[38]

Norman liked his job as governor of the Bank of England despite its high visibility. Banking was in his blood, on both sides of his family. His father was a banker, and his maternal grandfather had served as a governor of the Bank of England. Elected as governor himself in 1920, Norman had been a director of the bank for more than a decade. His reelection to a second term as governor broke with the tradition of a single two-year term. Norman was determined to stay at the top post as long as it took to establish an international organization of central bankers, which he passionately believed the postwar world required.

In his opinion, the Balfour Note had been a horrible mistake. He believed that repaying the British debt to the United States was vital to maintaining the superiority of Britain's credit in international financial markets. He also knew that cooperation with America—particularly with its Federal Reserve—was vital to the functioning of international trade and stable currencies.

To Norman's delight, his American counterpart, Ben Strong, shared his vision. They had become good friends and had corresponded regularly for the past six years. Norman had visited with Strong during his May visit to the United States and expected Strong to meet him when the *Majestic* docked.

The *Majestic* received much attention on account of the famous people traveling aboard, but also because of its refined interior and furnishings. Designed by the firm of Mewès & Davis, which had done the drawings for the interiors of the Ritz hotels in Paris and London, the *Majestic*'s décor followed the same elegant style. Both partners in the firm had studied at the École des Beaux-Arts in Paris and employed the quiet symmetry of the Louis XVI style in most of their work for the lounges, dining rooms, salons, and palm courts.

The *Majestic* had two orchestras aboard, one with seven musicians that played in the first-class dining room, and a smaller ensemble in the à-la-carte restaurant. By New Year's Eve, Baldwin and Norman had discovered that they shared a love of classical music. Under the twenty-foot ceiling of the elegantly furnished first-class lounge, there was a grand piano on the stage. There they rang in the new year at sail on a tempestuous sea by listening to the renowned German pianist Wilhelm Backhaus, who had toured that fall and played in London for the first time since the war. Baldwin wrote from the ship to friends that Backhaus had "played gloriously" on the ship that evening and "gave us five Chopins, a beautiful Schumann, and two Liszts, including the 'Second Rhapsody.'"[39]

In the same letter, Baldwin wrote, "We are completing a record passage, the longest ever taken by this ship . . . and all the time with high seas." He added, "but with all that, it has been a wonderful rest and I feel as fit as a whole orchestra of fiddles." Norman, Baldwin reported, felt the same way and "like me, enjoyed the rest so much, and looked pounds better already."[40]

∽

The British delegation had no written instructions from the Cabinet as to the terms for the debt settlement with the United States, although Prime Minister Bonar Law had given Baldwin "oral authority to settle within an annual annuity of £25 million" (approximately $166 million). This was based on the 2.5 percent refunding concept that Ambassador Harvey had led the British cabinet to believe was possible, far below the 4.25 percent rate set by the US Congress. While storms tossed the *Majestic*, there had been some positive movement on war debts in Washington.[41]

Mellon understood from the beginning that Congress would act politically rather than practically. He also knew that Britain could not agree to the terms set by Congress. Not only did Mellon agree with Leffingwell that the commission would be going into the negotiations with its hands tied, but President Harding now recognized that difficulty as well.

On December 28, Harding sent a letter to Senator Henry Cabot Lodge, chairman of the Foreign Relations Committee, to express his opposition to the idea of convening an economic conference to deal with the condition of war-torn Europe. The president also commented on the restrictions Congress had put on the World War Debt Funding Commission.

"If Congress really means to facilitate the task of the government in dealing with the European situation," Harding wrote, "the first practical

step would be to free the hands of the commission so that helpful negotiations may be undertaken." The president's admonishment of the legislative
body for having set unworkable terms was read to the Senate on the following day.[42]

The Times of London editorialized: "The President's suggestion to Congress is eminently practical. It is also a welcome and gratifying gesture to
Mr. Baldwin's mission."[43]

The members of Baldwin's mission apparently did not learn of Harding's
statement while aboard the ship, but later interpreted it as the administration "preparing American public opinion for the fact, now fully realized
by everyone concerned, that it would not be possible to make a settlement
within the provisions of the Act."[44]

As the *Majestic* approached New York on the evening of January 3, a heavy
snowstorm prevented it from docking in the harbor, and the liner was required
to anchor off Sandy Hook, New Jersey, for the night. Andrew Mellon had
sent his assistant secretary, Eliot Wadsworth, to New York to meet the British
delegation. When Wadsworth learned that the ship could not reach port,
he boarded the Coast Guard cutter *Manhattan*—assigned to the Treasury
Department for revenue patrol—to retrieve the Baldwin delegation and take
them "down the Bay" so that they could catch the late train to Washington.
Weather however delayed Wadsworth's mission until the next morning.

Ben Strong joined Wadsworth aboard the *Manhattan* the next day. The
New York central banker wrote to his friend Basil Blackett that Baldwin
and Norman "were honored by a visit from more newspaper representatives and camera men than I have ever seen on shipboard."[45]

Only a portion of the press contingent, however, was there for the British
delegation. Also traveling on the *Majestic* was Émile Coué, the French
exponent of positive thinking, who was about to begin a lecture tour of
the United States and had been promoting it by sending news releases by
wireless stating that he had "cured sea-sick passengers by auto-suggestion"
while the giant liner "was fighting her way through the Atlantic gale."[46]

Another group of reporters was at the New York dock to welcome the
Moscow Art Theatre. Its director, Konstantin Stanislavsky, remembered

The Baldwin delegation arriving on January 4, 1923. Left to right, Assistant Treasury Secretary Eliot Wadsworth, Undersecretary of the Treasury Parker Gilbert, British Ambassador Auckland Geddes, Governor of the Bank of England Montagu Norman, Chancellor of the Exchequer Stanley Baldwin, Lucy Baldwin. *Courtesy of the Library of Congress, Washington, DC.*

that the journalists arrived "like a flock of rooks" and started photographing him from every direction. The large press contingent waiting at the New York pier to cover the arrival of the three different contingents hired a tugboat to take them out to the moored *Majestic*. When the press tug arrived, Wadsworth was ready to depart with the British delegation, but Baldwin decided that they should delay in order to make themselves available.[47]

Asked by reporters about the proposal he was bringing to President Harding, Baldwin answered, "Of course, I can't say anything on that subject until I present my credentials to the President." But he declared that he was hopeful about the outcome, and, when asked, stated that there was no question about paying his country's obligations. "We English," he stated with a tinge of official pride, "have always paid our debts. My ambition is to effect a deal which brings satisfaction to the American people and the British."

Asked if the outlook for success was promising, he answered: "I am of a hopeful temperament. I don't see how anybody who hopes to help finance Europe at this time can be of anything *but* a hopeful temperament."[48]

Aware that Norman had met with President Harding, on a "secret mission," the press contingent hunted for the mysterious banker. Once trapped, Norman did his best to tell them almost nothing. While denying that his visit last May had been secret, he confirmed that it had taken place and that he had spoken with Harding, Mellon, and others.

Asked if he had discussed "America's participation in a general plan to settle the international debt question," with President Harding, Norman replied, "I do not believe there is any question relating to finance that I did not discuss with him." Questioned about whether he considered reparations and debt to be inseparable topics, Norman answered with a question of his own: "Is the world all one? If the world is all one, then those two questions are inseparable. If it is possible to separate the world into little compartments, then those two questions may be separable. It depends on how you look at it." And when queried about the feasibility of the plan Congress had made law, setting interest at 4.25 percent, Norman answered: "That is for Congress to say. Congress knows a great deal about what is feasible.

But it may change its mind. There have been many diverse opinions on this subject."

Norman did give reporters one straight answer.

When asked whether he knew that President Harding wanted the interest rate and other terms to be modified by Congress, he replied: "I understood this much, or did when I was here before, that the terms of that act of Congress were not what Secretary Mellon asked. He asked for bread, and they gave him a stone."[49]

After their arrival in Washington, the British delegation had several opportunities to socialize with members of the American debt commission, including a courtesy call at the White House to present their credentials and a dinner reception at the British embassy. It was a weekend of pomp and protocol intended to allow them to get to know one another before their formal discussions began.

As chairman, Mellon greeted the British visitors in the commission's meeting room at the Treasury Building on Monday morning, January 8. The group of eleven sat together around the oval conference table for the first time. Mellon was not one for making speeches and, in his usual businesslike manner, he stated that they all knew why they were there. "He wished at the moment," it was reported, "only to say that the prompt payment by Great Britain of one hundred million dollars of interest during the past three months . . . was, to his mind, conclusive proof of the right spirit."[50]

Under the three-year moratorium granted by the Wilson administration, the first interest payment on the British debt had become due in May 1922, and was paid in October in advance of the canceled Horne mission. Baldwin had insisted that the second $50 million due in November be paid on time, and it was.

As the head of his delegation, Baldwin began with a reassuring statement in the same spirit: "We have come with the express intention of repaying our debt, and it is owing to the practical difficulties of making international payments that we are about to consult with you in order to accomplish the end which we both have in view." He then noted the historic nature of their joint mission, "We meet to settle the largest single financial transaction, I believe, between two friendly nations in the history of the world." As Baldwin read the rest of his long, prepared statement, he made a reasoned case for the war debts to be considered on a moral basis, asserting that "the debt was contracted in common cause."

Adding facts to principle, he pointed out: "The money was all expended here, most of it for cotton, wheat, food products and munitions of war. Every cent used for the purchase of these goods was spent in America. American labor received the wages; American capitalists the profits; the United States Treasury the taxation imposed on those profits."

In contrast to the "shame America" policy permeating the Balfour Note, Baldwin took a more positive approach. He recognized the United States for its financial contribution to the war which saved "free peoples being brought under the destructive rule of military autocracy," and for American manpower, "whose soldiers who fought so gallantly with ours and those of our Allies for the same purpose." He saluted "the generosity of America," but assured the commissioners that "we are not here to ask for favors or to impose on generosity." Instead, in language he knew Mellon would especially appreciate, he asserted, "Our wish is to approach the discussion as businessmen seeking a business solution of what is fundamentally a business problem."[51]

According to the British mission's log, his prepared statement had been written "with a view to appealing to the minds of the American public," but also in part for the readers back in England. The text was distributed to correspondents representing both American and British newspapers.[52]

The idea of making information about their negotiations public was not the way Mellon was accustomed to doing business. As chair, he suggested that no notes of their discussions be put in writing until the two groups had been able to talk freely and frankly in private. There would be no stenographer present, nor any daily press conferences. Mellon and his fellow commissioners, however, took note of the shift in British policy from advocating cancellation to promising repayment and asked the president to consider making a public statement to set the stage for a settlement.

From the White House the next day, the *New York Times* reported that President Harding was convinced that "it would be impossible to make a settlement with the debtor nations under the terms of the debt commission act as it now stood." The announcement signaled that he would support a call for Congress to change the law to allow for a lower interest rate and more favorable terms for a settlement. Finally, it seemed that the hands of Mellon and the commission might be untied by Congress, or at least loosened a bit.[53]

The British delegation regarded Harding's effort as "a statement of the greatest importance." The Washington correspondent of *The Times* of London agreed, calling it "the most important announcement yet made in regard to the British debt to America." The article also reported that Baldwin's opening speech "has made in official and other circles here the happiest impression."[54]

⧢

With optimism in the air, deal diplomacy—Mellon style—began in earnest the following day, at the third meeting with the British delegation. That afternoon, Mellon led an informal discussion of "the possible methods of accomplishing a refunding." Having set the negotiation table, Mellon and his top lieutenants at the Treasury Department, Eliot Wadsworth and Parker Gilbert, built on those discussions at the dinner table. Mellon's point man on war debts, Wadsworth, and his bride, Nancy, entertained Stanley Baldwin, his wife, Lucy, and Montagu Norman at an intimate supper in their Georgetown home that evening. Gilbert, the brilliant banker who was once rumored to be engaged to Ailsa, was tasked with escorting Ailsa, Betty Baldwin, and junior members of the British delegation, around town to dinners and dances, which also provided opportunities for him to talk informally with the distinguished visitors and members of Congress.[55]

The following evening at Mellon's Dupont Circle apartment, Ailsa and A. W. hosted a dinner party for the entire group of British and American negotiators, including spouses, former president William Howard Taft, and a bevy of noted socialites. Serving liquor during Prohibition was not unlawful in private homes and Mellon's had an impressive selection to offer. Baldwin's private secretary, P. J. Grigg, would later write that"at Mr. Mellon's, we were done extremely well." He described the scene that evening: "There were vast bowls of silver, filled with the most exotic flowers which come daily from Pittsburgh of all places . . . Mrs. Marshall Field and other ladies were covered in ropes of pearls." Grigg also noted that they "were surrounded by Old Masters," from Mellon's stellar art collection. These were mainly British and Dutch in origin, and included works by Rembrandt, Hals, El Greco, Gainsborough, and Constable. One painting that his British guests could not miss was Sir Henry Raeburn's vivid and life-size portrait of Colonel Francis James Scott, in a red tunic and gold epaulets, hung prominently in the dining room where, Grigg recorded, the guests enjoyed "bowls of strawberries out of season" for dessert.[56]

Back in the commission's designated meeting room on the third floor at Treasury the next day—where the artwork consisted mostly of bland portraits of former Treasury secretaries—Mellon got down to business and proposed specific settlement terms for the first time.

Mellon said that Congress would probably approve a settlement of the principal at 3.5 percent interest over a term of sixty-one years, with the deferred interest calculated at 5 percent. This would amount to an annual payment of $187 million.[57]

Baldwin countered, telling the commission that the most he could offer was an annual payment of $140 million for a period not to exceed fifty years. This was $26 million below the top level set by Bonar Law based on an interest rate of 2.5 percent.

Mellon responded by offering to halve the interest rate for the first five years to allow the British economy time to recover. The difference, however, would be added to the outstanding principal balance, with interest.

Baldwin explained that even the modified offer was beyond what he had been authorized to accept and that he would have to communicate the commission's offer to his government. Given that it was 4:30 on Friday afternoon and that it would require some time for Baldwin to hear back from Prime Minister Bonar Law via telegraph, Mellon suggested that they reconvene on Sunday, at his residence at 5:00 P.M. All agreed.

Bonar Law responded to Baldwin's telegram on Saturday, but not with the message the British delegation had hoped to hear. According to the mission's log, he said "it was quite impossible that the Government should accept the American offer," and called the terms "exceedingly harsh." He believed that the interest rate should not exceed 2.5 percent—a notion that stemmed from his misunderstanding of comments made by Ambassador Harvey the previous summer. "If a settlement is not attainable on terms which seem to us reasonable," Bonar Law wrote, "you have no alternative but to ask for further time to consider and to return."

In a second round of transatlantic telegrams, Baldwin told Bonar Law that Montagu Norman and Ambassador Geddes agreed with him that the British government should offer to settle at 3 percent, arguing that even if that rate was rejected, it could be made public that Britain had made "a fair and reasonable offer."

In reply to Baldwin's plea, Bonar Law reiterated his strong belief that they should not settle for more than 2.5 percent but proposed that if the United States would remit the back interest—approximately $600 million—he would call a Cabinet meeting for January 15 and recommend acceptance of the offer. "Bear in mind," he wrote, "I believe we both think the proposal is most ungenerous" and a big price to pay for "a momentary increase of goodwill between the countries."[58]

Before the scheduled Sunday negotiation session at Mellon's apartment, Baldwin met with Mellon privately. After that discussion, he telegraphed Bonar Law: "Immediately on receipt of your telegram I had confidential conversation with the chairman of commission whom I am persuaded is not only anxious for immediate settlement but is genuinely friendly to Great Britain but whose position is such to preclude separate negotiations with me."[59]

Mellon appreciated the chancellor's gesture to signal the desire of the British delegation to reach a settlement but he resisted the urge to negotiate independently of the commission. More importantly, the conversation showed that both men saw one another as honest brokers.

Sensing that an agreement was within their grasp, both Mellon and Baldwin knew, however, that time was running out. There would be no point in proposing a settlement that neither Congress, nor the British cabinet, would approve. Mellon needed terms that Senator Smoot and Representative Burton could steer through Congress. Once he had those, Mellon knew that the commission would be able to persuade President Harding to put the weight of his office behind the settlement. For his part, Baldwin, by telegram, somehow needed to overcome Bonar Law's belief that a deal was possible at 2.5 percent. It would be a difficult needle for both statesmen to thread.

∽

When the British delegation met with the American commissioners, as planned, in Mellon's apartment at five o'clock that Sunday evening, Baldwin proposed the British government's terms, but he left out the prime minister's condition that the United States remit the back interest. Baldwin knew that would amount to cancellation, which Mellon would have to reject because there would be no hope of getting Congress to approve it. Acting beyond his authority, the chancellor proposed that if the US Commission would agree to a settlement at 3 percent, the British delegation would ask the prime minister to put the matters before the full cabinet meeting.

To Mellon, this was a realistic proposal.

Wadsworth's minutes of this session—like those of the previous ones—said little. He recorded only that the meeting continued from five to six thirty P.M., then adjourned until ten that evening, when it reconvened.[60]

There was no explanation for this unusual recess or the continuation of the talks at such a late hour on a Sunday night. The confidential British mission log, however, noted two critical facts: the commission was recessing to consider the British proposal in private; and to then consult with the president.

During the three-and-a-half-hour recess, Mellon, Hughes, Hoover, Smoot, and Burton finalized the terms on which the group agreed, and then conferred with President Harding, who gave his consent to make the offer to the British delegation.

When the meeting reconvened at ten that evening, Mellon proposed a counteroffer of 3 percent for the first ten years, and 3.5 percent over the remaining fifty-two years. The commission would also recommend lowering the rate on Britain's accumulated deferred interest from 5 percent to 4.25. This translated into an annual payment of $161 million for the first ten years and $184 million thereafter.

For both countries, a settlement would be more a political matter than an economic one. To put the proposed offer into context, the funding would increase the American government's receipts, and the British government's spending, by approximately the same amount, 4 percent, on an annual basis in the early years.

To make the offer even more attractive to the British delegation, the commission suggested that if a settlement could be reached immediately, they believed that the Republican leadership would agree to Britain's longstanding appeal for the United States to recognize the linkage between war debts and reparations. This inducement was particularly remarkable because it contravened the long-standing, and seemingly intractable US policy established during the Wilson administration, which Britain and the Allies believed was responsible for preventing a resolution to either war debts or reparations to be reached.

After the meeting adjourned at 11:00 P.M., Baldwin began drafting a telegram, the fourteenth that his delegation had dispatched to London. Sent early the following morning, it strongly urged Bonar Law to accept the American terms without delay and stressed that he was also speaking for Norman and Geddes.

"We are all three convinced that these are the best terms we can obtain," he asserted. "They represent a tremendous advance in American opinion."

The alternative, he argued, would be for the US government to invoke the original terms of the loans—payable on demand at 5 percent interest to be repaid in twenty-five years. If this negotiation ended without a settlement and was "followed by a request to His Majesty's Government to pay," what alternatives would the British government then have?

Baldwin added that time was of the essence, as the current session of Congress would end in March, and they had been told that the incoming members were likely to further divide the American parties and result in the British debt being debated in an even more "bitterly partisan spirit."

Acting on the opportunity at hand, Baldwin explained, was imperative given that "public opinion . . . has moved in our favor partly because of the action of France." By this, he meant the seizure of the Ruhr by France and Belgium, following the Reparations Commission declaring that Germany was in default on its reparation obligations, and the failure of European leaders, including Bonar Law, to resolve the conflict. But perhaps even more importantly, Baldwin advised, the moment was critical because "the American public has come to believe we mean to pay."

Baldwin then reminded his prime minister of the big picture, saying that, without an Anglo-American agreement, there would be no economic recovery in Europe. "We feel very strongly," he said, "that a settlement is well-nigh essential and that without it we cannot expect improvement in general financial conditions." The question then, he asked, "is whether settlement now proposed is so burdensome as to outweigh all these advantages. In my opinion, it is not."

"All of us who are working here," he concluded, "are convinced of necessity of settlement and I urge cabinet to accept. It appears to me in all circumstances that honestly and expediency for once go hand in hand and I gravely fear . . . by trying for shadow we lose the bone."[61]

These arguments did not move the prime minister. The next day, he informed Baldwin that the British cabinet had unanimously concluded that the commission's offer could not be accepted.

Bonar Law explained: "It was difficult for them to believe that American opinion should permanently regard the offer as fair. It was tantamount to more than three-point-four percent interest over a long period" and "the proposal offered no concession, even if the debt were regarded as an ordinary business transaction." With that, Bonar Law advised Baldwin to make it clear that the British government had been willing to accept 3 percent, and to return to London.[62]

When the debt commission and British delegation met again on the afternoon of January 16 at Treasury, Baldwin announced that "his task at this time was not an easy one." His government "had refused to empower him and his colleagues to accept the terms" and "had instructed them to return home at once for consultation." Baldwin asked the commission to "consider his departure as a postponement of negotiations and not as a rupture."[63]

On the following day, much to the surprise of the British delegation, the Washington correspondent of *The Times* of London reported the exact terms of the American proposal: an interest rate of 3 percent for the first ten years and 3.5 percent for the remainder of the period. "This suggestion," the article stated, "was a compromise between a three-percent interest charge, which had been mentioned by Mr. Baldwin, and three-and-a-half percent, which for some time the Americans had held to."[64]

The British delegation's dismay was recorded in the mission's log: "The publication of the terms offered profoundly altered the situation. After the first meeting right up to the sixteenth, the Commission had been insistent that nothing should be put down on paper—no notes on proceedings, even, were taken until the sixteenth—lest Congress should call for papers or ask questions . . . but once the American offer had been published, it ceased to be a basis for possible future discussion . . . it would have been impossible for the Commission to have given us better terms later on, even if they had wished to."[65]

The final meeting of Mellon's debt commission with Baldwin's funding delegation was held on the morning of Thursday, January 18, a few hours before they would leave on the one o'clock train for New York. In the only official joint statement issued during the eighteen days in Washington, it was announced that "progress had been made . . . and discussions had now reached the point at which the British Government thinks it desirable that the chancellor of the exchequer should return to London for consultation . . . and therefore the discussions have been adjourned and Mr. Stanley Baldwin will sail on January 20."[66]

Before they left Washington, however, Mellon had Wadsworth meet with Norman to discuss the form of the bond that the US Treasury Department would issue for settlement. The Treasury secretary believed that the American offer was fair and that, in the end, the British government would come to see it as so and accept it.

Despite the issuance of a joint statement that the talks were merely an adjournment, many newspapers in America, and several in England, immediately labeled the Baldwin mission a failure. One report stated: "Mr. Baldwin has failed to negotiate even a provisional agreement with the United States."[67]

Support for the proposed settlement, however, sprung up in influential British and American circles. Financial firms in the City found the terms wholly acceptable, especially since they had the backing of Norman. Likewise, the New York banking community, as well as Washington political leaders, thought the offer was both fair economically, and politically feasible. That President Harding believed that Congress would accept the lower rates was an important factor.

All recognized though, the need for Great Britain to accept the US debt commission's offer promptly, otherwise Congress would not be able to pass the required legislation before its session ended on March 4. No one worked harder to make this clear than Secretary of State Hughes.

After the negotiators final, but very brief meeting, the British log recorded that "Mr. Hughes again laid great emphasis on the desirability of reaching a settlement during the run of the present Congress." The secretary of state had also told them that there "was quite definitely no body of opinion in America—as there certainly was in England—which thought that the next Congress would be likely to accept a more favourable settlement than the present." Rather, Hughes believed that, if no settlement was reached, "the attitude of Congress would stiffen." The British log also noted, "He stated most emphatically that he regarded this as one of the critical points in history."[68]

Baldwin believed that they had negotiated the best deal they could. He also realized that his own reputation was at stake. The chancellor went to America having announced that Great Britain would repay its debts on a businesslike basis. Now, his government was dithering at the critical moment when a fair offer was on the table.

Baldwin dreaded the difficult discussion ahead with Bonar Law. He knew that two key former British Treasury officials respected by the prime minister, Reginald McKenna and John Maynard Keynes, had counseled Bonar Law against accepting Mellon's offer. Even more daunting, the cabinet had already rejected the deal. The mission was looking increasingly like a disaster, and perhaps one that would result in Baldwin having to resign. It stung that he had gone to America hoping to successfully negotiate what he had called "the largest single financial transaction . . . in the history of the world," and now he would not be allowed to close the deal.[69]

Coincidentally, Robert Horne, the former chancellor of the exchequer who was originally to have led the British delegation, was in New York representing the Baldwin family business when the British delegation arrived in New York. After hearing about the delegation's negotiations, Horne concurred that they had worked out the best terms possible with the Americans. He offered to telegraph the prime minister to express his support for the settlement and to urge Bonar Law to accept it, a proposition Grigg remembered as a noble act.[70]

Horne sent the telegram two days later. The British log recorded that "he urged the Prime Minister that the terms should be accepted at once" and that he and other friends of Great Britain in New York believed "we should never get such good terms again and that nothing, but harm could come from delay."[71]

Before they sailed, Baldwin and Norman spent the day on Wall Street doing what they could to finesse the impasse. While Baldwin went to see J. P. Morgan Jr. Britain's financial agent, Norman visited his friend, Ben Strong, in lower Manhattan at the Federal Reserve Bank of New York's offices. Like Horne, Strong supported Baldwin and Norman, and believed that Mellon and the debt commission had made the British government an offer it should not refuse. The alternative was to be subject to the statutory terms of the loan agreement at 5 percent interest, or worse, to default. They all recognized that Britain's standing and credit in the world was at stake.

✍

On Saturday morning, when the British delegation sailed for home, the weather—thankfully—included no forecast of storms or high seas. As Stanley Baldwin boarded the *Olympic*, he was, however, prepared for another type of tempest, anxious newspaper reporters vying for color on the debt negotiations before the ship sailed at noon.

"I cannot at this time say anything on the Debt Commission," he told them good naturedly. "The situation is too delicate. But there is one thing I would like to say." This was to thank "the American people for the extraordinarily cordial reception which they gave us," and to "acknowledge thanks to the American press for the great kindness shown." He added his hope that on his return to England "the British press is equally fair."

He closed with something of a plea: "There should be a calm view of the whole situation," he said, "especially during the next ten days or two weeks, and I hope that nothing will be said on either side that would be liable to misinterpret the actual situation when described across a distance of three thousand miles."[72]

The White Star liner departed on time from Pier 60, heading out on the North River, but without one passenger who had planned to travel back to England with the British delegation—George Harvey, the American ambassador to Great Britain. It had not been his decision to return on a different ship.

Harvey and Secretary of State Charles Evans Hughes were not friendly. Although he had been President Harding's guest at the White House during the two weeks of the Mellon-Baldwin negotiations, Harvey had been largely kept away from the British delegation in Washington. Hughes had been "especially opposed" to Harvey's appointment as ambassador, acknowledging that while he possessed certain capabilities, he brought "one notorious failing" to the job—his drinking. This often resulted in Harvey, according to Hughes, talking "recklessly" and in making it evident that "he was intoxicated and hardly knew what he was saying." Harding, as Hughes understood it, felt that he owed Harvey the position and that he had extracted a pledge from his ambassador that the drinking would stop. It was clear though, that it was a pledge that Harvey could not keep.[73]

Now, with the situation so delicate, Hughes had no choice but to send Harvey back to his post in London to report on British developments, but he wanted to avoid the risk that the hard-drinking ambassador might further compromise the fragile state of Anglo-American relations during a five-day voyage. Therefore, he had Harvey sail from Hoboken, New Jersey, on the same day as the British delegation, but aboard a different ship, the *America*.

The *Olympic* and the *America* crossed the Atlantic Ocean at the same time, but not for the same port in England, nor within sight of one another.

The window to get a bill through Congress by March 4 was growing shorter as the two ocean liners traveled eastward. Although the Harding administration had been preparing the way for the legislation, there was little time to spare. Hearings would need to be held in both the House and Senate, followed by conference committees, and then floor votes.

As they sailed for England, the British delegation—and particularly Stanley Baldwin—had a more accurate understanding of the nature of the American Congress than they did when they arrived.

ℐ

While the ships carrying the British delegation and Harvey were crossing the ocean, unbeknownst to anyone involved in the British-American debt negotiations, Prime Minister Andrew Bonar Law was trying to get London's most influential newspaper, *The Times*, to support his opposition to the proposed settlement terms that Baldwin and his delegation had negotiated.

The prime minister believed that the American proposal should be rejected and put off until some later date, but he had little support in Britain for its rejection. On January 17, the same day that the leaked terms had been published by the Washington correspondent of *The Times* of London—3 percent interest for the first the year, and three and a half for the remainder—Bonar Law called the new editor of the paper, Geoffrey Dawson, to 10 Downing Street for a discussion about why the American proposal should be rejected and why *The Times* should support his position.[74]

Dawson, however, did not agree with the prime minister's argument, nor did he feel comfortable in the paper putting it forward as its position. Instead, he suggested that the prime minister put his thoughts down on paper. A week later, Bonar Law had drafted his argument, but since he had admonished his cabinet not to comment on the debt negotiations just a week earlier, he and Dawson decided that the article should be published anonymously.[75]

It appeared in *The Times* as a dispatch "From a Colonial Correspondent" on the morning of January 27, the same morning the *Olympic* docked in Southampton. Dawson's diary, published years later, revealed the prime minister as the true author and recorded, "I was all for letting the world know his arguments in a very difficult case but would not myself undertake to support them. He seemed a little sad at this, but we parted friends, and I carried out my undertaking."[76]

One of Bonar Law's biographers attributed the unusual and duplicitous publication to his subject's "desperation to bring his colleagues around to this perspective."[77]

The article proclaimed: "What our Government should do is to refuse to fund while conditions are at present. If America insists upon payment of the debt in full, I do not suggest that we should repudiate it. What I suggest is that we should pay the interest year by year, and I cannot believe that any American Government would demand that the rate should be higher than that at which they themselves can borrow."

"In taking this course," the article went on, "the Government would be appealing to the fair play of the American people, and in the long run I am certain that that people, who are as fair-minded and as little grasping as any nation in the world, would, if they understood the position, refuse to make such demands as are made now."[78]

This was Bonar Law's appeal, based on his belief that the morality of the issue would move American opinion over time to better terms. Yet it would be a difficult position for those involved in the negotiations to understand. How was it a moral offence at 3 percent, but perfectly acceptable at 2.5, especially when the alternative was to pay the full 5 percent?

Reporters at the pier in Southampton were eager to talk with Baldwin that Saturday morning just after breakfast when the *Olympic* docked. The chancellor invited about a dozen of them aboard to talk in his luxurious stateroom, which, he explained, had been provided by the White Star Line at no expense to the British taxpayer.[79]

As careful as he had been with the American press when he left New York, he seemed completely at home with the British reporters and took time to answer their questions. He was not in a rush, as the boat train to London would not leave until 11:30 A.M. He wanted the reporters to know why he believed so strongly that proposed settlement terms should be accepted.

He explained that as far as the Americans were concerned, the US debt commission had issued the British delegation a take-it-or-leave-it offer, with the approval of the president of the United States. It would soon expire, however, should there not be enough time for the 67th Congress to pass the requisite legislation by the end of its session at midday on March 4. To help the reporters better understand the nuances of the situation, Baldwin expounded on the role of Congress in the settlement process.

"The great difference between America and this country," he told them, "is that the settlement of the debt, in America, is in the hands of politicians." Baldwin was implying that many American politicians were naïve about foreign matters. "If you look at the Senate," he explained, "you will find that the majority of its members come from the agricultural and pastoral communities, and they do not realize the existing position with regard to the meaning of the international debt."[80]

After his two-week visit, Baldwin was now lecturing the British press as an authority on US politicians, the country's population, and Americans' scant knowledge of the British debt situation. "The bulk of the people in America," he explained, "have no acquaintance with it. Great Britain lives on international trade, but in America this is not so. The people in the West merely sell wheat and hogs and other produce and take no further interest in connection with the international debt or international trade."[81]

Baldwin's comments made the afternoon papers that day. The chancellor had also made mention of the negotiations, saying, "We had reached the stage when, according to the present outlook, we could not hope for better terms." Baldwin did not, however, tell the reporters the actual terms, or if he did, they were not reported accurately, for he was quoted as saying that "on the Commission terms of three-and-a-half percent, it would mean we should have to pay about thirty-one million pounds a year." He added that there was "no earthly chance" of the debt commission putting new proposals to Congress before it rose on March 4. "They have gone the limit of what they are likely to propose."

When asked if the matter was now shelved until Congress met again in December, Baldwin answered, "Yes. If no agreement is come to now, the whole thing falls to the ground."[82]

The American reaction to Baldwin's remarks was swift. That afternoon, the US Treasury officially released the actual "suggestions," as it called the terms, stating that they were "made available here today in an official quarter, following the cabled dispatches of an interview with Stanley Baldwin, chancellor of the British exchequer, in which Mr. Baldwin made reference to the so-called American terms." It noted that the terms stated by Baldwin "are not exactly the nearest approach to an arrangement arrived at, although correct in some particulars." Mellon's terms were now officially public.[83]

Several US senators took offense at Baldwin's remarks. One denounced the British chancellor's "pastoral" reference as a clumsy attempt to "cast odium" on the many American senators representing agricultural regions. Another stated that he had hurt his own cause: "Congress is quite unlikely to indulge in an outburst of pro-British sentimentality over the suggestion that a majority of senators and representatives are 'rubes,' who have no competent knowledge of international questions." An article in the *New York Times* was even more blunt, calling Baldwin "indiscreet" and "blundering" in his interview: "In laying the blame upon Congress for the failure to offer terms for debt funding which the British Government could accept, Chancellor Baldwin states a certain amount of undoubted truth. Whether it was wise for him to say it publicly is another question."[84]

*

When Stanley Baldwin reached London later that Saturday afternoon, he was met at Waterloo Station by several friends and Bonar Law's private secretary, J. C. C. Davidson. Baldwin did not need the secretary to tell him how the prime minister felt about the American terms. A remark attributed directly to Bonar Law had appeared in London newspapers that day: "If I sign the terms suggested at Washington, I shall be the most cursed man in England.[85]

Given Bonar Law's admonition to his cabinet not to talk publicly about the debt settlement negotiations, this remark, in addition to the anonymous article in *The Times*, suggested that perhaps the prime minister was preemptively trying to undermine his chancellor before the rest of the cabinet could hear from him on Tuesday.

From Waterloo Station, Baldwin went promptly to 10 Downing Street promptly to meet with the prime minister. It was a brief meeting.

Baldwin understood his friend's torment over the debt settlement. He would later recall that in the settlement, Bonar Law "saw the blood of his two sons," who had been killed in the war. He remembered Bonar Law saying, "We paid in blood; they did not. You can't equate that with a cash payment."[86]

Tensions escalated Monday morning when an editorial in *The Times* refuted the argument made by Bonar Law in the anonymous article the paper had published at his request. The editor asserted that the American terms for settling Britain's debt should be accepted. "Taking everything into consideration—the importance of every reasonable settlement in this world of chaos, the immeasurable harm which may arise from too protracted bargaining, the legal strength of the American case and the manifest goodwill of its spokesman—we are definitely of opinion that a supreme effort should be made this week to reach an agreement."[87]

Other news editors concurred. "The majority of opinion as expressed in the London papers this morning favors acceptance of the American terms for funding the debt," reported a round-up story that included excerpts from the *Daily Telegraph, Morning Post, Daily News, Westminster Gazette, Daily Mail,* and *Herald.*[88]

That afternoon, Ambassador Harvey met with Bonar Law to convey the American case. Baldwin sat in on this, but "remained silent." The chancellor would make his case to full the cabinet the next day.[89]

By all accounts, it was an unusual and dramatic meeting on Tuesday, January 30. After Baldwin strongly recommended that the American terms be accepted, Bonar Law "did an extraordinary thing," Lord Derby, the secretary of state for war, recorded in his diary. Rather than asking each of the members for their opinions as he usually did, he expressed his own right away, saying that "his mind was quite made up, and that nothing would induce him to remain the head of a government which consented to sign."[90]

The entire Cabinet understood that he was threatening to resign as prime minister if he did not have his way.

"We were all aghast at this," Derby wrote, adding that the lord high chancellor "really voiced our opinions when he made in a very tactful way a remonstrance against a pistol being put to our heads."

This made the normally democratic prime minister see that he had acted imperiously. In short order, he corrected himself and sought their opinions. Derby recounts that, with one exception, "we were absolutely unanimous in saying that we ought to accept the terms, and it looked at the moment as if there would be a break of the government there and then, but luckily somebody—I cannot remember who—suggested that we might adjourn and meet again the next day."

The prime minister's behavior had upset several of the cabinet members, particularly the Duke of Devonshire, who was serving as the secretary of state for the colonies. Derby described him as "indignant" and that "there was not a Cabinet but a Dictator," which was precisely what they had disliked about the Lloyd George government. Derby himself said that he did not see how he "could remain a member of a government which repudiated a debt."[91]

On the following day at noon, the members of the cabinet met without Bonar Law, but with his knowledge, in Lord Cave's room in the House of Lords, to discuss how to deal with the situation. The threat of Bonar Law's resignation created the possibility of a major political crisis and the end of their new Conservative government, which had been in office for only three months. It had been difficult enough to convince Bonar Law to lead them, and they knew that no one else had the gravitas to form another government. Baldwin, Lord Cave, and the Duke of Devonshire were deputed to speak to Bonar Law and convince him to withdraw his threat of resignation before the cabinet was scheduled to meet again later that afternoon.

While the members of the cabinet were meeting to decide how to approach their prime minister and avert a crisis, Reginald McKenna, who had initially counseled Bonar Law to reject the American terms, visited 10 Downing Street to inform him that City opinion was now overwhelmingly in favor of acceptance.

When the Cabinet reconvened that Wednesday afternoon, there was little discussion. According to Derby, "Bonar said he had slept on it and had come to the conclusion that he was asking his colleagues to make too great a sacrifice." The proceedings despite "a full attendance of ministers," lasted only a few minutes. When the last three arrived, "there had been barely time for them to discard their overcoats" before the cabinet, including Bonar Law, voted to accept the American terms.[92]

Bonar Law left no account explaining his change of heart. Whether it was due to persuasion or duty, is not known. Either way, the prime minister's decision kept the new government together. He had not yet been diagnosed with terminal throat cancer, but he would not live out the year.

∽

Baldwin's skill in influencing public opinion remained underappreciated until many years later, when a biographer commented: "One is left wondering whether Baldwin's interview with the journalists on the *Olympic* was quite the accidental indiscretion that it seemed. Baldwin had carried the whole Cabinet with him over an issue on which they had been unanimously against him only a few days before, and he had forced the prime minister into complete capitulation. Someone who can do this is either very strong or very lucky or both."[93]

Five days after he returned to English soil, Baldwin delivered, through diplomatic channels, the British government's acceptance of the American offer. This gave Mellon, the debt commission, and Harding thirty-one days to move the legislation through Congress.

The US House of Representatives voted in favor of the debt settlement on February 9, with many Democrats voting with the Republican majority. Likewise, the Senate followed suit and President Harding signed the legislation, named the Smoot-Burton Act, on February 28. There was no ceremony at the White House. The president and Mrs. Harding left Washington on March 5, as planned, for a month's vacation with "a party of friends" on a special train en route to Florida. It was reported that he was "glad to be rid of Congress."[94]

The *New York Times*, in an editorial published after the Senate vote, wrote, "It is not yet known precisely what arguments led Mr. Bonar Law's government to reverse its position within two days" but added, "Whatever the ins and outs leading up to the decision, it has happily been made." In appraising the Mellon-Baldwin agreement, the editorial concluded that it was "the greatest financial transaction between two nations that was ever completed."[95]

Montagu Norman, for his part, offered his opinion of it all privately, in a letter to Basil Blackett on February 26, writing: "I don't know what your view is of the US debt settlement, but I should like to know. I feel sure you are well content." Norman believed the settlement was good, but as he told Blackett, it might have been better if Baldwin had not been called home so soon and "had been allowed a freer hand on the spot, helped as he was by a rising tide throughout the United States and by the French madness on the Ruhr."[96]

5

WESTMINSTER ABBEY

While Stanley Baldwin was in the United States meeting with Andrew Mellon and the debt commission, Winston Churchill was in the South of France with his family, enjoying the warm climate and the winter sun over the Mediterranean. For him, it was a working vacation, and his goal was to complete at least the first volume of his war memoir, and perhaps the second.

He had been writing it in fits and spurts since 1919. After losing his seat in Parliament in the November 1922 general election, his friend and former adviser on Arab affairs, T. E. Lawrence, advised him to "rest a little—six months perhaps," reminding him that "there is that book of memoirs." It was advice that Churchill could appreciate. For the first time in twenty-two years, he had no governmental responsibility. The Balfour Note and the British debt to the United States no longer commanded his attention, nor did he make any public comment about Baldwin's refunding mission to America.[1]

In addition to writing his war memoir, Churchill had recently taken on another project, the restoration of a country house on a hill in Kent, about twenty-five miles south of London. He had purchased Chartwell Manor, as it was known, in September 1922, during the same week that his daughter Mary was born. He was enthralled by the estate from the moment he first toured its grounds and saw its stunning view over a quiet valley. He knew immediately that he wanted to make it his permanent home.[2]

This would require substantial time and money, and it would mark a profound change for him and his family. The large country house would give him space to work, paint, and entertain. During the renovations, Winston and Clemmie gave up their London house in Sussex Square and rented a villa in Cannes for six months. They shared a fondness for the French Riviera, having vacationed there before, sometimes separately. They arrived with their family on December 2, less than two months after Winston's defeat in Dundee.

During their winter *séjour* on the Côte d'Azur, Winston returned to London several times to deal with matters related to his book, as well as to check on renovations to Chartwell and to take his ten-year-old son, Randolph, back to school. The journey of almost nine hundred miles was neither difficult nor unpleasant, especially since *Le Train Bleu*, which was named for its deep blue cars with gold trim, serviced the route between Calais on the North Sea to Menton on the Mediterranean. The first-class-only train suited Churchill to a tee, with its French chefs serving meals in the Pergola restaurant car.[3]

On one trip in late January, Winston reported on his war memoir's progress to Clemmie, "I have been working steadily at the book and there is practically nothing now to do except to read the final page proofs." He added that the title was still in doubt, but this too would be settled soon. The best suggestions so far, he told her, were "Within the Storm," "The Meteor Flat," and "The World Crisis," but he found "none of them very satisfactory."

At that time, Stanley Baldwin had just returned from America and had caused a stir with his remarks to the press upon his arrival at Southampton. Churchill, however, held his tongue and did not engage in the ensuing public controversy. He did comment privately though to Clemmie: "Baldwin has returned empty handed from America. There is no doubt they are finding the problem no more easy to settle than we did." Winston closed his letter with "tender love my sweet—a very nice photo in the *Times* yesterday of your hitting a back hander." Clemmie, playing in competitive lawn tennis, was now the Churchill making news, while Winston was temporarily out of the public eye.[4]

Inevitably though, sightings of Churchill in and around Whitehall led to speculation in the press. "Rumour is again busy with the name of Mr. Winston Churchill," said one report. "Two months have elapsed since he sustained a sensational defeat at Dundee, and during that period little or nothing has been heard of him."[5]

Another story attributed to Churchill reported that "he is prepared to consider an offer from Mr. Bonar Law to place him once more in a position of Ministerial responsibility." When asked about this, Churchill replied dismissively that "the story is totally devoid of foundation" and explained that he was merely in London for a brief period, at the end of which he would complete his "rest cure in the South of France."[6]

For more than a week, London's Ritz Hotel, with its impeccable service and lush surroundings, was Churchill's base of operations. Opened in 1906, it was one of the first buildings in London with steel framing, which allowed its weight to be carried by the strength of the steel rather than by bulky stone and concrete. This permitted higher ceilings and wider interior spaces without the need of supporting columns. Its architects, Mewès and Davis, the same men who had designed the Hôtel Ritz in Paris and the *Majestic*'s interiors, had again created a special atmosphere of elegant restraint through the consistency and unity in their design.[7]

On Tuesday, January 30, 1923, Winston wrote to Clemmie, "The week is passing very rapidly away and I am so busy I hardly ever leave the Ritz except for meals." Those meals, however, were seldom taken by Churchill alone. "On Thursday, the Prince is lunching with me at Buck's Club . . . to talk polo and politics," he wrote. Churchill was referring to Edward, the Prince of Wales, who would become King Edward VIII thirteen years later, only to abdicate the throne after holding it a little less than a year.

Winston also met with Geoffrey Dawson, editor of *The Times*. The paper was paying £5,000 to run a series of sixteen excerpts from his forthcoming book, which would begin running on February 8. Dawson had read the proofs and made some suggestions about the book and potential titles. Winston told Clemmie, "*The Times* is very friendly and helpful. They have turned some of their best men on to try to find mottoes for the chapter headings I have been unable to fill."

J. L. Garvin, another influential London editor, and a longtime friend, had also been given a full set of proofs and was "absolutely satisfied with it." Winston confided to Clemmie that Garvin would be writing "a tremendous review" in the *Observer*, "when the time came."[8]

∞

Churchill left London on February 4 and returned to Cannes on the Blue Train. While little but rumors had been written about him for several months, all of that was about to change because of the serialization of his book. On February 8, *The Times* touted, "The book is not a mere chronicle of the military and naval operations, but a complete account, from Mr. Churchill's point of view, of the whole movement of events—political and diplomatic, military and naval—which led up to the war and marked its opening phase."[9]

Winston arrived back in Cannes to find thousands of mimosa trees on the Côte d'Azur in bloom, turning the hillsides golden. His daughters Diana and Sarah had watched the annual parade known as the *Bataille de Fleurs*, in which horse-drawn carriages and open automobiles filled with sweet-smelling mimosa blooms and beautiful women in festive costumes paraded along La Croisette, the town's main boulevard bordering the Mediterranean, throwing bouquets of the fluffy yellow flowers at the spectators. Diana, thirteen years old, and Sarah, seven, had been photographed by London's *Sunday Pictorial*, wearing dresses, hats, and clutching bouquets. The caption described them as "the charming little daughters of Mrs. Winston Churchill." Clemmie had sent the press cutting to him.[10]

With excerpts of the book running in *The Times*, and the page proofs delivered, Churchill could relax now, at least until the April start of the London season, when he would be feted during the swirl of social events. He "spent many happy sunlit hours painting," and played polo, perhaps to show that he had recovered from his surgery and was back in form, enjoying himself.[11]

Churchill sent advance copies of the book, which now had a title, *The World Crisis*, to several of his friends, including his cousin, the Duke of Marlborough, whom he fondly called Sunny. In his letter from Cannes, Winston wrote: "It has been vy pleasant out here & such a relief after all these years not to have a score of big anxieties & puzzles on one's shoulders. The Government moulders placidly away. But I must confess myself more interested in the past than in the present." He repeated this same sentiment to others as well.[12]

The Prince of Wales, who had received a copy, wrote back, remarking: "I'm so glad that you've had a lot of polo & are fit enough again to enjoy it. It's great news to hear you are playing in London this coming season & I hope we'll get lots of games together."[13]

Churchill, too, began looking forward to the coming season in London, especially after good reviews of the book had started to appear, including his friend Garvin's, which claimed, "Amongst the shoal of other narratives and apologies on the British side, it is like a whale amongst minnows."[14]

∽

Winston soon accepted several invitations to social events and speaking engagements. He also began to think about a return to politics, albeit on his own schedule, as he promoted the book and enjoyed his newly enhanced reputation as historian, author, and government leader in troublesome times.

He left Cannes for London on the morning of April 18. Clemmie and the children would follow. The London season was beginning earlier than usual because of the Duke of York's wedding. Albert, the second son of King George V and known to friends as Bertie, was to be married in Westminster Abbey on April 26 to Lady Elizabeth Bowes-Lyon. The ceremony promised to be memorable, as it would mark the first time in over five hundred years that a prince of the royal house would be wed in the Abbey.

The press predicted that the event would ring in the "most brilliant week of the London season," and one that was likely to be "the most brilliant enjoyed since the war."[15]

Winston and Clemmie, of course, were on the guest list. No one then had anticipated that Bertie would later become the king of England, let alone that his bride would become the future queen mother. Even so, the unusual Abbey wedding was cause for grand pageantry and a joyous celebration. A London journalist wrote, "The vivid scarlet of military dress, the lustrous gold of heavy shoulder-knots, the streaming white feathers of the helmets of the Gentlemen-at-Arms, and the subtle combinations of beautiful colour in the gowns of the ladies set against the great grey pillars of the old Abbey made a picture fit only for a master hand."[16]

The following month, Churchill gave a speech to the Aldwych Club in London, his first since his defeat at the polls in November. Promoted as a speech about "the present political situation," it signaled to political watchers that he was eyeing a return to government.[17]

He began on a humorous note. "After seventeen rough years of official work," he told his business-minded audience, "I can assure you that there are worse things than private life." This brought laughter from the friendly crowd. His main theme, socialism, was a serious matter that he believed would take hold of the country if the Liberals and Conservatives continued to battle each other. "So bitter against one another are the groups and parties which are opposed to Socialism," he said, "that the official leaders and managers—both of the Conservative and Liberal Parties—vie with one another in dulling and deadening the public to the danger which is approaching."[18]

His speech was widely covered and commented upon, with one columnist writing, "It is not at all clear from this speech whether Mr. Churchill considers himself a Liberal or a Conservative or is pledged to remain a Coalitionist for all time." Another was quite certain of what to make of it. "The speech," he wrote, "was a very emphatic political reentry by the late Member for Dundee."[19]

The retirement of Bonar Law as prime minster injected a major surprise into the London season. He had also surprised many by not resigning in person to the king as was traditional—instead, he informed King George by letter, without suggesting a successor, and let it be known that he did not wish to do so. This left the decision to the sovereign. Lord Curzon, the secretary of state for foreign affairs was believed to be the favorite due to his extensive experience. When the king asked the opinion of Arthur Balfour, now a peer, Balfour counseled in favor of Stanley Baldwin, who was a member of the House of Commons, and would be a more popular choice for the democratic times than Curzon, a member of the House of Lords.

Only seven months into the job of chancellor of the exchequer, Baldwin did not expect to be chosen for the top post. With such brief ministerial experience to his credit in comparison to Curzon, and without Bonar Law's endorsement, Baldwin himself viewed Curzon as the more likely successor. Yet it was Baldwin who was called to Buckingham Palace by the king.[20]

After accepting the king's invitation to form a government, Baldwin responded to the cheering crowd awaiting his arrival at Downing Street, saying, "I want your prayers more than your congratulations."[21]

The change in the premiership raised speculation that Baldwin would make changes in the cabinet. He made few, however, leaving Curzon as the head of the foreign office. For his own replacement, Baldwin wanted Reginald McKenna, who had served as chancellor in Lloyd George's coalition. McKenna, however, wanted to stay in City finance. Baldwin's second choice was Robert Horne, who also turned him down. The delay in making key appointments to the cabinet raised concern that his government might be short-lived.

There was also speculation that Churchill might return to the Conservative Party, in which he had begun his political career before leaving it in 1904. His Aldwych speech had made that possibility seem more likely, especially now that Baldwin was prime minister. On May 26, the "Londoner's Diary" column in the *Evening Standard* opined, "The time may not be ripe for him to make his final decision, but I will risk the prophesy that in the fulfillment of time, Mr. Churchill will return to the camp from which he came and to which he instinctively belongs."[22]

Days later, Horne suggested to Baldwin personally that "he would be wise to invite Winston to join the Government, as he would thus secure a powerful colleague and an excellent debater." The new prime minister found the idea unappealing at the time.

Horne was on solid ground in making the suggestion, as he had lunched with Churchill to ask him where he stood politically. Churchill had told him: "I am what I have always been—a Tory Democrat. Force of circumstances has compelled me to serve with another party, but my views have never changed, and I should be glad to give effect to them by rejoining the Conservatives."[23]

The "rumor that Winston Churchill may become a supporter of the Conservative Government" appeared in the *London Sunday Times*, on June 3, and was quoted in the *New York Times* on the same date. "What is being said in the Unionist press," another report explained, "seems to point to a desire to make the party familiar with the idea that the process of Conservative reunion which Mr. Baldwin is very anxious to promote, may include the absorption of Mr. Churchill in the party which he deserted on the Free Trade issue nearly twenty years ago."[24]

As the subject of all this speculation, Churchill quietly considered where he might run for a new seat in the Commons and began increasing his visibility. On June 6, he and Clemmie attended the Epsom Derby, a fashionable horse race; he spoke at Harrow, the prep school he had attended, on the evening of the annual pageant acted by students; and he also attended an investiture at Buckingham Palace as one of the thirty-one Elder Brothers at Trinity House, a royal corporation that maintains buoys, beacons, and navigational aids.

Since 1921, Churchill had been president of the English-Speaking Union, which sought to bind the United States in friendship to England and the British dominions. When he officiated at one of its events the previous year, he had told Clemmie, "It was uphill work to make an enthusiastic speech about the United States at a time when so many hard things are said of us over there and when they are wringing the last penny out of their unfortunate allies."[25]

This year, the leadership of the English-Speaking Union, which included Lord Balfour and Lord Grey, were honoring Walter Hines Page, the American ambassador to Great Britain during the Wilson administration. Page had pushed for the entry of the United States into the war long before President Wilson would even hear of it. The former ambassador had died in December 1918, and the group would be unveiling a tablet in his memory in Westminster Abbey on July 3. Page's widow was arriving from America for the ceremony; and Churchill would be a guest at a dinner in her honor, as would his friend J. L. Garvin of the *Observer* and the American painter John Singer Sargent.

The Churchills received several more invitations, including one to a garden party at Buckingham Palace and another to a dinner-dance to be thrown by Mrs. Cornelius Vanderbilt, the American socialite who regularly appeared in the social columns of New York and Washington newspapers. Her cousin, Consuelo Vanderbilt, had been married to Churchill's cousin, Sunny, and Winston was close to both of them. Mrs. Vanderbilt had planned the July 2 event at Brook House, a mansion in London's West End, in hopes of finding a suitable husband, for her twenty-two-year-old daughter, Grace, preferably a British nobleman. The calculating mother had rented the fashionable Mayfair mansion for the 1923 season from Lord and Lady Mountbatten expressly for that purpose.

The star-packed guest list included European princes and princesses, British dukes and duchesses, counts and countesses. The new prime minister, Stanley Baldwin, attended with his wife, Lucy, and daughter, Betty. Another dozen or so eligible young women did so as well, including the daughter of Lord Curzon, and the daughter of Otto Kahn, the wealthy New York banker. The music was provided by Benjamin Baruch Ambrose and his popular seven-piece band, which played regularly at the Embassy Club, an exclusive society haunt of the time, and one of the best dance clubs in London.[26]

The *Daily Telegraph* published a list of "those present" the next day that numbered almost two hundred, including the Churchills, and several of their close friends and colleagues, including John Lavery, Winston's painting instructor, and his wife, Hazel. Austen Chamberlain and his wife were also in attendance as was Eddie Marsh, Winston's former private secretary.[27]

Sometime during the evening, Winston Churchill may have met one of Mrs. Vanderbilt's social friends from America, Andrew Mellon, the secretary of the Treasury of the United States.

If not, they would meet the next day.

∞

Outside Westminster Abbey on Tuesday, July 3, a late afternoon thunderstorm sent a large crowd scurrying into the magnificent, twin-towered church, where kings and queens had been crowned for centuries, and where royalty had recently married. Hundreds had come to attend a memorial service in honor of Walter Hines Page, the US ambassador to the Court of St. James's during the war, who, in the eyes of many, had been "one of the best friends that Great Britain ever had, and a far-seeing and practical crusader in the cause of Anglo-American cooperation."[28]

Some six months earlier, several former prime ministers had made a public appeal to memorialize Page, a proposal readily endorsed by *The Times* of London. The paper's editor asserted that "no man of our times had had a more vivid and more inspiring conception of what Great Britain and the United States might achieve by acting together," and he urged that the America ambassador "should be permanently commemorated by some such means as a tablet in Westminster Abbey."[29]

The Abbey leadership promptly took the appeal under advisement and shortly thereafter decided to organize a lasting tribute to Page in cooperation with the English-Speaking Union. They commissioned a sculptor to incise lettering in a tablet to be made from white marble. They specified that it was to be placed near the Chapter House, a medieval part of the church where Britain had honored another US ambassador. The decision to commemorate Walter Hines Page with an eternal memorial in Westminster Abbey made him only the third American to be so honored.[30]

Landing outside the double-arched entrance to the Chapter House, Westminster Abbey, where Mellon and Churchill met on July 3, 1923. The plaque memorializing Walter Hines Page can be seen at the lower right. *Credit: The Historic England Archive, London.*

While the congregation took their seats in the nave and transepts of the Abbey in anticipation of the service, a private ceremony to unveil the Page tablet was taking place just outside the nearby Chapter House. Built in the twelfth century, it was, like the church, a stunning piece of Gothic architecture. Ever since its completion, the octagonal building had appeared to be supported by a single column in its center with struts that vaulted out like a gigantic umbrella in support of the massive ceiling which spanned almost six hundred feet. The structure's vastness, and its huge stained-glass windows, gave it a luminous and divine aura.

The small unveiling party of fewer than twenty milled about in the Chapter House and outside it on what had long been thought of as its entrance porch, where the ceremony would take place. The porch was in fact a landing at the top of nine wide stone steps at the end of the inner vestibule.

As they were called to assemble, Andrew Mellon and Winston Churchill found themselves together, standing in the intimate space on the landing. With them were the Page family, Prime Minister Stanley Baldwin, and a handful of dignitaries, facing a stained-glass window crowned by angels heralding Anglo-American unity.[31]

While diplomatic protocol called for them to be introduced, neither Mellon, nor Churchill, had any business with the other. The American secretary of the Treasury was on vacation, and the famous British statesman was no longer in government. Mellon was attending as a representative of the US government and Churchill was there as an officer of the British chapter of the English-Speaking Union.

While this was perhaps their first meeting, Mellon and Churchill were not unknown to one another. Ambition had brought each of them onto the world stage. The press covered their respective personal comings and goings as closely as their quips—mostly Churchill's—and silences—mostly Mellon's—all the while keeping records of their individual political wins and losses.

Mellon knew Churchill was regarded as an accomplished military officer, respected author, and influential political figure. In reviewing his new book, the recently launched *Time* magazine had put him on its cover. It lauded him as a literary genius, and dubbed him "the Suzerain of the Seas," while noting that his political style often "caused no inconsiderable alarm among his colleagues."[32]

There was less for Churchill to know about the publicity-shy American Treasury secretary. But while he was in London, *Time* put Mellon on its cover, writing that "his arrival is anticipated with no little speculation," given that "the United States is Europe's great creditor."[33]

The significance of their meeting was not lost on Baldwin who could observe them up close as they interacted. He knew firsthand that Mellon, like most Americans, believed that Britain and the Allies owed the United States not only money, but gratitude for having come to Europe's aid. Baldwin also knew of Churchill's resolve to make America see that it had an obligation to write off the debts in recognition of the Allies having fought in common cause in defense of democracy and freedom. It boiled down to Mellon being as determined to settle the debts as Churchill was to have them canceled. The prime minister likely appreciated the irony of the moment knowing that the ancient crypt lying right below where they were meeting had once served as the Royal Treasury.

Promptly at 5:30 P.M., Herbert Ryle, the dean of Westminster, and the Chapter canons, a select constituency of priests from the Church of England, entered from the nearby cloisters in procession, "wearing their robes, edged with black, scarlet and purple." The clerics joined the small party huddled together on the landing above the wide stone stairs, while the choir remained below.[34]

Lord Grey of Fallodon, who had worked closely with Page as Britain's secretary of state for foreign affairs, officiated, and spoke briefly. In a low voice, with his eyes directed at the tablet, he paid tribute to his former colleague, "We in this country feel a deep gratitude for the sympathy and moral support which Walter Page gave us in the greatest crisis in our history." He also cited the bond that Page had wanted others to feel. "It was very near his heart," Grey remembered, "that there should be between his country and ours a true knowledge and understanding, each of the other."

He then stepped forward and drew away the white covering to reveal the tablet. The emblazoned name, WALTER HINES PAGE, stood out in gold letters, as did the last words on the plaque, "The friend of Britain in her sorest need."[35]

After Dean Ryle accepted the Page memorial on behalf of the Abbey and promised that it would always be "preserved, tended, and regarded with affectionate veneration," he led the unveiling party down the centuries-worn steps. Veiled in black, Mrs. Page took the arm of the prime minister. Together, she and Baldwin filed out as the choir sang the hymn "Hark, the Sound of Heavenly Voices," with the rest of the party following in procession. Through the cloisters, they made their way to the main Abbey where the packed congregation waited. The music from the Abbey's organ heightened the grandeur of the occasion.[36]

Behind the Page family, Mellon and Churchill walked from the dimly lit, arched passageway out into the sunlight of the cloisters, where the rain had let up and the scarlet cassocks of the choir blazed in contrast to the soft green lawn of the central garth. The two future rivals entered the Abbey through the west cloister door and passed through the nave between the north and south aisles, where they could hear strains from the hymn: "Walk in golden light, . . . marching with thy cross their banner, . . . reign in heavenly glory."[37]

When they arrived at the section normally occupied by the choir, they turned in opposite directions to take their seats. Churchill sat down in the first row on the right with Baldwin, Lord Grey, and former prime ministers David Lloyd George, Herbert Asquith, and Bonar Law. Mellon took his place in the first row on the left, facing Churchill, alongside the Page family and a few American embassy officials. Neither Mellon nor Churchill, had any speaking part in the service; they could both focus on the dean's address celebrating the Anglo-American bond—or each other.

From where he was seated, Mellon could observe Churchill, looking like he belonged, as he sat alongside the elite club of current and former prime ministers. Mellon knew that it was widely expected that Churchill would soon return to government. What he could not know was that when

Churchill did, he still intended to put America in an invidious position before the world.

Across the aisle, Churchill could see Mellon, who hardly fit the picture of a man with the world's economy in his pocket. Britain had stood atop the pinnacle of financial power for centuries. Now, it belonged to the American looking back at him.

After some prayers, the service ended with the choir singing "a combined National Anthem" in two verses—"God Save the King," followed by "My Country 'Tis of Thee"—to the same melody. An American attendee remembered the service as "memorable and affecting." *The Times* of London called it "a singularly moving close to a most impressive service." The *New York Times* agreed, observing that the service "was one of great beauty and impressiveness."[38]

Mellon and Churchill may have been impressed with the service celebrating the Anglo-American bond of friendship, but there was no indication of them having had friendly inclinations toward one another.[39]

⁂

With the London season in full swing, Americans, including A. W. and Ailsa, enjoyed invitations to the whirl of luncheons, garden parties, and dinner dances it occasioned. They celebrated the Fourth of July at an afternoon reception hosted by the American embassy at Lansdowne House and later a banquet at the Savoy Hotel thrown by the American Society.

The highlight of the Independence Day celebrations in London for Mellon, though, took place in the House of Commons, when Prime Minister Stanley Baldwin spoke about Britain's settlement of its indebtedness to the United States. "Whatever may be said about the terms agreed upon," he began, "I am convinced that regarding them as business terms, they are fair and honest terms." This received cheers, as did his statement that the American debt commissioners "did everything in their power to make the payment of those terms as easy and convenient to us as they were able."[40]

Baldwin's comments may have been directed at Mellon, who had been greeted by the prime minister on the terrace of the House of Commons earlier that day in a manner described by a member of Parliament as "that of two old schoolmates."[41]

In the House of Commons that day, a member of Parliament asked Baldwin about the Allies' debts to Britain, and the prime minister reiterated his government's policy, "Those who owed us money still owe us money." He added that the French government's decision to reject the offer Britain had made in January—which, notably, did not contain any conditional language related to American policy—has now left "our hands perfectly free to deal with all these matters as we may deem best." Securing a settlement with the French government ranked high on Mellon's to-do list as well.[42]

The prime minister continued, asserting that he viewed the settlement he had negotiated with Mellon as the "first step towards the settlement of the world's problems." He explained to the House that he was convinced that it would pave the way for America "to work hand in hand with us wherever any work is to be done for the regeneration of this world."[43]

The following day, July 5, back in Washington, Parker Gilbert, Mellon's able undersecretary, oversaw the delivery of the financial instruments that would conclude the refunding of Britain's debt to the United States. The British embassy delivered "1,000 bonds of $4,600,000 denomination each, dated December 15, 1922, and maturing December 15, 1984, covering the 62-year period of the funding arrangement." The agreement provided that the bonds be payable in United States gold coin or its equivalent in gold bullion, or with any bonds of the United States issued after April 6, 1917, the date that the United States had declared war against Germany. The first payment had already been made before the agreement was executed and paid in US Liberty Bonds. Upon receipt, Gilbert marked "received" on the demand obligations—which had been held by the Treasury since the loans were made—and relinquished them to the British embassy.

With that, the greatest financial transaction in modern history was concluded without fanfare, and as a routine Treasury matter, exactly as Gilbert knew Secretary Mellon preferred.[44]

Reassured that Britain and the United States were in alignment, and the transaction concluded, A. W. could now enjoy the rest of the London season with Ailsa.

The Mellons were received on the afternoon of July 5 as guests of the prime minister and Mrs. Baldwin at the first large social gathering at 10 Downing Street since Baldwin had taken the premiership. Ailsa and A. W. inched their way along with hundreds of other guests, from the cabinet room to the gardens behind Numbers 10 and 11, which abutted the Horse Guards Parade. It was a perfect summer day for the visitors to enjoy tea and band music.[45]

During Mellon's visit, Joseph Duveen, the enterprising London-based art dealer, was determined to capitalize on Mellon's first trip back to Europe in ten years. While Mellon had previously purchased a few Old Master paintings from his gallery, Duveen was determined to increase his influence over the wealthy art collector. His tactics of choice: flattery, surveillance, and bribery. A master of ingratiation, he arranged for Mellon's portrait to be painted by the popular artist, Oswald Birley, and he brokered requests from "people of great taste in art" to see Mellon's collection in Washington. Duveen also had presents delivered to the cabins of Ailsa and her chaperone aboard the *Majestic*. He even tried to outmaneuver American embassy personnel in making reservations for the Mellons at Claridge's where several of the hotel staff that he tipped generously would keep him informed of Mellon's movements. His efforts resulted in a visit from A. W. and Ailsa to his showroom on Old Bond Street, where they enjoyed "a very interesting hour's talk." Mellon liked two of the paintings he saw, enough for Duveen to quote prices and alert his New York office of the development.[46]

On July 20, the Mellons and the Baldwins found themselves seated together at the Lord Mayor's annual banquet for the bankers and merchants of London at the Mansion House. In representing the business interests of the City, the Lord Mayor operated independently of the elected mayor of London. The setting for the dinner was the eighteenth-century building's "Egyptian Hall," a curious misnomer as there was nothing Egyptian about its architecture. The vast Palladium-style auditorium could accommodate more than three hundred under its eighty-foot ceiling supported by twenty-four white Corinthian columns with gilded capitals.

Joining the prime minister and American Treasury secretary at the head table was the colorful and enigmatic Montagu Norman, who had been part of the delegation to America to refund the debt.

Following tradition, Baldwin, as prime minister, gave the keynote address and reported positive economic news: "We have maintained unimpaired the credit of this City and of our country—a credit that is the life blood of commerce and on which our lives and the food of our people depend." The audience understood that this had been achieved by the settlement of Britain's debt to the United States. Baldwin then spoke more personally about the settlement: "I know my friend Mr. Mellon would agree with the Governor of the Bank of England and with me, that no business arrangement could have been carried out more fairly, more honorably and more pleasantly in its details than the settlement of our debt to America which was negotiated in Washington last January." This brought cheers, with Baldwin adding that it had been possible because neither he, nor the governor of the Bank of England, nor Mr. Mellon, had ever been members of the legal profession but were all businessmen. That remark brought even more cheers from the audience. [47]

While Mellon and Churchill were traveling in the same orbit during the month, neither seemed to have made an effort to socialize with the other, nor to communicate in any way. Nor was there any evidence of even a polite nod during the king and queen's garden party at Buckingham Palace. It marked the end of London's social season and the last day that Mellon would be in the capital. Both the Mellons and the Churchills were on the guest list, but perhaps one or both of them preferred to blend into the crowd of two thousand. [48]

On July 27, Mellon arrived in Paris for the French leg of his vacation amid a din of speculation in the press about the nature of his visit. He gave reporters his usual story, saying that he was on vacation and that his mission in Paris was "strictly private and personal business."[49]

These statements were no longer believed, and his visit was interpreted as "a desire to sound France out on her war debt to the United States in connection with coming reparations discussions." This was partially true. But before taking any part in such discussions, Mellon wanted to visit French battlefields to see for himself how badly France had suffered in the war and the state of the country's devastation.[50]

The logistics for Mellon's motoring tour and his accommodations were overseen by Theodore Rousseau, the manager of the Paris branch of the Guaranty Trust Company of New York. Born in Savannah, Georgia, Rousseau had moved to Europe during the war.

On Tuesday, July 31, they set off from Paris in a dismal rain, and headed east toward Verdun, where one of the deadliest battles on the Western Front had taken place. Mellon wanted to come back through Rheims, where the great cathedral in which French kings were once crowned had been heavily shelled during the first year of the war.

The entourage returned in time for Mellon's meeting with Premier Raymond Poincaré on Friday morning, August 3, at the French foreign office at the Quai d'Orsay. Planned to be a courtesy call, instead Mellon learned that President Warren Harding had died.[51]

∽

News of the death of the American president shocked the world.

"In a twinkling of an eye." wrote Washington's *Evening Star*, "the political situation has been changed."[52]

In Calvin Coolidge's first act as president, he issued a statement that he planned to carry out his predecessor's policies and to keep "those who have given their efforts to assist him" in his cabinet. The new executive set a course for "meticulous continuity."[53]

Parker Gilbert met with President Coolidge "for some time" on the first day of his presidency. They both knew that Mellon would not be able to return from Paris in time for Harding's funeral in Marion, Ohio. Gilbert learned that Coolidge expected all the members in his cabinet to continue their work in the same way and with the same policies. Gilbert cabled Mellon saying that he had had a "good talk with the President and that Mellon need not attempt to change his itinerary." He also conveyed to Mellon that Coolidge was "sound" on the Treasury Department's agenda.[54]

Coolidge held his first cabinet meeting on August 14, four days after Harding's funeral. He reaffirmed his position on the major policy issues, including war debts. It, like others, would remain unchanged. He intended for his administration "to do everything it can do honorably, to collect every dollar that is due to the United States from foreign countries," but with "no intention of bearing down on those countries that find themselves wholly unable to pay." Coolidge reiterated, "The policy of 'fund and collect' has been decided upon."[55]

The *New York Times* reported similarly: "The policies of the Harding Administration, not some of them, but all of them . . . will be the policies of President Coolidge." On war debts, the new administration "will continue its efforts to refund all the European debt and to collect the sums due as rapidly as circumstances will permit."[56]

When Mellon arrived on the *Aquitania* in New York on August 17, Gilbert was there to meet the ship at quarantine and take him off on a revenue cutter to Manhattan's Pier A, and then to the Biltmore Hotel located over Grand Central Terminal. Gilbert updated the Treasury secretary that evening and on the train to Washington the next day.

Mellon went to the White House to meet with Coolidge on Monday, August 20. Following an hourlong conference, it was announced that Coolidge's cabinet "with Mellon's acceptance, is brought over intact from the administration of the late President Harding." It was also made known that "in Mr. Mellon's opinion, conditions in Europe show considerable improvement along business and other lines, but that the Ruhr situation still overshadows all other conditions, both political and economic, and that no assurance of returned stability can be looked for so long as this problem remains unsettled."[57]

Mellon and Coolidge had few differences on policy or approach, and they were known commodities to one another. Their worldviews were similar, and they were both quiet men who respected one another's style and manner.

The settlement of the Allies' war debts to the United States that had begun during the Lloyd George government and the Harding administration had now become a matter between the Coolidge administration and the Baldwin government. With the British settlement completed and the goodwill that it seemingly had engendered, Andrew Mellon had achieved a major accomplishment.

Winston Churchill, meanwhile, would soon return to parliamentary power, and believed that the matter of the British debt to the United States needed more interpretation.

6

THE RISE OF THE RIVALRY

W hile the Mellon-Baldwin agreement had settled Britain's war debt as far as the United States was concerned, many Britons harbored misgivings.

Not long after the agreement had been signed, Parker Gilbert was warned by his predecessor at Treasury, Russell Leffingwell, that "it would be a mistake for you to conclude, as I fear you do, that the British like the settlement." Leffingwell explained from personal experience that it was characteristic of the British "to put the best possible face on a bad matter," and warned that "there is practical unanimity among Englishmen in the view that we should have canceled the debt."[1]

Even as the British press was reporting broad approval across England for the settlement when it was announced on February 1, 1923, several newspapers noted a general feeling that the terms were harsh and ungenerous. The government has "unquestionably done the right thing," wrote *The Times* of London, acknowledging that "the American Commission had made considerable concessions" and that Britain "was not likely to get better terms." But the editorial added, "We still hold that interest at two-and-a-half percent would have been a fair rate for Great Britain to pay."[2]

The consequences of the settlement terms, wrote the *Manchester Guardian* that same day, "will probably touch the pocket of every English taxpayer for the rest of his natural life." The editorial writer stated that Britain would still be paying the United States in 1982 for "loans contracted in a war, as remote to those days as the Crimean war is to ours, in which America was herself our ally and for which no other ally will have ever paid a penny . . . it is ridiculous on the face of it, but we must leave the recognition of this absurdity to the unaided perception of the American people."[3]

Shortly after Coolidge took office, syndicated columnist David Lawrence returned from Europe with a similar message for the new president and his administration. "About the most unpopular thing the British government ever did," he wrote, "was to agree to pay the American war debt and about the most unfavorable opinion that could possibly be held of the American government is held by the average man in the street because he believes the United States insisted on its pound of flesh at a time when the British are staggering and stumbling." Lawrence argued that the United States needed to take part in the process of Europe's recovery: "America need not agree in advance to cancel or reduce war debts but cannot refuse to discuss with other governments measures that would relieve them of the strain."[4]

Nine months later, unease with the settlement negotiated by then-chancellor of the exchequer, Stanley Baldwin, had hardened into reproach. WHY DID HE DO IT? asked a newspaper in the industrial town of Stockport, reminding its readers that it had declared the terms "impossible" even before the settlement was made. "His hasty and unfortunate settlement of the terms of payment of our debt," the paper asserted, was now "becoming a serious contributory cause of unemployment." In Stockport, more than 10 percent of the town's population was out of work.[5]

There was also a sense of injustice at the refusal of the United States to consider the loans it made to the Allies as a contribution to the common cause. "The moral side of the problem presented by the Allied debts has not yet sufficiently been explored," said the Stockport editorial, which raised the question of "whether the attempt of one Ally to collect from another Ally money spent in the common cause is not immoral."[6]

The American perspective on the morality of the Allied debts needed no further exploration as far as Calvin Coolidge was concerned. On

December 6, 1923, he addressed it directly during his first address as president to a joint session of Congress.

In his calm and concise manner, he spoke about the wartime loans: "I do not favor the cancellation of this debt, but I see no objection to adjusting it in accordance with the principle adopted for the British debt." With officials from virtually every nation present in a reserved section of the House chamber, he told the packed gallery, "Our country would not wish to assume the role of an oppressive creditor but would maintain the principle that financial obligations between nations are likewise moral obligations which international faith and honor require should be discharged."[7]

His message expressed the opinion of many Americans, including his Treasury secretary, Andrew Mellon.

Mellon's continuing efforts to settle war debts, however, were stalled, as economic and political conditions in Europe remained uncertain. The occupation of the Ruhr by France and Belgium had failed to force Germany to make the required reparation payments. Instead, the German government stood by as spiraling inflation devastated its economy and destroyed the value of its currency.

One German mark, quoted at 12 cents American at the end of 1918, had fallen to below a penny in June 1922. By November 1923, it had become too expensive to print banknotes, being worth, as one writer put it, "something more ridiculous than zero," at 42 billion marks to one US cent. Germans who had no access to foreign currencies had to rely on selling possessions or barter. One eyewitness recalled buying food from farmers with "new and worn clothes, hats, scarves, stockings, cutlery, cigarettes, pipe tobacco, or books with pictures in them—anything but banknotes."[8]

The introduction of a new currency that month helped to restore some semblance of financial order when a reconstituted German central bank, the Reichsbank under the direction of Hjalmar Schacht, took charge of the economy. Reparations, however, if they were to be paid at all, needed to be put on a practical basis. Until they were, the American debt commission would not be able to secure repayment of the loans outstanding from France, Belgium, Italy, and six other debtors.

Five days after his speech to Congress, Coolidge surprised everyone. He announced his plan for the "unofficial participation by Americans in a general European effort to solve the reparations tangle." This marked a significant, but nuanced, departure from the long-standing policy of the Wilson and Harding administrations to avoid any involvement in the resolution of German reparations. For years, the State Department had been using bankers and business leaders as quasi-members of the diplomatic corps. They worked largely behind the scenes and outside normal channels to represent American interests overseas.

Coolidge's plan subtly sanctioned that practice. Sending American financial experts to participate in the Reparations Commission's study of Germany's economic situation would allow Coolidge to diffuse the political risk of involvement. Many believed that it would also introduce an objective source of economic expertise into the fray of competing national interests. The president explained that the United States, "in view of its direct interests as a creditor and the importance of the economic recuperation of Europe," would find the study "of great value." Whether intentional or not, it was a tacit recognition by the Coolidge administration of the connection between war debts and reparations.[9]

On the same day as the Coolidge surprise, British Prime Minister Stanley Baldwin announced one of his own in London. Support for his government had plummeted since Mellon's summer visit. To bolster his political standing, Baldwin had made a bold proposal to reverse Britain's policy of free trade—dating from 1846—by imposing tariffs that he argued would remedy the country's widespread unemployment. The autumn debate over the proposal had evolved into a referendum on his leadership. To the surprise of many, voters in the general election did not believe Baldwin's protectionist plan would alleviate the unemployment crisis and rejected it. The startling defeat left his Conservative government with the sudden likelihood of not having the parliamentary support to continue—after being in power only eight months—and consigned Baldwin to the humiliating consequence of having to resign as prime minister. All that remained was for him to announce it.

With the king and all of Britain anticipating Baldwin's immediate resignation, the London correspondent of the *Guardian* reported the next day, "Nothing so pretty has been seen by way of a political gesture as Mr. Baldwin's return today to Downing Street with a load of holly on the top of his car, to signify that he intended to spend Christmastide at that homestead." The report also included an observation of Baldwin at the scene: "There was no apparent diminution of his cheerfulness, and his pipe was drawing well." The report added, "If it turns out that this is his farewell to Downing Street, nothing will have become him so much as the manner of it."[10]

Late that Tuesday evening, Baldwin announced that his cabinet had decided unanimously that it was their constitutional duty to stay in office until Parliament next met in January. Then, the Liberal and Labour Parties could jockey for control. The unusual and unanticipated decision would prolong the humiliation of the Baldwin government's defeat, but it would allow for a more orderly transition.

Six weeks later, on January 21, 1924, Baldwin resigned, having "met his fate in manly fashion," according to London's *Evening Standard*. Many felt he had made "a good end" to his premiership.[11]

※

The committee of international experts detailed to study the ability of Germany to pay reparations got underway in Paris that January. Charles G. Dawes, a brigadier general during the war, and a former director of the bureau of the budget under President Harding, was chosen by the Reparations Commission as one of its ten members and made chairman.

Tasked with "the stabilization of German currency and the balancing of the German budget," the committee developed "a comprehensive plan for readjustment of the entire reparation burden." Intended to be temporary, the plan took into consideration Germany's ability to pay—in keeping with the approach to war debts in the Treaty of Versailles—and authorized payments to be increased or reduced based on Germany's current economic condition. Its broad provisions included installation of the

Reichsbank as an institution independent from the German government, establishment of the Reichsmark as a new currency, and the conversion of the German National Railroad into a corporation to guarantee a source of revenue for reparation payments. It became known as the Dawes Plan, was approved in April, and adopted in August by the Allied and German governments. None of it would be easily executed. [12]

One scholar put it clearly: "The interrelated problems were the reconstruction of the German monetary system, the withdrawal of France from the Ruhr, and the raising of a foreign loan both to back the new German mark and to rebuild the economy so that Germany could pay reparations." J. P. Morgan and Company would underwrite the loan in the United States and Europe, with more than half of the money coming from the US. [13]

To manage the Dawes Plan, the committee created the position of "agent general for reparations." One foreign correspondent called it the "most important job in Europe, and maybe the world," as the agent general would be required to "liquidate Germany's payments without ruining the other countries' exchanges and without flooding them with German-made goods." [14]

Dawes by this time had been picked to be the vice presidential candidate on the ticket with Coolidge in the 1924 election, which took him out of the running for agent general. Owen D. Young, president of the General Electric Company, who was one of the American representatives to the Dawes Committee, agreed to take the job, but only temporarily, until a permanent replacement could be found.

Among the leading candidates that surfaced immediately was Dwight Morrow, a Columbia Law School graduate who had joined J. P. Morgan in 1913 and had been sent to France during the war by President Wilson as a civilian aide to General John J. Pershing, commander of the American Expeditionary Forces. When Montagu Norman asked Jack Morgan who would be the best person for agent general, Morgan named Morrow. The Morrow candidacy soon ended, though, when reports appeared that foreign governments would not approve a Morgan appointee. In addition, there were objections from Coolidge. Morrow was a close friend and college classmate of the president. Coolidge did not want to be accused of cronyism, nor did he wish to have his campaign and administration appear so favorably inclined toward Wall Street.[15]

The suggestion of Parker Gilbert for agent general was likely put forward by Russell Leffingwell, now a partner at J. P. Morgan. They had worked closely together at the law firm of Cravath and Henderson in New York before Leffingwell had recruited Gilbert to the Treasury Department as a member of the war loan staff. After five years of living on a government salary, Gilbert had returned to his highly remunerative law career.

Gilbert's selection was announced on September 3. Ever industrious and efficient, he promptly got engaged to Louise Todd, whom he had been courting for some time. Three days after their wedding, the newlyweds set sail from New York for a honeymoon in Paris before Gilbert took his post as agent general in Berlin on October 31, 1924.

The German press had already given Gilbert the title of "'emperor' of Europe."[16]

As unexpected as Baldwin's departure had been, his return nine months later was equally unforeseen. The short-lived Labour government of his successor, Ramsay MacDonald, had continued the series of fragile coalitions and minority ministries in Britain that began during the war. It was brought down by a scandal that had raised fears of a Communist threat. The second Baldwin government, however, commenced in November with a sense of hope and higher purpose. One observer described it as a longing for "the reestablishment of the Empire."[17]

Baldwin knew that it would require some daring for his second government to succeed. Despite having taken political risks that caused his own downfall, he did not hesitate to act boldly once again. On November 6, 1924, he appointed Winston Churchill—a Liberal Party member and Baldwin critic—as chancellor of the exchequer.

Reaction from the press involved a scramble for adjectives to describe the momentous decision. A "bombshell in political circles," wrote one newspaper. Another called it an "audacious decision." Yet another commented, "Surprise decisions are becoming quite a habit with Mr. Baldwin."[18]

Churchill was as shocked as everyone else, especially in the wake of recent publicity surrounding his overspending during the 1921 Cairo conference—charges of which he had been cleared—and disclosures related to his troubled personal finances. The *Sunday Mirror* remarked, "Certainly there is something novel in the spectacle of Mr. Churchill in charge of the purse-strings."[19]

Churchill, however, found his appointment to be quite a pleasant surprise. His long-held aspiration to hold the office still burned. The black silk robe with gold embroidery that had been worn by his father as chancellor and kept in storage for him by his mother, was now his to wear.

More than a hundred people gathered outside the main gate of Buckingham Palace on the morning of November 7 to witness the ministerial changeover from the MacDonald to the second Baldwin government. This involved the transfer of the seals of office, a royal affair carried out by strict protocol. As the former ministers departed after having surrendered their seals of office to the king, members of the new Baldwin cabinet arrived to accept them. "There was little demonstration when the new ministers arrived," one reporter observed, until Churchill, clad in a black silk top hat and fur-collared coat, "drove up in an open car, was cheered, and raised his hat to the crowd."[20]

∽

The elections of November 1924 in Britain and the United States stabilized the government of Stanley Baldwin and the administration of Calvin Coolidge. It also resulted in casting Churchill and Mellon in comparable positions at their respective Treasuries.

Simmering misgivings over Allied war debts resurfaced soon after, in both the United States and Great Britain. Frustration in Congress over continued insinuations from the Allies of American greed as a creditor had heated up at the same time that news reports of Andrew Mellon's

Winston Churchill leaving Buckingham Palace, with the car window raised, after receiving the seal of the office of Chancellor of the Exchequer, on November 7, 1924. *Courtesy of the Library of Congress, Washington, DC.*

discussions with the French government about a debt settlement surfaced. Calvin Coolidge, having been elected to a four-year term of his own, raised the temperature, albeit unintentionally.

Instead of delivering the traditional "President's Annual Message to Congress" in person, Coolidge sent his report on the state of the union by courier. He stressed his theme of economy in government by traveling to Chicago, not in a special railway car, but in a "public Pullman." Without the pomp and glamour normally associated with the occasion, clerks read his words simultaneously in both the House and Senate chambers on December 2. One reporter observed that economy had been applied to the message itself, describing it as "notable for its brevity and directness of expression."[21]

In addressing war debts, Coolidge affirmed that the US policy established by President Wilson, and practiced by President Harding, would continue in his administration:

> I am opposed to the cancellation of these debts and believe it for the best welfare of the world that they should be liquidated and paid as fast as possible. I do not favor oppressive measures but unless money that is borrowed is repaid, credit cannot be secured in time of necessity, and there exists a moral obligation which our country cannot ignore, and no other country can evade. Terms and conditions may have to conform to differences in the financial abilities of the countries concerned, but the principle that each country should meet its obligation admits of no differences and is of universal application.[22]

In three declarative sentences, Coolidge reiterated the long-standing American policy on war debts and endeavored to present the United States as a principled, but considerate, creditor.[23]

Two of its debtors demurred.

In France, the message was clearly understood to mean that America would not annul its debts. As the French government had led the public to believe that the debts would ultimately be canceled, the press treated Coolidge's message as "startling news." Fears spread that Britain would also demand payment from France. Unsurprisingly, editorial columns expressed "decided hostility" toward the idea of making any payment on any of its debts during the first five years of German reparations being paid.[24]

Across the channel, Coolidge's statement about future settlements also created "a stir in financial circles" and "caused deep feeling in London." There it had been interpreted to mean that America intended "to sanction a more favorable debt settlement to France than was accorded Great Britain." The British press reported this as an objectionable development. "Coolidge's dictum that differences in the financial abilities of debtor-nations may justify inequalities of treatment" was discriminatory, grumbled the *Daily Telegraph*. The British protests had crossed into disingenuous territory. The methodology chosen by the American debt commission—capacity to pay—had been developed originally by Britain and prescribed in the Treaty of Versailles. The method factored a debtor's financial circumstances into the determination of settlement terms. It seemed that the idea of giving such consideration to France was an objectionable matter as far as Britain was concerned.[25]

It was especially objectionable to Chancellor of the Exchequer Winston Churchill. When news of Mellon's discussions with the French government broke, Churchill warned the cabinet that the question of inter-Allied debts "is bound to loom very largely." Britain had not yet called for repayment from its debtors, primarily because it had few solvent ones, but France was both a major debtor and financially sound, although its government leadership was increasingly unstable. If France was going to repay America, Churchill wanted to make sure that Britain would be repaid as well. In an alert to the cabinet, Churchill recirculated his memorandum from August 1922, in which he had advised that "the financial effects hoped for from the Balfour Note cannot possibly be produced unless that note remains for two or three years the unaltered policy of the Great Britain."[26]

It was time—on Churchill's watch—to bring back his collect-if-you-will-America-but-shame-on-you policy, as Stanley Baldwin had once summarized it.

Days before Coolidge's statement on war debts, Churchill had begun preparations to speak on the same issue in his first address to the House of Commons as chancellor. He wrote to his principal adviser at Treasury, outlining "the argument and policy which I wish to sustain," point by point. He planned to reassert the Balfour Note as the policy of the British government, but his reasoning would be based on "the greatness of the British contribution to the War." He noted, in point number five, that France would be dealt with "in the strongest possible terms."[27]

It had been two years since Churchill last addressed the House of Commons. Since then, unease with the unrelenting burden of war debts had given way to anxiety. British taxpayers were realizing that the debt payments being made to the United States, as set in the Mellon-Baldwin agreement, were largely coming out of their own pockets. Parliamentary opposition leaders were calling for the new Baldwin government to state its policy on inter-Allied debts. Churchill had made it known that he would address the issue on the evening of December 10.[28]

When the time arrived, the chamber was packed in anticipation. With cheers resounding, Churchill worked his charm on the members. He coyly asked for their consideration, in part because he was "very new to the office," but also because of his anxiety about "causing offense to friends and Allies."[29]

Once he sensed that all eyes were on him, Churchill launched his argument, stating, "The British burdens in the War were not inferior to those borne by any other Allied nation." He asserted that once the entirety of contributions to, and since, the war were "computed, weighed and measured," the sum of them would show that Britain's "financial burdens have been incomparably greater than those of any other victorious Power." A bit of mischief found its way into his argument when he twice invoked a misrepresentation previously made by the British government. This was the claim that if Britain had not lent to the Allies, it would not have incurred its debt to the United States. As far as US Treasury officials were concerned, that misrepresentation had been debunked long ago. To bring the full measure of Britain's financial contribution up to the present moment, Churchill declared that "no other victorious nation is making similar or equal sacrifice" in meeting its postwar liabilities.[30]

Churchill's greater sacrifice argument marked a significant departure from the principle of common cause which had underscored the Balfour Note. The new argument reflected a British sense of injustice in response to Coolidge's suggestion that France deserved better terms than those meted out to Britain. It also provided the context for Churchill to introduce his new policy to protect British interests. That policy had only recently been adopted by the Cabinet. "Any payments made by our debtors in Europe to their creditors in the United States," the chancellor told the House, "should be accompanied simultaneously pari passu with proportionate payments to Great Britain." If France paid the United States, Britain expected to be paid as well.

As a critic of the Mellon-Baldwin agreement, Churchill had to finesse his previous opposition to the settlement into one of support. "Opinions had differed about the settlement," he readily acknowledged, then paused, and added that that had included his own opinion as well. The disarming admission drew laughter from the House. With his audience on his side, he took his new stand: "The settlement has been made and it must be made good."

Churchill made the pivot complete by contending that the settlement "has placed us in an extraordinarily strong position." He based this on the fact that Britain had "met all its liabilities as prescribed," and had regained its financial freedom and independence. But this, he intoned, had not been done "without great sacrifice." The debt settlement, the confident chancellor concluded, was indispensable to "the increasing establishment of our credit throughout the whole world."

Churchill continued, arguing that the Balfour Note needed to play an important part in all future discussions of inter-Allied debts. Knowing that the controversial policy had been absent from the national dialogue for years, he reminded his colleagues that it proposed to "obliterate and delete all war debts" owing to Britain if the United States would act similarly in canceling all debts owed to America. Should, however, the United States reject all-around cancellation and insist on repayment, Britain would only collect "as much and no more" from Europe than the United States demanded of Britain. Instead of provoking reservations as it had in 1922, the Balfour policy now dispelled them. To cheers, Churchill declared that the Balfour Note "remains the settled policy of the government and is now affirmed for the third time—in three successive administrations."

Next, the chancellor turned to "the Dawes reparation scheme," stating that prospects for German reparations had become more real and prospectively more valuable.

Despite the possibility of greater than expected remittances, Churchill said the British government did not feel it could depend on the fruition of the Dawes Plan to achieve its goal of "parity in payments from Europe to Great Britain and from Great Britain to the United States," as set forth in the Balfour Note. Churchill was announcing, ever so artfully, that the British government intended to begin collecting from its war debtors. It went without saying that the chancellor of the exchequer of His Majesty's Treasury would lead the effort. Loud cheers ensued.[31]

In less than thirty minutes, Churchill had reopened the issue of war debts in Britain and around the world. In so doing, he had also stirred resentment toward the United States, and put both France and the United States on notice.

Prime Minister Stanley Baldwin reported to King George that Churchill's speech "was obviously intended for international consumption and was not addressed to the House of Commons alone." He complimented his chancellor's "conscious restraint and absence of gesture," which helped convey "a grave sense of responsibility." Baldwin added that Churchill's self-control revealed "his consummate skill in exposition and debate" and resulted in a delivery that had been received "with the warm approval of all parties in the House."[32]

Churchill's speech received worldwide press coverage. Reporters had one question for Mellon. Had it put his negotiations with France in jeopardy?

Suddenly, Andrew Mellon found himself in direct competition with Winston Churchill to reach settlements with many of the same governments. The largest of those, for the United States and Great Britain alike, was France.

The US Treasury Department issued a terse statement on December 11, 1924, saying that it found Churchill's "declaration on allied debts" to be "obvious and logical," and that it would be making no further comment.[33]

7

BEST INTENTIONS

Despite the fact that he was approaching seventy, Andrew Mellon had no thoughts of retirement. He had achieved an eminence in Washington that few experienced and one he likely never imagined for himself. Hailed for the swift turnaround in the American economy from the severe recession of 1921 to widespread prosperity in less than two years, Mellon received honorary degrees from Dartmouth, Princeton, and New York University. Columbia University not only awarded him a degree but made him the guest of honor at a dinner celebrating Alexander Hamilton, Mellon's exemplar, who was considered one of the school's most illustrious alumni.[1]

The dinner had been held in New York on December 3, 1924, a week before Churchill's speech on war debts. Over a thousand guests filled the ballroom of the Hotel Commodore where Columbia's president, Nicholas Murray Butler, presided. Women in a colorful rainbow of long, beaded gowns, over-the-elbow gloves, and glittering jewels hovered above in the balcony, eyeing those dancing to big-band music. Will Rogers, the popular vaudeville performer and humorist entertained. Radio stations broadcast interviews and speeches from the evening's festivities.

Hamilton, considered the greatest American Treasury secretary, funded the foreign debt of the United States to establish the United States as an honorable and trustworthy borrower. In a book Mellon had authored earlier that year, he hailed Hamilton's genius in establishing the financial system of the US government. He specifically cited the fundamental values Hamilton instilled in Americans—a commitment to "keeping expenditures within income," and to "the payment of debt." Those values, deeply rooted in the American ethic, were held reverentially, even by Congress.[2]

Eliot Wadsworth, Mellon's seasoned assistant secretary, delivered the keynote address, praising the service of both Hamilton and Mellon. He added to Butler's assessment of Hamilton's genius, saying, "his theories, largely of his own creation . . . were converted into practical, successful practices by the alchemy of his extraordinary leadership." Wadsworth went on, "In the light of an ever expanding knowledge of economics and national finance, the prestige of his accomplishments has grown greater, not less." He gave a special salute to Mellon by relating that President Coolidge "has said that under the present Secretary the finances of this nation have been managed with a genius and success unmatched since the day of Hamilton." While this accolade for Mellon had been expressed before in select political circles, it made newspaper headlines the following day.[3]

Mellon's financial mastery may have rivaled Hamilton's, but the taciturn successor still ranked among the poorest of all Treasury secretaries as a public speaker. Mellon admitted that he found making even short addresses "a painful ordeal." His discomfort in talking to either small or large groups remained as readily apparent as it had been when he first took office and his barely audible voice only worsened the effect. Even more disconcerting, Mellon's nervousness often resulted in awkward moments of silence and abrupt endings.[4]

In closing the evening's program, Mellon kept his remarks brief. Despite his whispery utterances, Mellon's reverence for Hamilton was evident. A reporter with good hearing was able to quote Mellon's words of praise for his most famous predecessor, as well as his comment about the comparison Wadsworth had made between Hamilton and himself. "I think that each successive Secretary of the Treasury," Mellon said, "at some time during his incumbency of office, enjoys the distinction of being the 'greatest since Hamilton.' However, he goes out of office and his glory has departed."[5]

The reporter noted one highly unusual aspect about Mellon's address that evening—the normally poker-faced secretary *smiled* as he spoke.[6]

Mellon possessed vast sums of money and remarkable power. Perhaps in that heady moment, the forty-ninth Treasury secretary indulged in a grin at the thought of his legacy including the kind of greatness that Hamilton had achieved, which had endured for more than a century. Hamilton had established the United States as an honorable debtor nation. Could Mellon achieve greatness by establishing America as an honorable creditor nation?

Achieving greatness, however, now involved dealing with a new French government and a reinvigorated Churchill.

∞

France, too, had undergone a change in leadership in 1924, when Raymond Poincaré lost support for his occupation of the Ruhr in parliamentary elections, and a leftist coalition took power under Édouard Herriot.

On December 27, three weeks after Churchill had declared the British government's intent to collect war debts from its European borrowers, Étienne Clémentel, the new French minister of finance, published a financial statement that detailed the country's assets and obligations. It notably omitted France's war debts to both Britain and the United States.[7]

The omission infuriated the American government, which interpreted it as evidence of "an intention to repudiate" the debt France owed to America. It particularly annoyed Mellon, who had a sober statement sent to France—the United States expected France to repay its debt.

Mellon's message was also communicated by Republican Senator David Reed of Pennsylvania on the Senate floor and forwarded to the French government by Secretary of State Hughes through the American embassy in Paris. It included a warning that France needed to understand that "with each day of delay in achieving a refunding of that debt makes it more difficult to grant her leniency of terms of payment." It also gave fair warning to France that its outstanding debt would impede its credit and make future French loans in America "impossible."[8]

Mellon was stern but not wholly unsympathetic. He recognized that France would likely need more generous terms than had been given to Britain. The destruction of critical French infrastructure—roads, bridges, canals, and railroads—and the damage done to its industrial and agricultural areas during the war exceeded that of all the other Allies, except possibly Belgium. Mellon suggested that a moratorium and lower interest rates would be appropriate. As one news correspondent summarized Mellon's position, that while the United States was insisting that "the debt must be recognized and paid," the American government had "no desire to be oppressive to France," nor did it "underate the sacrifice and spirit of France." It only hoped to deal with the debt question on a friendly and cordial basis.[9]

While most of the Senate agreed with Mellon's position, a few senators raised additional considerations in France's favor. One cited the aid that France had given to the American colonies in their struggle for independence. Another pointed to US tariffs, which made it nearly impossible for France and other countries to repay war debts to the United States by effectively pricing their goods out of the market. He argued that since France could only repay its debts by delivering goods to be sold in America, the Senate should contemplate removing "the high tariff wall which operates as a barrier to France and other foreign governments in paying their debts." Neither point elicited much discussion or empathy, but they raised the question of whether America had been fair in respecting its founding debt to France, or in setting a peacetime tariff policy that contravened its war debt policy.[10]

The *Boston Globe* noted that the French debt incident had "caused an unaccustomed holiday stir in Washington." It reported that the American government received the news of Clémentel's omission "with astonishment, amounting almost to disbelief." The article also included a denial from French embassy officials, stating that there was no intent on the part of the French government to avoid paying its debt: "all fears of repudiation were not only groundless, but absurd." The *Globe* pointed out some signs to the contrary. Hadn't French officials recently suggested a "breathing spell" before being pressed to repay? Hadn't they had also tried to persuade US cabinet members that France's "sacrifices were so great they should be taken into consideration" in any discussion about war debt payments? No one, however, was more frustrated with France's continued efforts to evade an official discussion on the issue than the chairman of the US debt commission.[11]

On December 30, France responded to Mellon's warning, albeit unconventionally. Instead of communicating through diplomatic channels, the Herriot government—the fourth French ministry since Mellon had taken office—distributed a memorandum from Clémentel to the press.

Edwin L. James, the Paris correspondent for the *New York Times*, reported on January 3, 1925, that France was requesting a ten-year moratorium, eighty years to repay, and an interest rate of one half of one percent. He noted that the French proposal "represents a desire to meet the American sentiment for the moment rather than intention for immediate negotiations." Recognizing concerns about the instability of the French government, James stated that the Herriot government believed that any successor government would likely "stand by any statements of the present government to Washington."[12]

A *Baltimore Sun* correspondent reported that the Coolidge administration was hopeful that France might, at last, be signaling a willingness to begin official discussions about a settlement.[13]

News of the French proposal returned the issue of war debts to the front pages of newspapers across America. The *Los Angeles Times* observed, "Not since the World War ended, not even when Stanley Baldwin negotiated the funding of the British debt to the United States, has there been more newspaper discussion over inter-Allied debts and the financial aftermath of the war." The press coverage also stirred up tensions in Europe, where hostility toward the United States was growing. In Paris, the newspaper *La Liberté* charged, "the claims of the United States are holding up the economic recovery of Europe." It also used the epithet "Shylock" in referring to American senators. In a private communication to the State Department, the US ambassador in France warned that the United States is increasingly viewed is "a merciless creditor."[14]

In his January 3 article, James also reported that France had made it clear that it wanted to settle its debt to Great Britain before beginning negotiations with the United States. He surmised that if France could secure a virtual reduction in its debt to Britain, it would better France's position in negotiating with the American government.

James included one other news item in his influential report. The upcoming conference in Paris of Allied finance ministers was being postponed in order to allow Churchill time "to discuss inter-Allied debts in their relation to payments by Germany on the reparation account" with the French finance minister.[15]

∞

Before the Churchills had been able to move into the chancellor's quarters at 11 Downing Street, Winston left for Paris on January 6 to meet with Clémentel, before the conference. Speculation about the outcomes of their anticipated dialogue on war debts overshadowed the original purpose of the conference which was to settle claims for reparations.

The United States had declined to take part in the conference officially, despite having submitted a claim to recover its military costs and war damages incurred during the occupation of the Rhineland. The American government would be represented instead by observers. They included James A. Logan, the "unofficial" US representative to the Reparations Commission, as well as the American ambassadors to Britain and France.

One reason for American sensitivity toward official participation at the conference had to do with US policy on reparations. The Coolidge administration, like its predecessors, had continued to maintain that the United States had no stake in reparations and therefore it was a matter for European leaders to resolve. By making a claim for reparations, the US government opened itself up to charges of hypocrisy. The claim was also inflammatory in the face of the refusal of the United States to officially acknowledge any connection between reparations and war debts. This stirred the resentment of European leaders toward the United States. Since the Wilson administration, the US government had maintained the deceit out of fear that its European debtors—the Allies and Germany—might decide to band together against their American creditor.

An additional reason the United States was hesitant to attend involved the Treaty of Versailles. The 1919 treaty set out an agreed-upon framework for the determination of the amount Germany and the defeated powers would be required to pay to the European Allies in reparations, as well as how that compensation would be allocated. The United States had declined to sign the treaty and therefore had no legal standing in the proceedings. It was now asking the Allied finance ministers, however, to grant America a share of the reparations derived from a treaty that the United States had declined to ratify.

Of all the reasons behind the reluctance of the United States to engage in the Paris conference proceedings, the most serious one had to do with Andrew Mellon. Under pressure from Congress to recoup wartime expenses, Mellon had sent Eliot Wadsworth, his assistant secretary, to Europe in 1923 to present a US claim for the reimbursement of its army costs incurred during the Ruhr occupation. Wadsworth succeeded in pushing British and French finance ministers into an agreement to compensate America, but not without engendering a degree of ill will. The fact that America was looking for more money from the Allies, in addition to the repayment of the war debts, offended European sensibilities.

In subsequent years, the Allies had made only token reimbursement payments under the "Wadsworth agreement." The US Treasury saw the conference as an opportunity to address the impasse by submitting a claim. Dated November 24, 1924, it included not only the costs covered in the agreement, but also damages which effectively doubled the original demand.[16]

The US claim galled Churchill. A week after the United States submitted it, Churchill wrote a seven-point memo to the cabinet, titled "American Claim to Reparation," which he marked SECRET. In it, he stated, "we have been advised that legally America has no claim." He argued, therefore, that the United States should not be allowed to benefit from a treaty in which it had refused to become a signatory. He pointed out that if the US claim was allowed, it would reduce the funds available to the legitimate parties to the treaty.

By the time he left for the conference a month later, however, Churchill had come to see that the American demand created an opportunity for Britain. He informed the cabinet on December 30 that he planned to take the position that while Britain would "not accept the American view either in law or in equity," the British government would be willing to arbitrate the American claim. He reasoned that Britain should do so because French officials would be under pressure to accede to the US demand for reparation, due to France's debt to America and its need for capital from American banks. Churchill believed they would do this even though they knew it to be "a wrongful American claim." As for the Americans, he believed they would be willing to accept British assistance, especially as the hypocrisy behind their claim became more apparent and necessitated a graceful retreat. He reasoned that Britain's strong and independent position would allow him both to optimize the "possibilities of agreement" and to press France on its outstanding war debts with Britain.[17]

Most importantly, the memo revealed Churchill's vision of the conference as a golden opportunity to broker a settlement to the US demand that would result in the official engagement of the United States in the European resolution of German reparations.

And he promptly seized it. On January 10, dispatches from newspaper correspondents in Paris heralded a breakthrough agreement achieved by Churchill. London's *Sunday Mirror* announced, MR. CHURCHILL MAKES REPARATIONS PACT WITH U.S. In his first international financial negotiation, he had persuaded the United States to become an official partner in a fifty-year agreement with the Allies to collect reparations from Germany. He did so by building support among the finance ministers to grant the United States its full claim, which represented less than a 3 percent share in German reparations. The press reported that virtually all the European financial ministers said that they considered it a small price to pay for securing the official partnership of the United States in the postwar economics of Europe.[18]

The press also trumpeted Churchill's statesmanship and the innovative method to rely on private conversations in place of the usual subcommittees and large roundtable discussions. The American ambassador to Britain, Frank Kellogg, whom Coolidge had appointed to replace George Harvey, said, "I particularly desire to thank the chancellor of the Exchequer for the broad view and most generous spirit which he has shown in these negotiations." French Premier Herriot was reported to have said that Churchill had "combined statesmanlike qualities with a chivalry which had won the affection of all those with whom he had to deal." A London dispatch to the *New York Herald* declared: "Winston Churchill, British Chancellor of the Exchequer, arriving here tonight from the Paris conference, was hailed by the press as a conquering hero. Not since the palmy days of Lloyd George has any British statesman come out of a conference with such glowing tributes as Mr. Churchill is now receiving. Antwerp and Gallipoli are quite forgotten, and the prospects of Churchill as a possible future Premier are now bright."[19]

Churchill had also made progress on the war debt issue at the conference. He wrote a cabinet memorandum a few days later, informing his fellow ministers that at "the spontaneous initiative of the French"—meaning Clémentel, and future finance minister, Louis Loucheur—he had learned of France's desire to make a proposal on settling its British debt on friendly terms. "For the moment, there is no resentment towards us," Churchill wrote. "All that has passed over to the United States. The wisdom and justice of the Balfour Note enables me to stand here as a debt collector without odium."[20]

Clémentel even complimented his British creditor publicly: "We found in Mr. Churchill a courageous man with an open mind and a realist who desired to find a practical solution of the Inter-Allied debt question."[21]

While the United States left the Paris conference with an agreement for the reimbursement of its $600 million in war costs and damages, it was no closer to securing the repayment of more than $4 billion of the French war debt. With all indications pointing to a harmonious Anglo-French deal soon being struck, Mellon had a message sent on January 15 through the State Department to the French foreign ministry, stating that "the terms suggested in Clémentel's memorandum for dealing with the debt of France to the United States do not seem to offer a practical basis upon which negotiations might be begun." The diplomatic cable said, in addition, "Mr. Mellon adds that he will appreciate receiving any information that may have come to you respecting any discussions that may have taken place in Paris respecting inter-Allied debts."[22]

∽

By the spring of 1925, it was clear to Mellon that France had no intention of settling its debt with the United States. A revised offer to the American debt commission from French finance minister Clémentel had been rejected, not only for still lacking negotiable terms, but also because it had introduced a provision to make payments to the US conditional on receipt of German reparations to France. As France well knew, such a safeguard clause would run afoul of US policy, which did not permit conjoining war debts and reparations.

Even worse for Mellon, Belgium, Italy, Czechoslovakia, and Rumania seemed to be waiting for France to settle before responding to his debt commission's summons. To break the impasse, Mellon instituted a new policy prohibiting the origination of American loans to debtor nations with unsettled obligations. Any country that had not settled its war indebtedness would not be able to access new capital in the United States.[23]

The embargo compelled Belgium to begin negotiations with the debt commission. The State Department had delivered the message from Mellon informing Belgian officials that approval for the loan of $50 million they were seeking from J. P. Morgan and Company would be withheld until Belgium arranged to settle its obligations with the debt commission. The Belgian finance minister protested, reminding

US officials that under the Treaty of Versailles, Belgium's war debts were to be repaid through German reparations and that "authorized American representatives" of President Wilson had been present at those negotiations. He argued that while the United States had not ratified that treaty and was "not legally bound by its terms," he felt that, "at least morally," any negotiation with the United States should begin by recognizing that promise.

Mellon held firm. The State Department issued a stronger reply, stating that the Belgium response was "unsatisfactory," and that the US government would await word "before taking any action on the loan sought by Belgium from J. P. Morgan and Company."[24]

Mellon prevailed. A Belgian delegation arrived in Washington on Monday, August 10, to meet with the debt commission. "The funding of your debt to us within your capacity to pay," Mellon told the delegation, "means far more than mere payment by you and the receipt by us of a certain number of dollars each year. It is a recognition of the integrity of international obligations and the settlement of a question which might disturb the long friendship of our two nations." The moment illustrated the larger point that debt between nations can only be settled by mutual agreement. The alternative, as the seizure of the Ruhr had shown, was military force.[25]

Mellon wanted the Belgian officials to understand that "capacity to pay" meant striking a fair balance between how much the United States, as creditor, would lose, and Belgium, as debtor, would repay. Like Hamilton, he believed that the international financial system depended on the responsible management of credit and debt by governments. The objective of the negotiations, as far as Mellon was concerned, was to set repayment at a level that would uphold the credit of Belgium without impoverishing its economy.

With all of Europe closely monitoring the parley in Washington, the principals agreed to withhold from commenting to the press during the course of their negotiations. Unlike the British settlement, no socializing had been arranged, nor any diplomatic functions scheduled. All seemed to recognize that making a settlement promptly and discreetly was in their common interest.

By Friday, August 14, the debt commission and the Belgian delegation had worked out the basic terms for a settlement agreement. The terms were more attractive than those granted to Britain. The agreement also included an artful accommodation of the pre-armistice borrowings that the Belgian government believed would be assumed by Germany, which allowed the United States to honor the treaty pledge made to Belgium. While the agreement would likely encounter congressional opposition, Mellon knew that the president would give it his support due to its fairness and feasibility. The Coolidge administration operated "within the limits of the practicable and the possible" and the agreement fit within that range.[26]

Before the close of the meeting, Mellon announced that "the settlement had to be approved by the President before it could be finally accepted by the commission," and, therefore, he and his fellow commissioner, Senator Reed Smoot, would travel to Plymouth, Vermont, where the president was vacationing at his family homestead. All agreed to reconvene on Tuesday, August 18.[27]

Mellon's summer plans had already involved considerable transportation and communications logistics before a visit to the hills of New England complicated the mix.

After the debt commission meeting, he left for Long Island, New York, where he had rented the home of a Pittsburgh friend for the season. A. W. had decided to forgo taking Ailsa and Paul on a European vacation because of continued overtures from French government officials who professed an intent to travel to Washington to begin settlement talks. A reporter with a taste for mordant humor, writing for *Time*, described Mellon's Southampton refuge as "a little bungalow of perhaps twenty rooms," noting that "the Secretary, if he wills, may romp directly from his dressing room into the surf." The closest to the surf that press photographers would catch Mellon that summer, however, was on the veranda of "Villa Rea," with Ailsa, where he appeared perfectly coiffed and clad in a sportscoat, tie, vest, and light-colored shoes and slacks.[28]

Mellon had arranged for "airplane dispatch services" between Washington and his summer enclave so that he could be kept informed of important "foreign debt developments" while he spent weekends with his family "on the dunes." Just as Mellon had foreseen the transformative commercial potential of aluminum and industrial abrasives such as carborundum, he was intrigued by the possibilities of commercial aviation. With the US government now pioneering the infrastructure to advance it, Mellon readily took advantage of the developments. This involved Garrard Winston, his new Treasury undersecretary, who Parker Gilbert had recruited to succeed him. Like Leffingwell, Gilbert had honored the ethos of ensuring that the best minds were brought to the US Treasury. Winston had likely not imagined flying as part of his job, and most certainly he had not anticipated shuttling between the Treasury department and Mellon's seaside cottage.[29]

Winston did not drop in over the weekend of August 15, but the US ambassador to France, Myron Herrick, did. During lunch with Mellon on Saturday, he disclosed that the French officials, who for months had been intimating that they would come to Washington, were instead going to London during the following week to meet with Churchill.

In addition to the disappointing French news, Mellon had little time to enjoy the beach that weekend. He left Sunday afternoon aboard one of the Treasury's revenue cutters, which ferried him on the first leg of his expedition to Vermont.[30]

At ten o'clock on Monday morning, Mellon and Senator Smoot arrived, via special train and presidential car, at the home of President Coolidge's eighty-year-old father. One correspondent described their arrival, "With sumptuous automobiles and liveried chauffeurs standing by and representatives of the press of the world waiting tense for the decision which may affect the economics of two continents." Most remarkably, he noted, the conference with the president took place on the porch of the farmhouse.[31]

Mrs. Coolidge and her husband had tacked up three linen bed sheets and pinned the sides together that morning to serve as a sun awning and a screen to block the curious eyes of the sheriffs, onlookers, and reporters who had gathered less than two hundred feet away. One of the reporters commented that "this porch in an out-of-the-way village on the mountaintop"

Right—REVIEW BELGIAN
OFFER. Senator Reed Smoot,
President Coolidge and Secretary
of the Treasury Mellon met at the
home of the President's father in
Plymouth, Vt., Monday to confer
on the terms for funding the Belgian debt. The meeting took place
on the porch.   *Keystone*

The visit of Andrew Mellon and Senator Reed Smoot to Coolidge's father's home in Plymouth, Vermont, on August 17, 1925, to obtain the president's approval of the Belgian debt settlement, is recorded in a mounted photograph on newsprint in the files at the Calvin Coolidge Presidential Library and Museum. *Courtesy of the Forbes Library, Northampton, Massachusetts.*

was perhaps "the oddest place for such a gathering ever selected by a president."[32]

It was, however, also a pleasant and productive one. Mellon presented the settlement terms proposed by the debt commission waiving all interest on money borrowed by Belgium during the war, in recognition of the "weighty moral obligation" posed by the pledge of President Wilson. Mellon was right that Coolidge would view the agreement as honorable and realistic. The president approved the settlement plan just before noon and then took the commissioners out for lunch at an historic inn and on a drive through Woodstock. While Mellon and Smoot were enjoying the president's hospitality, Garrard Winston at the Treasury Department received word of an important foreign debt development. It was not from France though. Italy had cabled that it wanted to meet with the debt commission to discuss settling its debts. The loan embargo seemed to be working.[33]

⁂

Three days after the announcement that President Coolidge had approved the Belgian debt settlement, the *New York Times* reported that the Senate Irreconcilables who had fought against the League of Nations were not only preparing to "make an onslaught" against the terms of the agreement, but against the debt commission "especially." They did not view Wilson's promise to allow Belgium's debt to the United States to be paid through German reparations as a weighty moral obligation, and they strongly opposed its use as the rationale for cancelling the interest on Belgium's pre-armistice debt. Mellon was now facing opposition from a constituency he had underwritten before entering government.[34]

The forces mounting against Mellon took a dramatic turn during the following week when Churchill unexpectedly struck a tentative deal with Joseph Caillaux, the new French finance minister in yet another new French government. Churchill did so by lowering the interest rate on French indebtedness to 2 percent over the sixty-two-year term of the agreement, which reduced the terms Britain had previously proposed by almost 40 percent. He also granted two concessions that France had sought—a partial moratorium allowing France to pay smaller sums for the first five years, and, even more significantly, a provision that would release France from making payments to Britain should Germany not make reparation payments to France. There was one important caveat to the British offer: it was contingent on the United States agreeing to fund the French debt to America on the same terms.[35]

Churchill had once again succeeded in putting the United States in an unenviable position before the world, just as he had when the Balfour Note was issued. Mellon, already encountering Congressional opposition to the Belgian settlement at 3.5 percent, would have to match Britain's generosity to France at 2 percent, or risk validating the Allies' charge of American greed as a creditor nation.

8

ROUGH PASSAGES

The promised onslaught of opposition to the ratification of the Belgian debt settlement erupted on the floor of the Senate on December 16, 1925.

Seeking ratification, Reed Smoot of Utah, the chairman of the Senate Finance Committee and a member of the debt commission, put the pact, and five others, before the Senate. Each had been passed unanimously by the commission and approved by President Coolidge. Four of them, Estonia, Latvia, Rumania, and Czechoslovakia, had been settled basically on the same terms as Great Britain. However, Belgium and Italy had been granted significantly easier terms.

Senators "hurling jibes over the leniency of the settlements" took aim at Smoot using the recently negotiated agreement with Italy as ammunition. It was even more generous in its terms than those granted to Belgium. It called for Italy to repay the principal of the debt in full but at such a low interest rate, and over so long a period, that it practically amounted to a cancellation of more than 75 percent of the debt.[1]

Senator James Reed, Democrat of Missouri, opened fire.

"We are in effect being asked to cancel the Italian debt," he argued, charging that the interest rate of one eighth of one percent, was essentially a "whitewashed repudiation" of Italy's debt to the United States. One of the "Irreconcilables" in opposition to the League of Nations and a foe of internationalism, Reed had also been the most vocal opponent of

The US Senate chamber, as it appeared between the period when the Treaty of Versailles was rejected, and the war debt settlements were ratified. *Courtesy of the Library of Congress, Washington, DC.*

granting Mellon sole power to negotiate the settlement of the foreign debts during the 1921 Senate Finance Committee hearings. He continued to be a critic.[2]

Now, the attack intensified as a Republican senator from Nebraska contrasted the Italian rate to the 4.25 percent "paid by the American taxpayer on the loan."[3]

In defense of the settlement, Smoot insisted that Italy would be paying every penny that it could be expected to raise from its people who had not only survived the war, but who were already highly taxed.

The other Republican senator from Nebraska, George Norris, pointed out that after the Italian delegation had reached a settlement with the debt commission, Italy had immediately sought out a new loan of $100 million with J. P. Morgan and Company.

Norris asked, are they going to pay Morgan "on the same basis on which they are going to pay us?"

Smoot disclosed that the Morgan loan had been negotiated at 7 percent, citing the postwar credit risk Italy now carried due to its financial weakness. After being pressed further on the particulars of the deal, he added that the rate had been discounted from the original 9 percent. It was an attempt to validate the assessment of Italy's capacity to pay made by the debt commission. It failed to satisfy the indignant senators.

Senator Hiram Johnson, Republican of California, quickly calculated that "the interest given the people of the United States on their debt is one twenty-eighth of what Italy pays to the House of Morgan."

To which Norris added, Mr. Morgan has set out "to get 100 cents on the dollar" while Uncle Sam is proposing "to get 40 cents on the dollar."[4]

Smoot bravely weathered continued attacks. Senator Pat Harrison, Democrat of Mississippi, read a section from the Republican national platform that stated that future debt settlements would be based on the British settlement, and asked, "Do these settlements conform to that?"

Replying gamely, Smoot explained that they conformed to the British settlement "as much as possible," adding that all the pacts had been "based on capacity to pay."

Senator Reed argued: "We are not applying the same principles to American farmers as we are to European countries. If the farmer can't repay a loan, we don't let him pay according to his ability or income. We foreclose the mortgage, take his land and his home. That's business, they say."

By this point, the snarl over the debt settlements had become so heated that Smoot "was forced to postpone their consideration indefinitely."[5]

Meanwhile, members of the House of Representatives were arguing that any legislation concerning the foreign debt settlements "must originate in the House" under the provisions of the US Constitution, and let it be known that if the Senate acted first, "the House would not accept such measure."[6]

⁂

Mellon was not about to let time kill the deals. On January 4, he went to Capitol Hill to explain to the House Ways and Means Committee in an executive session why opponents of the debt settlements should, as the *New York Times* put it, "draw in their horns and ratify the compacts without unfortunate controversy."

For the closed-door session in the committee's large room in the House Office Building, Mellon was accompanied by Garrard Winston, his undersecretary, and Representative Theodore Burton of Ohio, a member of the debt commission. It would never occur to Mellon to make an argument without including a profusion of facts and figures. Having dealt with Congress for five years had not changed that. He presented a quantitative analysis of the comparative debt burdens borne by England, Belgium, and Italy as well as the impact of the respective burdens on their standards of living. His intent was to emphasize the role that the principle of "capacity to pay" had played in the debt commission's efforts to achieve fairness.

Mellon gave something of a master class on the facts and principles of settling the debts within the authority and terms set by Congress in creating the debt commission. He explained that it had adopted the tenet "that repayment of principal is essential in order that the debtor might feel it had paid its debt in full and that we might know that we had our capital returned to us." Therefore, each debtor nation would be required to repay its principal obligation in full, but the interest on it would be adjusted based on its capacity to pay.

Mellon argued that the British settlement was "not a fixed formula to which all others, irrespective of capacity, must conform." Each debtor nation had, in fact, been required to pay its principal obligation in full, per congressional legislation. Mellon pointed out that "England itself in dealing with its European debtors has made settlements more favorable to one than another."

Regarding the Italian settlement, he explained the "quite material difference" between Italy and the other debtor nations. "Italy has no natural resources and no productive colonies," he said. "Its balance of trade has always been adverse; a large part of the country is mountainous and it must import food for its rapidly increasing population." While it owed the United States more than $2 billion, it also owed England about 25 percent more. "An insistence of a settlement of the Italian-American debt on the British-American basis would have been entirely futile," he reasoned. "Italy could not have paid, and such an instance would have meant only that the United States would receive nothing."

He also responded to the consternation over the Morgan loan to Italy expressed during the heated debate in the Senate. Mellon asserted, "The American Commission has not recommended settlements of the debts to profit from those who wish to loan money abroad." He explained that banks do not extend credit to nations with outstanding debts. Without credit, those nations do not have the ability to access capital to purchase American products, such as wheat and cotton. He argued that the debt commission's settlements enable debtor nations to obtain the private loans which make US exports possible. "The entire foreign debt is not worth as much to the American people in dollars and cents as a prosperous Europe as a customer."

Mellon then explained the special situation of Belgium at length, and the circumstances that had influenced the settlement. This involved an agreement sanctioned by the United States at the time of the negotiations of the Treaty of Versailles whereby "the pre-armistice debt of Belgium would be assumed by Germany and Belgium released." Subsequently, the United States had declined to honor the agreement because it did not want to accept Germany as substitute for Belgium on the debt. "The American Commission felt that the equities were with Belgium," Mellon explained. In justifying their decision, Mellon showed that the commission had navigated a middle road. "We would not agree to substitute Germany as our debtor," because it would violate US policy. But Mellon added, "We did not think it just, however, to ask Belgium to repay more than the principal of the pre-armistice advances." The solution was to use the flexibility in setting the interest rate, granted to the debt commission.

Fairness, based on the principle of capacity to pay, was one of the debt committee's basic tenets. "No nation," he said, "except by the pressure of public opinion and the necessities of its own credit, can be compelled to pay a debt to another nation." Insisting on an agreement in excess of the country's ability to pay was not fair or productive. "None can do the impossible," Mellon continued. "If the debtor is to be able to pay and if the creditor is to receive anything, a settlement fair to both countries is essential. It follows that those who insist on impossible terms are, in the final analysis, working for an entire repudiation of the debts. The only other alternative which they might urge is that the United States go to war to collect."

Mellon rested his argument for the ratification of the six agreements on one key point in particular. The settlement of "interallied debts constitute the principal item," he stressed, that was essential to the reconstruction of Europe. "We have learned the folly of imposing indefinite and impossible terms from the experiment with Germany before the Dawes Plan," he said, referring to the seizure of the Ruhr by France and Belgium.

Mellon stood by his commission's debt settlements. "While some may believe our recommendations too lenient and others too harsh, I know it is the honest judgment of the commission that they are just settlements in the real interests of our country."[7]

That the Ways and Means Committee was insisting that the House originate the debt settlement legislation was reported as "highly pleasing to President Coolidge and Secretary Mellon, who believe the decision means a business-like consideration of the problem rather than an out-and-out political fight from the start" as had been threatened by the Senate.[8]

∞

Later that month, Churchill faced criticism in Parliament regarding the leniency he had extended to Italy in striking an agreement with Count Volpi, Italy's finance minister, on January 28. By setting annual payments at roughly £4 million ($20 million) over sixty-two years, Britain was effectively cutting Italy's debt in half.

Lord Arnold, a former Cabinet official, denounced the Italian settlement as "a thoroughly bad one." He railed, "It must now be recognized that the plan of the Balfour Note has gone completely awry." The influential peer was regarded as one of Britain's soundest financial and fiscal experts. In criticizing the settlement, he charged, "It is scarcely conceivable that any British government could have accepted worse terms." He based his judgment on the fact that the British Treasury had estimated the Italian capacity to pay at one-third that of France while the American Treasury's corresponding assessment had been one sixth. Putting the settlement into context, he concluded, "Whatever the present government does or settles or professes to settle . . . it is always the British taxpayer who has to pay."

Invoking the provisional agreement that Churchill had struck in late August with French Minister of Finance Joseph Caillaux, Lord Arnold directed his most severe criticism to Churchill personally, charging that the Italian and French settlements "would shatter the reputation of any business man" and that the chancellor had mortgaged Britain's future to address present shortcomings.[9]

The chamber of the House of Commons in the British Parliament. *From* An Outline of Christianity: The Story of Our Civilization, *1926.*

In the House of Commons on February 2, Churchill's debt settlements drew more criticism. Former Prime Minister David Lloyd George mocked the Italian settlement, projecting that it would never reach "the sublime altitude of a penny" against the six pence per pound income tax. Like Lord Arnold, he too referenced the Churchill-Caillaux agreement, asking facetiously when payment, if any, from France would begin?[10]

The references to the French provisional agreement reflected the indignation still felt in Parliament. Churchill had been criticized at the time for being overly generous then too. How did offering to "write off two-thirds" of France's debt to England benefit British taxpayers, some had demanded to know.[11]

Churchill's largesse had also fueled speculation in the United States about his motivations. Had he offered France lenient terms to once again shame the US Congress for its insistence on full repayment? Senator William Borah, chairman of the Senate Foreign Relations Committee and one of the resident Senate critics of the debt commission, believed he had: "The terms suggested to the United States through the courtesy of England may be satisfactory to England," he huffed, "but I don't think they will be satisfactory to the taxpayers of the United States. The manoeuvre which is being made in this matter in London is perfectly transparent and need not mislead anyone."[12]

The suggestion of a British attempt "to put America in the wrong as a more hard-hearted creditor than England" had resulted in an uproar that played out in newspapers across the United States. The *New York Times* published commentary from ten different papers, including the *Los Angeles Times*, *Kansas City Star*, and *Providence Journal*. The realization that Britain could afford to be generous to France because of the proportionate debt payment policy Winston Churchill had established the previous winter, fueled American indignation.[13]

Edwin James, the *New York Times* correspondent in Paris, characterized the British maneuver as a plan to leave "the dirty work of settling interallied debts" to the United States. To help stateside readers understand, he summed up the British policy on French war debts: "Pay us at the rate you pay America, and we will call it square." James noted further that "the authorship of the debt plan is freely attributed to the British Chancellor of the Exchequer."[14]

With Churchill "having dealt so generously with Italy," attention quickly turned to France, where the falling franc and continuing crisis had forced Caillaux to resign as finance minister. The *Guardian* reported on January 29 that the new French government intended to resume negotiations with the chancellor, which they interpreted to mean that France hoped to better the terms set out in the Churchill-Caillaux provisional agreement.[15]

Another report speculated that France would endeavor to "clinch a new debt funding agreement" before the French government resumed talks with Treasury Secretary Mellon. This would be Mellon's second attempt at securing a settlement with France. The previous fall, he had entered into a generous gentlemen's agreement with Caillaux, only to have it leaked to the press by a member of the French delegation before he could obtain the support of his fellow debts commissioners and the president. The best that Mellon could do in light of the humiliating defeat was to send Caillaux back to France with a temporary agreement that included much harsher terms.[16]

At the time, it was not widely known that Mellon had had "a long private conversation" with Henry Bérenger, a wealthy newspaper editor serving as an observer of the Caillaux delegation, before the French negotiators left Washington to return to France. Nor were many aware that Bérenger's subsequent appointment to the post of French ambassador to the United States with special plenipotentiary powers, had come about as a result of a "circumspect request of the American government." In a February 4 editorial, the *New York Times* revealed the backstory and also reported that Bérenger had met with Mellon upon his return to Washington in January. Reports then circulated that the ambassador would reopen negotiations with the debt commission only after certain events took place. Some cited a settlement between France and Britain, others the ratification of the six debt settlements pending in the Senate.[17]

The issue of the debt commission's pending settlements heated up again that week when Robert Howell, a Republican senator from Nebraska, assailed them during a Senate debate on a Mellon tax reduction bill. Howell charged, "The terms resulting from the commission's refunding operations, so far as the American people are concerned, are discouraging, if not disheartening." He presented some statistics to substantiate his claim that "the debts have really been canceled" and argued that "it is probable that every other debt will also be canceled."[18]

With the debt settlements now in greater jeopardy than before, Mellon sent a letter to President Coolidge on February 10, urging him to pressure the Senate to ratify the Italian debt settlement. It was an unusual step, but one Mellon was willing to take because Italy had complied with US policy for settling its debt. It had sent a delegation to Washington, presented its case to the debt commission, facilitated an assessment of Italy's capacity to pay, and negotiated a settlement in good faith which Mellon added, "was approved by you and was passed by the House of Representatives."

Mellon warned: "If now the Senate failed to approve the settlement, I think it would be obvious to the world that the reason was political and not fiscal. Italy, within its capacity to pay, has met its international obligation in view of the expert American commission. Neither in America nor in Europe would her moral credit be hurt if she refused to renegotiate."

Mellon argued that the consequences of the failure to ratify the Italian settlement "would render doubtful the possibility of an early settlement with France. We would certainly be placed in an undesirable light in Europe and we might retard the reestablishment in that continent of sound fiscal systems." Mellon closed his letter by citing the economic consequences for the United States: "We can ill afford to hamper the customers which alone permit our large exports. Without a market to dispose of our surplus, our own prosperity would be threatened."[19]

Coolidge readily agreed to apply his influence to the cause. The Mellon-Coolidge campaign for ratification of the debt settlements got underway on February 19 when President Coolidge defended the Italian agreement to reporters at a White House press conference that day. Despite suffering from a cold that had weakened his voice, Coolidge explained—at length—why the Senate should approve the settlement which, he pointed out, had been reached by a nonpartisan commission "that represented the best thoughts of able men." His central reason was that the settlement would facilitate the economic restoration of Europe and benefit US trade. One reporter noted that the president had canceled his morning cabinet meeting on the advice of his physician, but had "left the seclusion of his sickroom long enough today" to meet with the newspapermen. Coolidge was all in.[20]

After reports that a group of senators had met in a secret conference the following day to discuss making the Italian settlement a party issue for the Democrats, Mellon and Smoot conferred with the president, who was feeling much better. The following day, Coolidge made it clear to callers at the White House that he wanted the Senate to act on the issue. Failure to ratify the settlement, he warned, would affect his economic program.[21]

Mellon was taking no chances. Despite reports that Coolidge had converted some Senate debt foes by linking the Italian settlement to the economy, the *New York Times* published excerpts from the letter Mellon had written earlier that month in seeking Coolidge's support. With Mellon's full argument for the Italian agreement in print, senators made pleas over the radio for and against its terms. On March 7, it was reported that Mellon had been assured that the Senate would ratify the Italian settlement. The question, though, remained when.[22]

∽

In addition to having been accused of being too generous in settling war debts, Churchill was also under fire for the ills in the coal industry that were now being attributed to his decision to return Britain to the gold standard. The judgment vindicated John Maynard Keynes, who had been one of the few to oppose the return to gold. The economist had turned his opposition into a personal attack, publishing an article titled "The Economic Consequences of Mr. Churchill," an allusion to his bestselling book,

The Economic Consequences of the Peace, that had argued for an all-around cancellation of war debts.

Churchill knew that more controversy over the outstanding war debts would come his way in late April when he presented the annual budget. It would show that Britain had not received in German reparations and Allied war debt payments even half of what it had to pay to the United States. Basil Blackett's admonition years earlier that Britain would not collect enough from its debtors to pay its creditor had been right on the money.[23]

At an energy low from the mounting criticism, Churchill had an Arnold "Alpine Sun" lamp installed in Downing Street at the suggestion of Walter Guinness, the minister for agriculture. This involved retrofitting a space in the chancellor's living quarters for the electric-powered artificial sunlight apparatus to create a treatment room. Some viewed the idea of indoor sunbathing as an amusing fad; others regarded it as a remedy or "tonic." One reporter jested that "the public could look forward now with happy hopes to Budget night" because the chancellor would have "sunshine in his heart" after taking regular doses of the light treatment. Another reported more practically that the treatments would help keep him fit for the "long hours of hard work in the House of Commons."[24]

While Churchill wished he was with Clemmie "reviving in Riviera brightness," he wrote glowingly to Guinness about his new sunbaths "I have had two doses, and already feel more energetic."[25]

Recharged, Churchill went on the offensive in a speech on March 24, in the House of Commons.

Once again, he blamed the difficulties over war debts on the United States for having refused to adopt a policy of all-around cancellation. "We have undertaken to pay what the United States so insistently and incessantly demanded," he asserted. According to his calculations, the undertaking involved paying £100,000 (approximately a half million dollars) daily to the United States for more than three generations. "To pass that immense sum continuously across a frontier, across an ocean, across the Exchange," he seethed, "is one of the most stupendous tasks and burdens ever undertaken by any country in the whole financial history of the world."[26]

Churchill also reminded the House: "There has been from the very beginning of these controversies, a very marked difference of view in Great Britain and the United States in regard to War debts. We have never taken the view that the cost of shot and shell fired in the common cause can be considered, morally and sentimentally, whatever it may be legally, as on exactly the same footing as ordinary commercial debts."

To further set in relief the difference between British and American war debt policy, he invoked the magnanimous approach taken by Britain as set forth in the Balfour Note: "The principal was that we should not take or ask, not only in debts but in reparations, more than was paid by us to our creditors across the Atlantic."[27]

Churchill saved his most pointed recrimination for America's approach to the debt issue for his closing. He charged that "the amount that the United States is receiving from Europe . . . is approximately equal to the whole amount of reparations which Germany is paying." Looking into the future, he saw that "the pressure of debt extraction will draw reparations through different channels from the devastated and war-stricken countries of Europe, which will flow in an unbroken stream across the Atlantic to that wealthy and prosperous and great Republic."[28]

The *Evening Standard* made note of "the entrancing exhibition of Mr. Churchill deploying his arguments as if they were armies."[29]

It had been a field day for the chancellor, everywhere but in Washington. The *Baltimore Sun* reported reaction from the Senate to Churchill's speech, headlining the article WAR REMARKS DRAW FIRE. Describing Hiram Johnson, the Republican senator from California, as "vigorous and caustic," the paper reported, "He declared he resented the remarks of 'men across the sea speaking of our attitude during the war, stating that this country devoted itself merely to making money.'" The account quoted Johnson further: "No man who is Chancellor of the Exchequer of another country has a right to refer to the selfishness of this land. We did our duty in those days as Americans in the American way just as we will always do our duty in every crisis."[30]

One editorial expressed the representative indignation felt by many Americans: "This country has sins enough in its postwar policy to answer for, God knows; but there is no particular reason why it should bow in humility before the moral grandeur of any nation of Europe." It also responded directly to Churchill's call for cancellation, saying that if Europe hoped to persuade the United States to soften its war debt policy, it should understand that seeking to shame America would fail. Furthermore, the editorial made a reasoned argument to show that the vaunted Balfour policy actually benefitted Britain's coffers more than her European allies.[31]

In a strange coincidence, Churchill's speech blaming America for the debt burden and its consequent hardship to Britain was delivered in London virtually at the same time as a speech given by Mellon in Philadelphia defending the US Treasury for not having extracted the last cent from her debtors.

On March 24, Mellon's seventy-second birthday, he spoke to a group of hardline Philadelphia businessmen who were inclined to admire him personally, but who disapproved of the forbearance extended by the debt commission to the Allied debtors. Mellon's job was to use his considerable prestige in his home state to persuade them that the settlements were just and fair, as he believed they were.

Deploying Mellon as a Treasury spokesman reflected the pressure the Coolidge administration was under on the issue of war debts and the intensity of the campaign the secretary and the president were waging against Senate opposition to the settlements. The campaign was designed to address the change in American attitudes toward Europe and intransigence in Congress. Opinions on war debts had evolved into three general groups: those calling for a revision of debt settlements on more favorable terms, those supporting outright cancellation of all war debts, and the hardliners continuing to demand full repayment of foreign loans.

Revisionists included industry leaders who believed that more lenient settlement terms would open foreign markets to improved trade in American goods. Cancellationists, largely comprised of Wall Street bankers and a growing number of academics, abhorred the ill will engendered in Europe by US insistence on debt repayment. The largest constituency, however, remained the Hardliners. They included not only most of the American population who had been led by politicians to see the debts as valid commercial loans, but more importantly, a majority of the US Senate, which still resented the intrusion of the executive branch in setting foreign policy.

Mellon based his argument to the businessmen on the moral principle of fairness. While recognizing that the United States had an obligation to help Europe recover from the devastation of war—"we do, and we will carry out this duty"—he asserted that the Coolidge administration believed "not in charity, but in help, and our financial policies towards Europe are backed, not by sentiment, but by sense."

He explained why the reconstruction of the European economy was so difficult: "A nation's effort to win the peace is much less effective than its effort to win the war." Mellon made an analogy to a flood disaster where every effort is made to fight the flood, but only grudging attempts are made afterward, during "the drudgery of clearing the land and the stones left by the retiring waters." He made it clear that "this work must be done."

Invoking the argument made by Russell Leffingwell at the time of the formation of the debt commission, Mellon portrayed the European Allies not as debtors but as America's "best customers." Knowing that his audience of businessmen was most concerned about their ability to sell products abroad, he argued that "Europe cannot continue to be a great consumer unless it is restored to health." He warned that without help to revive their economies, Europeans would not be able to purchase American products. Mellon acknowledged the criticism of his commission for "our failure to collect the last cent," but he argued, "I should rather have solvent customers in the future which permit me to run a profitable business than insist upon terms to debt settlement which will again force my customers into bankruptcy."

With his case made, Mellon stated that "we have, I believe, made for the United States, the most favorable settlements short of force."

The *Philadelphia Inquirer* reported that Mellon's statements were "diamond clear in their lucidity."[32]

To British minds, however, they were inflammatory.

London papers contrasted Churchill's reaffirmation of Britain's generous Balfour policy with the greed of the American policy on war debts. They also took note of Mellon's "short of force" statement and criticized his satisfaction with the US settlements.[33]

Despite the bitter resentments fueled by Mellon and Churchill in their respective speeches, both soon achieved significant victories. On April 22, the Mellon-Coolidge campaign prevailed in getting the US Senate to ratify the Italian settlement, and those for Belgium and the four others.[34]

Churchill announced on April 26 that Britain would receive a payment of £4 million from France to demonstrate its intent to settle its indebtedness to Britain. France settled with America in an agreement made between Mellon and French Ambassador Henry Bérenger on April 29.[35]

While these were major milestones in the settlement of inter-Allied war debts, the two Treasury titans set off a storm of resentment in the process, fueled by a sense of injustice in Britain, ingratitude in the United States, and bitterness in France.

9

ANDREW MELLON'S SUMMER VACATION

The artificial sunlight therapy was working.

Not only was it energizing Churchill, but it was also saving him money. Facing a personal financial crisis that spring of 1926, he decided to forego his annual summer vacation to the French Riviera, where he enjoyed both basking in sunlight and painting its landscapes. The ongoing renovations of Chartwell, coupled with a hiatus in his writing career, had forced Churchill to borrow heavily earlier in the year from Lloyd's Bank and his family trust. With his personal credit exhausted, he decided to economize by spending summer weekends painting in the gardens of his country home. By the time the buddleia bloomed in late June, Churchill had come up with a clever plan to generate income from publication advances by resuming work on the third volume of his book, *The World Crisis*.

France was caught in a credit crisis too. It needed to borrow from the Bank of England in order to make the first payment on its war debt to Britain, per the agreement Churchill had negotiated in April. Britain's central bank, however, would not lend to France because the agreement was provisional and therefore, technically, its debt remained outstanding. Like the United States, the British government prohibited lending to any country that had not settled its war debts.

The French crisis presented a political problem for Churchill. He had negotiated the provisional agreement in response to parliamentary calls for the British Treasury to be more aggressive in collecting war debts owed to Britain. With the Churchill-Caillaux settlement from 1925 still unratified by France, Churchill had pressed in April for the new French government to settle, but he could only secure the provisional agreement. While the stopgap measure gave the appearance that France would begin making debt payments to Britain, the reality was that it only bought Churchill some time until France's first payment came due.

That though, was all the revitalized chancellor needed. Not only did Churchill craft a plan that June to solve his personal credit crisis, but he devised one for France as well.

Due to its financial crisis and the fall of the franc, the leftist French coalition governments had run through six finance ministers in the last two years. Aristide Briand, the coalition's third premier, brought Joseph Caillaux back again into the post on June 23, 1926, but only by promising him more power. This provided Churchill with the perfect trigger for his plan. He had developed a good rapport with Caillaux during their negotiations the previous summer. After signing the agreement at the French embassy in London, they had strolled through its small garden "arm in arm." The return of his amiable counterpart presented a second chance to get a Churchill-Caillaux settlement ratified by the French legislature. All attention, including Caillaux's, however, was focused on the ratification of the Mellon-Bérenger agreement with the United States.[1]

Despite fierce opposition to the settlement agreement with America, Caillaux announced that his top priority would be to seek its ratification by the Chamber of Deputies. He pleaded publicly for all to understand that the settlement was the key to stabilizing France's currency and to obtaining much needed foreign capital. Only that, he insisted, would quell France's political and financial woes.[2]

It was understood in top political circles that if Caillaux failed to get the settlement ratified, the current Briand government would likely fall for the second time.

News coverage in early July of the increasing hostilities and unrest in France over the prospective ratification of the Mellon-Bérenger agreement dominated headlines in Paris, London, and Washington. This signaled to Churchill that it was time to put his plan to work.

Over the first weekend in July, the British chancellor invited France's financial attaché in London, Henri Pouyanne, to Chartwell. The British Treasury had been in talks with Pouyanne about France's impending payment and potential default on its debt for weeks. Pouyanne had originally initiated the dialogue out of a sense of duty as disarray in the French finance ministry continued.[3]

Churchill's plan was subtle and ingenious. With Pouyanne acting as go-between, Churchill would offer Caillaux what Mellon had refused to grant Bérenger—a moratorium on debt payments, a safeguard clause, and a waiver on the form of the bonds France would be required to deliver, as Britain had no intent to sell them in the open market.[4]

Churchill believed the concessions would virtually guarantee the ratification of the Churchill-Caillaux agreement, although not without a political cost to himself. Some would view them as overly generous allowances made at the British taxpayers' expense. Others would see them as providing Caillaux with a means to pressure Mellon into revising the Mellon-Bérenger settlement to match Churchill's offer. Many would wonder how the chancellor's generosity benefitted Britain politically.

Churchill was counting on a few in Fleet Street to realize his larger objective in making the concessions—to force Mellon into revising, or preferably nullifying, the Mellon-Baldwin agreement. With resentment in Britain toward America growing because of the disparity in economic circumstances, some editors and political observers seemed inclined to support a new Churchill-Caillaux settlement and seize the opportunity to discredit the United States. As always, the press would play a key role in Churchill's plan.[5]

On Wednesday, July 7, several newspapers mistakenly reported that Caillaux, rather than Pouyanne, had met secretly with Churchill at Chartwell over the weekend. One of them commented that the secret had been "carefully—and successfully—kept," adding that it was obvious that "M. Caillaux did not visit Mr. Churchill to discuss the weather."[6]

The reports were promptly denied, and retractions published.

On Thursday, Pouyanne succeeded in returning to London from a consultation in Paris with Caillaux that went largely unnoticed by the press.

News then broke over the weekend that Caillaux had ordered "an aeroplane to be in readiness to take him at any moment" to London, expressly for a meeting with Churchill to sign a new settlement agreement. The revelation introduced a dramatic aspect to their rumored summit.[7]

In addition to warming to Churchill's inducements, the new Briand-Caillaux government authorized a demonstration to shame America for the terms set in the Mellon-Bérenger agreement. More than twelve thousand veterans demonstrated in Paris on Sunday against the ratification of the Mellon-Bérenger settlement. The veterans argued that the money had been lent in common cause and that France had already paid in blood. Agreeing to the settlement, they believed, would be the ruin of France and result in the loss of its independence. The protesters—including "a squadron of legless or crippled ex-soldiers pushing themselves along in their wheeled chairs . . . a large contingent of blind ex-combatants . . . and men with smashed faces"—marched the length of the Avenue des Champs-Elysées to the Tomb of the Unknown Soldier and then to the statue of George Washington. There, they left a stone plaque that said, in part: "Over the head of diplomacy and far from political and financial combines, the war veterans of France appeal straight to the people of the United States. After the deceptions of peace, the proposed debt settlement would consecrate the ruin of France and the loss of its independence."

The text of the inscription also called for reconsideration, asking "that the study of the question should be taken up once more.[8]

∽

The next morning, Joseph Caillaux went to Le Bourget Aerodrome, northeast of Paris, where he and his luggage were weighed for the flight to London. He was bringing a large suitcase, and because of his mission, a silk top hat. The nascent British airline, Imperial Airways, had been flying passengers between Paris and London since 1919. Its planes could now hold a dozen passengers who sat on wicker chairs in an enclosed cabin behind the open cockpit. At an altitude of less than six hundred feet, the plane's route passed over the French countryside of Picardie, the River Somme, and the Pas de Calais before crossing the English Channel and heading to the Croydon Aerodrome, south of London. The same trip by train and ferry took seven hours, more than double the time by air. Aircraft technology was steadily connecting the world.

Caillaux's arrival in London was a rare upbeat moment after eight years of constant bitter disagreement over war debts. Many press photographers and reporters greeted him with hopeful enthusiasm. He alighted from his plane dressed in a dark suit, a black bow tie, and a bowler hat, "looking as though he had just left his flat," one correspondent commented, instead of someone who had just spent almost three hours crossing the English Channel. He described Caillaux's demeanor as "bubbling over with high spirits, gay, and debonaire."[9]

The French finance minister confirmed for reporters that the flight had been his first. "I have had a splendid journey, but it was torture not to smoke," Caillaux told them as he drew his cigarette case. He posed for photographs, answered more questions, and shook hands with the dignitaries who had also come to welcome him. Several in the group accompanied him to the French embassy, where he arrived "still all smiles" as he walked up its front stairs to have lunch with Churchill.[10]

It took only an hour of private conversation for the second Churchill-Caillaux agreement to be made. There were no reports of a stroll through the garden this time, but both men had gotten what they needed politically to pursue their respective efforts to avert a French default to Britain.

European calls for revisions to the Mellon-Bérenger settlement in the wake of the Paris protests, coupled with news that Churchill had offered France concessions the American debt commission had refused to grant, prompted Mellon to issue a statement. He made it clear that the debt commission no longer had the authority to negotiate a new settlement or to make modifications to the Mellon-Bérenger agreement. He stressed that only Congress could do so, given that the settlement had been approved by the president, passed by the House of Representatives, and was pending before the Senate.[11]

Whether by design, or in a pique at Mellon's statement, Churchill seized the moment to chastise the American debt commission for its treatment of Britain in a speech he gave at the Lord Mayor's banquet at the Mansion House on July 14. Effectively, it was a personal rebuke of Mellon.

"We could no doubt have won a good deal of praise," Churchill charged, "if we had used the same rigour to our debtors as has been meted out to us." The general feeling that Britain had been treated harshly and unfairly had been expressed before. Now that it was being said publicly by the British chancellor, it was provocative.

Churchill criticized the war debt policy Mellon was carrying out as unwise, shortsighted, and designed "to win cheap cheers and a reputation for firmness." He denounced Mellon's debt commission for exalting its position as creditor "by making demands which would never be agreed to or by making agreements which would never be carried out."

Churchill told the Mansion House audience, which was largely composed of bankers: "The compact substance is worth more than the imposing shadow. The applause of the moment would be a poor compensation to us for the resentment, especially the suppressed resentment, of great nations across long periods of time."

He was not finished yet. Churchill took direct aim at the core tenet of US policy on war debts that Mellon had endorsed—that they were no different than commercial debts. "We have always held in this country that there are clear distinctions between war debts and commercial debts," Churchill explained. "The war debt is incurred for the purposes of self-preservation . . . but it leaves behind no fertile or reproductive instrument or possession. What is blown away in shot and shell is not comparable to a transaction which leaves behind it, let us say, a railway, a mighty reservoir, or a modern electric plant." Therefore, he argued, "an ordinary commercial debt . . . may raise the standard of living in both the lending and the borrowing countries, and consequently the general welfare of the world . . . the payment of a war debt . . . like all war expenditure, however necessary, can only depress the standard of living of the borrowing country."

Churchill took one last jab: "Much may happen in two generations, and it may well be, in the best interests of the world, that a different view may prevail before that period is completed."[12]

∽

Churchill's provocation did not upset Mellon, but it infuriated his undersecretary, Garrard Winston. He confided in a letter to Ben Strong, "If Mr. Churchill believes that the American people will become more friendly to England by his stirring up antagonism, I disagree with him." He went on to say: "Who would not be willing to release a bankrupt debtor if one's creditor would release us in a like amount? This may sound a bit warm tempered; it is. But I do think England is making a mistake, and in her own interests ought to behave more friendly."[13]

Undersecretary Winston's remark was understandable. He and Strong had recently returned from Europe where, in May, they had observed firsthand the hostilities directed toward the United States because of its policy on war debts.[14]

Mellon had turned over responsibility for handling most war debt issues to his undersecretary by then. Beyond serving as secretary of the debt commission, Garrard Winston had played a principal role in drafting and negotiating many of the later settlement proposals. On his May trip to Europe, he had met with various government leaders in London, Paris, and Rome, including Mussolini, to discuss the settlement agreements. Approaching forty-four and with a stocky build, Winston was characterized by the London-based correspondent for the *Chicago Tribune* as Mellon's "sentry . . . to guard yank finance." A profile by a syndicated columnist back in Washington, described him as having "a twinkle about his eyes that suggest a kewpie come to life . . . and a sort of boyishness which seems strangely incongruous in the treasury."[15]

Before Mellon left Washington on Friday, July 16, he delegated a task concerning war debts to Winston—one which had come to the Treasury secretary directly from President Coolidge.

An obscure attorney in Massachusetts named Frederick Peabody had sent a long letter to Coolidge and others in Washington, insisting that the war debts must be canceled because America was being "betrayed, dishonored . . . and made odious in the estimation of mankind . . . as a merciless, money-grabbing extortioner." Peabody's effort to change American public opinion became clear after it was reported in the *New York Times* and other newspapers on Sunday, July 4.[16]

When asked about the letter in his last White House news conference before leaving for his vacation in upstate New York, Coolidge replied that he had not seen any communication from "a Frederick Peabody about the British debt," only some reference to it in the press. "I took it," the president said, to be from "someone that wants to get a communication published so as to get their ideas before the public—they write a letter to the President."[17]

Retired, Peabody was something of a crank. He had dogged Mary Baker Eddy, the Christian Science religious leader, for years, accusing her of immorality in books he had written and published. Unsatisfied by their impact, he had continued his efforts to defame her in the press.

His letter to Coolidge, insisting on cancellation of all war debts ran on for sixty-five paragraphs. Coolidge had not wanted to dignify it with a White House response.

The president then left Washington for his "Summer White House" in the Adirondacks and sent the Peabody letter to Andrew Mellon to answer. Mellon, likewise, passed it on to his undersecretary to deal with before leaving on his own vacation almost two weeks later.

After drafting the response for Mellon on July 14, Winston told Strong about the letter from Peabody. The undersecretary described Peabody as an individual "who took occasion publicly to criticize our treatment of our debtors." He explained, "I purposely brought out England's situation," both as a creditor of the Allies and a solvent debtor to the United States, to differentiate it from that of the other Allies. He told Strong that he hoped his efforts would make the subject of war debts "better understood in this country."[18]

On Sunday July 18, Mellon was out at sea, bound for Cherbourg aboard the *Majestic*, 545 miles east of its port in New York, when the administration's reply to the Peabody letter from the Treasury Department was released to the press.

Instead of politely responding to Peabody in a few sentences, the Treasury undersecretary's temper got the better of him. He replied not only in an argumentative tone, but at length, in some fourteen paragraphs. As Winston had told Strong, he did indeed single out England. His most inflammatory assertion—"It must be remembered that England borrowed a large proportion of the debt for purely commercial, as distinguished from war purposes"—was likely meant to counter Churchill's insistence that Britain had only borrowed from the United States to lend to the Allies, but instead, it was received as an accusatory statement on a new point.[19]

Garrard Winston's impolitic misstatement did not go unnoticed by the press. The Washington correspondent of *The Times* of London interpreted the US Treasury response to Peabody as a serious and calculated statement.

"Mr. Mellon's letter," said the article, "is substantially a counterattack to Mr. Churchill's speech, particularly the phrase 'rigour meted out to us' and his comparison of Great Britain's more favourable treatment for France." This was a reference to Churchill's speech of July 14. *The Times* report went on to say that "Mr. Churchill's remarks are understood to have caused no little pique in certain circles here, arousing the fear that they might induce France to cancel the Mellon-Bérenger agreement," or threaten to do so if the United States did not offer the same concessions that Churchill had.[20]

At noon on the Monday when *The Times* article ran, the *Majestic* was 1,115 miles east of the Lightship Ambrose, off Sandy Hook, New Jersey, where wireless reception was erratic but still possible. Mellon would, within a few hours, be in the middle of the Atlantic, and out of touch with both North America and Europe.[21]

Since he left port in New York, not only had the Treasury Department's reply to the letter from Frederick Peabody to President Coolidge been published, but Caillaux had failed to get the French Chamber of Deputies to ratify either the American or British debt settlements. The Briand government had fallen. It was the sixth French Cabinet to do so since Mellon took office.

While Mellon was largely incommunicado that Monday, Churchill was being criticized in the House of Commons by Philip Snowden of the Labour Party, for "being beaten on every point, at the expense of the British taxpayer" in debt negotiations. With the fall of the French government and the franc, he argued that Britain "was not getting from our Continental debtors a sum sufficient to pay our debt to America." France, Snowden said, now looked "incapable of putting her own house in order," and it seemed that the other countries of Europe "would have to come to her assistance."

Churchill took the floor to defend himself, contending "we have shown ourselves to be somewhat more conciliatory to French opinion than the United States has yet proved themselves to be." Then he changed the subject adroitly, saying that he believed he must "refer to the statement attributed to Mr. Mellon," which had appeared in the newspapers that morning. Churchill asserted that Mellon's statement charging that Britain had borrowed a large portion of its debt to the United States for commercial purposes was "a complete misapprehension," so much so that it almost made him "doubt the authenticity of the reports." He added, "There was certainly a good deal of feeling of resentment connected with payment of the war debt, but it was important that the feeling should not be increased by any misunderstandings arising as to the actual facts of the situation."

David Lloyd George, the former prime minister, took the occasion to join in and come to Churchill's defense by placing blame for that bad feeling on the Mellon-Baldwin agreement. Churchill, he said, "had put his finger upon the one mistake which has landed Europe in all this trouble, and that was the funding of our debt to America." Lloyd George concluded with a final swipe at Baldwin. "The Prime Minister," he said, "is alone responsible for the muddle in which Europe finds itself over this debt question at the present moment."[22]

That afternoon, Churchill's favorite press baron, Lord Rothermere, escalated his campaign to portray the United States as a rapacious "Uncle Shylock" and to quash any notion of the beneficent "Uncle Sam."

One of his popular newspapers, the *Daily Mirror*, noted that "Mr. Mellon, Secretary of the Treasury, is on his way to Europe from Washington," and commented that "the immense tribute now being exacted by the United States from her former Allies" was making American citizens like Mr. Peabody of Massachusetts "a little uneasy in their consciences about the manner in which 'Uncle Shylock' had claimed his blood money as a purely commercial proposition."[23]

A letter to the editor in the adjacent column titled "Unpopular Americans" asked, "Are our American friends having a good time in Europe just now?" It continued, "There can be no doubt that the whole history of the debt settlement has spread the impression—especially in France—that no nation is so avaricious as America. On a recent tour, I found that Americans are intensely unpopular on the Continent."[24]

British commentators were quick to point out that this was an attempt by the "Rothermere press" to fan anew "public antagonism to terms of the settlement of the British debt to the United States." The pro-Labour *Daily Herald* labeled the Rothermere outburst as "hate-mongering."[25]

The campaign being waged in London was also having an effect in France. A British columnist wrote, "Anti-American feeling, which has long been latent in Paris, is now flaring up there."[26]

Because of the fall of the franc, there were a large number of Britons and Americans in Paris that summer who were spending freely in shops and restaurants that Parisians could no longer afford. Americans were being insulted in restaurants and outdoor cafés, particularly in the popular tourist areas of Montmartre and Montparnasse, with reports of French patrons calling American tourists "profiteering pigs" and "sons of Shylock."[27]

Accounts of the French police intervening in demonstrations and drunken bar fights appeared in French, British, and American newspapers. Rocks were thrown at travel office windows, motorcoaches of tourists were met with boos and shouts of "Shylock, Shylock," and a brawl at the Place du Tertre near the Basilica du Sacré-Coeur was broken up with "several bloody noses and black eyes." An American columnist in London noted, "The gravity of the position in France is creating much anxiety here."[28]

⸎

On Tuesday, July 20, the day of the "Uncle Shylock" editorial, Andrew Mellon and the *Majestic* were in the middle of the Atlantic Ocean, and temporarily out of wireless communication with any continent.

Ben Strong and Parker Gilbert, now the agent general for reparations, were both in Europe and knew of Mellon's plan to arrive in France later that week. They soon became worried about Mellon's personal safety. The US secretary of the Treasury was now, due to the *Daily Mail*, another of the Rothermere papers, personified as "Uncle Shylock," the villain at the heart of the Europe's financial problems.

Turmoil in the leadership of the French government continued. Édouard Herriot, the longtime leader of the Radical Party, returned to form a cabinet after Premier Briand resigned, but had failed to stabilize the country. Two days into his premiership, the franc hit its lowest point ever, at less than two American cents. The Herriot government was reported on the "edge of the abyss," and was not expected to last the week.[29]

The *Majestic* moved within wireless range of England—some 797 miles west of the Lizard lighthouse marking the entrance to the English Channel—on Wednesday, July 21. The press sent Mellon messages requesting that he comment on the developments in France and explain the purpose of his trip. Mellon replied: "I do not feel that I can make any statement or comment for publication upon the situation, on the subject of your message, that would be useful in the present circumstances. The purpose of my visit is but for a short holiday."[30]

Another message asked Mellon to respond to Churchill's remarks about his letter to Peabody. The correspondent reported back that "Secretary Mellon is determined not to be trapped in a debate with Winston Churchill" and that he "dodged an invitation . . . to comment on Churchill's latest utterance that Britain had suffered 'adverse discrimination from the United States.'" The message also asked Mellon to comment on "agitation afoot in London to utilize his visit to Europe as an occasion for a new discussion of the inter-Allied debts question and of the *Daily Mail's* campaign for cancellation." Again, Mellon declined to comment, but the Mellon-Churchill debate had already become an international news story.[31]

By the time the *Majestic* arrived at the port of Cherbourg early on the morning of Friday, July 23, the French Chamber of Deputies had voted to reject its government for the second time in a week. The Herriot government had fallen in three days. With hopes of bringing stability, former premier Henri Poincaré had been asked to return and form a ministry. This was not entirely good news for Mellon. As premier, Poincaré had been responsible for the French invasion and occupation of the Ruhr in 1923. He had also been staunchly opposed to the ratification of the Mellon-Bérenger agreement without a safeguard clause and other amendments. Nonetheless, Poincaré's return broke the leftist coalition and its two-year parade of changing ministers and premiers. There was at least some hope of French stability.[32]

Mellon was met at Cherbourg by Theodore Rousseau, the Paris bank manager who had accompanied him and the Mellon party on its tour of French battlefields in 1923. Once again, he would handle travel logistics, but he would also take on the role of spokesman for Mellon. Well-connected and resourceful, Rousseau was a trusted source for the press. Before joining the Guaranty Bank and Trust Company of New York in its Paris office, he had been a newspaper reporter. He had also served as press secretary to New York Mayor John P. Mitchel, a Republican reformer. Rousseau understood both newspaper work and politics and had lived in Paris for the last six years.[33]

To Mellon's great relief, no French officials were there to greet the *Majestic*'s arrival in Cherbourg. His trip was officially unofficial, although

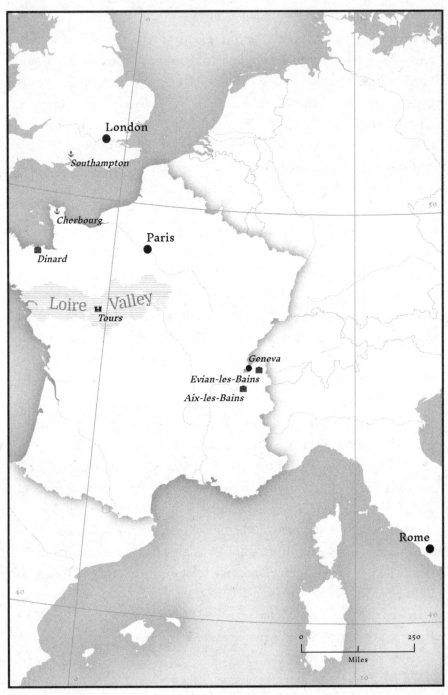

Mellon's travels across Europe from late July to September 1926. *Map by Morgan Kraft.*

few in the press believed that. Several reporters awaited him, mostly, but not all, from French newspapers.

Before disembarking, Rousseau had arranged a sit-down interview for Mellon, aboard the *Majestic*, with a representative of the *New York Times*. Mellon "made it quite plain that he had no intention of engaging in a controversy with Winston Churchill over the question of the British debt to America." He also discussed his response to the Peabody letter, saying, "I am sorry if what I said has caused a strong difference in view. What I said in regard to the purposes to which Britain put the money she borrowed from America was my own opinion, intended largely to explain the situation to Americans." Mellon did not deny authorship of the letter and echoed what his undersecretary had written to Ben Strong.

When Mellon said that he had not seen the complete text of Churchill's speech in the House of Commons, the *Times* reporter handed him a copy of it. Mellon started to say that he might have a comment after he read it—but then he corrected himself. "This, however, I very much doubt," he said, "for I do not wish to enter into a controversy over the British debt."

Nor did Mellon want to give the impression that he was there to talk with the French government about settlement terms. He gave "a very definite indication" that he saw "no prospect of a new Franco-American debt negotiations during his time in Europe." Nor would he comment on the possibility of France obtaining a no-commercialization clause, or the much discussed "safeguard provision" that would exempt France from payments if German reparations were not received.

Rather than trying to explain that he had no authority to renegotiate new conditions without the consent of the members of the debt commission and the US Congress, Mellon told the simple truth—that he was on vacation and had come to Europe for a rest and to see his daughter who was in Rome. He stressed that he had no appointments with French officials.[34]

When the *Times* interview was over, Mellon was approached by a group of French reporters who had driven over from Paris in hopes of extracting some comment about the situation in France from him. This they found difficult to do. Their encounter did not take place on the *Majestic*, but on the tender, a small boat that brought the liner's departing passengers to Cherbourg's inner harbor.

"Mr. Mellon is not a talker," reported Raymond de Nys, the well-known correspondent from *Le Petit Parisien*, a Paris daily, which, despite its name, had one of the largest circulations in France. After it became clear that Mellon was not going to answer any questions about the French debt agreement, the reporters questioned him about his destination. He replied that he was on a personal trip for pleasure—and he therefore was not inclined to tell the world where he was headed or when.

This prompted a guessing game. One reporter stated that it was understood that Mellon was to meet with Montagu Norman in Deauville, the seaside resort two hours east.

"Deauville?" Mellon asked thoughtfully. "Perhaps, but not today." He was not going there, but perhaps this answer provided a distraction.

"The chateaux de la Loire?" was another guess.

"Without doubt!" Mellon replied truthfully, for it was quite a large region and therefore not very specific, and he opened up a little, saying, "Then Italy, and on my return from Rome, where I'm going to see my daughter, I might stop, perhaps, in Paris."

Then, signaling that he would not be making any further comment, he took a few steps away from them to light a small cigar and admire the golden sunrise over the seacoast.

"Fine morning," he volunteered. "Fine country."

To make more from the very little information he had gathered, de Nys of the *Petit Parisien* added a few observations. "Useless to try to read something in his eyes," he wrote, "which are as blue as the sea and like her as bottomless. Mainly it is when he smiles that he is furthest from answering you." De Nys added that the man who possessed one of the "greatest fortunes of the new world" did not reveal it in his wardrobe, at least not in the opinion of the fashionable Frenchman: "He was wearing last year's same simple gray suit, the same overcoat, and good sturdy black shoes. His son accompanied him and was dressed as simply as he was."

Paul had just finished his freshman year at Yale College, and Mellon wanted his nineteen-year-old son to see more of the Loire Valley, just as he had as a young man. Joining them was Paul's friend from Pittsburgh, Jimmy McKay, who had been a classmate of Paul's at Choate, the prep school they had both attended.[35]

The Mellon contingent was ready to depart in "two powerful automobiles," which were waiting at the maritime port. Into the first climbed the American Treasury secretary. The second, de Nys observed—which was loaded with the luggage and perhaps Mellon's son and his friend—sported a hood ornament with "the head of Sioux Indian." The Pontiac automobile, equipped with a six-cylinder engine, had been introduced by General Motors that year and was on view at the company's Paris showroom on the Rue de Courcelles. Rousseau had likely figured that the boys would enjoy it.

Finally, at 8:35 A.M., reported the *Petite Parisien*, "Mr. Mellon sped away at ninety kilometers per hour, incognito, into the Normandy countryside."[36]

✤

The spiraling war of words between Mellon and Churchill was the subject of news articles, syndicated columns, and editorials in British, American, and French newspapers from the moment Mellon arrived in Cherbourg.

"The Mellon-Churchill duel has brought to the surface in England much latent ill-feeling in regard to the debt settlement with America," wrote an influential British columnist widely syndicated in the United States. He charged Mellon with discriminatory treatment of Britain as one factor fueling the controversy. Afterall, he wrote, "the money borrowed by Great Britain from the States was spent in the States, on the States' commodities."[37]

A London correspondent for the *Chicago Daily News* who was also widely syndicated wrote that weekend that Churchill was the cause of it all. "Cancellation of Great Britain's debt to the United States is the object underlying all of Winston Churchill's recent speeches in the House of Commons and all the abuse of America now a daily feature of certain

British newspapers." The correspondent conceded that Britons felt that the American debt was an "economic folly" and a "monstrous moral and historical outrage," but argued that Churchill was "going the wrong way" in pressing his case, not realizing that "abuse will retard rather than quicken any American disposition to reopen the debt question."[38]

From Paris, the Reuters news service reported, "The controversy between Mr. Winston Churchill and Mr. Andrew Mellon . . . about the American loan to Britain, assumed triangular formation this morning when Pertinax joined in with an article in the *Écho de Paris*." Pertinax was the pseudonym of André Géraud, an influential columnist who wrote largely from London and Paris on international affairs. His article was titled "The Anglo-American Quarrel," about which he wrote: "All spirit of prudence and reticence disappears. Epithets of 'Uncle Shylock' and 'usurer' are not spared. Messrs. Mellon and Churchill, through speeches and communiqués, engage in a kind of altercation."[39]

The Associated Press reported from London that "the Sunday papers devote much space to the debt controversy." While most deemed the dispute deplorable, they quickly declared that Churchill had "knocked the bottom out" of Mellon's contention concerning Britain's use of the debt for commercial purposes.[40]

The general conclusion was that Churchill had gotten the better of Mellon on the facts in the current round, and much of the rest of the controversy was due to the US Treasury's response to the Peabody letter.

A *New York Times* article that weekend, written by a seasoned correspondent in London, also had Churchill coming out on top. "The controversy between the London and Washington treasuries," he wrote, "is in its main features judged to have turned in favor of the British contention." The correspondent, however, questioned whether Mellon was the real author of the Peabody response: "Whether Secretary Mellon will add anything to it during his visit remains to be seen, but it is suggested by well-informed Americans now in London that the first statement to which he lent his authority was probably based on a rough draft submitted to him by Treasury officials on the eve of his

SKS
LEY
EMS

inistra-
itago-
d.

iference
ion to

Friday.
by the
an Bloc
second-
Amer-
uto the
resident
to-day
leaders.
ald at
in the

co, Pre-
ugh his
rumors.
cause of
he is
unusually
a a "re-
out that
ld last

HEAVYWEIGHTS IN WAR DEBT RING

MR. ANDREW W. MELLON **MR. WINSTON CHURCHILL**

These two men, who are likely to meet in London in the next few weeks, are the principals in the controversy between Great Britain and the United States concerning payment of war debts. Mr. Mellon, Secretary of the Treasury, is insisting on payment and Mr. Churchill, Chancellor of the Exchequer, is stirring up sentiment in Europe for modification of war debts.

Mr. Mellon, in France, Is Silent on War Debts

"MIN

FORN

*Paris O
Reflec
Ove*

The anxiety o
citizens by the
reflected in va
incidents. The
Commerce has
asking Parliam
party strife in
economic dange
the unsteadines
lead to suspens
ready it has obl
speedy settleme
restrict credit.
At Limoges
year-old man o
hanging, fearfu
the franc, whic
away most of hi
reduce him to
In Paris, mai
against foreign
night at the co
des Italiens an
a crowd gather
filled with tou
on a nocturn
through the cit
hissed and boo
police came, up
On the Boulev
tween the Ma

Front page of the *Paris Times*, July 23, 1926.

The New York Times.

SUNDAY, JULY 25, 1926.

CRITICISM OF AMERICA GROWS IN EUROPE

International War Debts a Bone of Contention in Which Finance and Sentiment Are Involved—Fall Of the Franc Is Closely Linked With Funding Operations—Basis of Europe's Grievance Set Out

Andrew W. Mellon, Secretary of the Treasury of the United States.   The Rt. Hon. Winston Churchill, Chancellor of the Exchequer of Great Britain.

TWO VIEWS IN THE CONTROVERSY OVER THE INTERALLIED DEBTS

MR. MELLON SAYS:

(From a letter dated July 24.)

MR. CHURCHILL SAYS:

(From a Speech to the Commons on July 19.)

THE INTER-GOVERNMENTAL DEBTS

departure and under less hurried circumstances would not have been issued at all."[41]

While the frenzy over the Mellon-Churchill clash roiled on, Rousseau settled his charges into a French seaside resort in Dinard, four hours west of Paris. There he knew Mellon and the boys would have some privacy. Rousseau may have had something to do with the false report that Mellon was on his way to Paris, which sent reporters in the wrong direction. Exchange Telegraph, another wire service, reported that Mellon is "expected to arrive at the Hotel Crillon late this afternoon."[42]

On Saturday, the Associated Press reported accurately that Mellon had spent Saturday walking the beach in Dinard with Rousseau, who "gave Mr. Mellon a brief synopsis of the events that occurred while he was still at sea." It was information Rousseau was happy to pass along to keep the press feeling informed.[43]

In his assumed role as Mellon's spokesman, Rousseau would continue to place strategic updates on Mellon's itinerary with the leading wire services. In a telephone interview from Dinard, he again informed the Associated Press: "Mr. Mellon is determined to say nothing respecting finance or politics during his vacation in Europe. He will, of course, receive newspapermen and callers courteously but would like to save them inconvenience by assuring them that he will under no circumstances permit himself to go beyond the decision he has made not to talk in Europe on public questions." Concerning his plans to meet with political leaders, Rousseau announced that "Mr. Mellon let it be known this evening that the one person he was principally interested in seeing in Europe was his daughter Ailsa," who now lived with her husband in Rome.[44]

Her marriage in May to David Bruce had been the social event of the year in Washington. Some society reporters had treated it as a fairy-tale romance—a supremely rich young woman marries a handsome but poor lawyer who proudly insists they will live on his salary. They scoffed at the idea of her living on her husband's earnings from his entry-level position in the State Department as vice-consul in the American consulate in Rome. A society reporter commented with glee that the heiress to unknown millions was "traveling like a humble schoolmarm on vacation" as she crossed the Atlantic on her honeymoon aboard one of the second-grade liners of the United States shipping board. Such a barb was not atypical. Since her parents' divorce, reporters had viewed Ailsa primarily as the spoiled and rich daughter of Andrew Mellon.[45]

To those who knew her, however, "there was more guile to Ailsa than most people suspected." Close associates of A. W. knew how proud he was of his daughter's business acumen and sense of dignity. Ailsa could enlist loyalty from those who worked in service to her, and "provoke intense, even incapacitating affection." She was also competitive and deployed "the incredible charm she could exert" to get what she wanted. All agreed that Ailsa did everything "with an air of distinction," yet also with an abject dread of calling attention to herself, just like her father.[46]

Ailsa's departure from their home in Washington had left A. W. forlorn. "The top of 1785 Mass Ave seems a very lonesome place," he wrote to her. "I do miss you!"[47]

As eager as he was to see Ailsa, Mellon had been persuaded to adjust his vacation itinerary in order to see colleagues who were already in France. Ben Strong was in Antibes, on the Côte d'Azur, with Montagu Norman, meeting quietly with other central bankers. They had invited Parker Gilbert to join them, but his wife, Louise, had fallen ill and the Gilberts remained in Paris for her surgery.[48]

Rousseau arranged for the three of them to meet in Dinard. Strong and Gilbert drove from Paris and met with Mellon on Sunday, July 25. Rousseau managed the accommodations in such a way that the press did not discover them or learn of their secret meeting.

The three men, and perhaps Rousseau, talked late into the night about the international financial situation. They had much to discuss.

The Dawes Plan was key to all their efforts. It set forth a comprehensive strategy for the reconstruction of the German economy to be overseen by the Allied powers. This involved recapitalizing Germany's central bank, restoring its currency, and raising money to fund reparations obligations. The planners had not intended for the entire strategy to be financed by loans

Ailsa Mellon and her father leave their Dupont Circle home for her wedding at the Bethlehem Chapel of the National Cathedral in Washington, DC, on May 29, 1926. *Credit: Carnegie Museum of Art, Pittsburgh.*

exclusively from the United States, but that was how it had turned out. The US was underwriting German reparation payments to the Allies, who then in turn were using the funds to pay their war debts to America. As the top Dawes official, Gilbert worried about the circular scheme's dependency on US loans and that, in the curious wheel of repayment, the money was largely coming from and going back to the United States.

Their most disturbing topic was the level of vitriol being expressed in the press regarding Mellon and Churchill. The dispute now permeated much of the political and financial news reporting in America and Europe.

That morning, two influential Sunday newspapers, the *New York Times*, and the *Observer* of London, featured in-depth articles about the Mellon-Churchill quarrel. The *New York Times* characterized it as "a sharp controversary" between two statesmen, one representing the United States, the other representing Britain. Written by P. W. Wilson, a British journalist and former Liberal member of the House of Commons, the article, headlined CRITICISM OF AMERICA GROWS IN EUROPE, filled the entire front page of its special features section. It was illustrated with hand-drawn portraits of Mellon and Churchill presented in interlocking ovals that took up half the page. Selections from their most recent statements on war debts were captioned below each of the images. Visually effective, the graphic and textual excerpts accentuated the head-to-head nature of the international controversy between the two Treasury titans.

Wilson asserted that while America's approach to collecting the debts was legally correct, "correctitude is not always enough." He argued that "the fact to be faced is that the war debts are challenged, not in law but in equity, by public opinion in Europe." Britain's widely publicized proposition that it was "ready at any time . . . to cancel debts and reparations by a stroke of the pen" had captured hearts and minds. Whether the British government was sincere about the proposition made no difference, because it effectively "gathered up the odium" of Britain's debtors and shipped it across the Atlantic. The metaphor underscored Wilson's explanation for the growing criticism of the United States—at every stage of European debt and reparations payments, the money was "all going to New York."[49]

The *Observer* of London called outright for a truce between Mellon and Churchill. Its editor, J. L. Garvin, wrote: "We ask Mr. Churchill and Mr. Mellon, 'Why can't you leave it alone?' Whatever they state publicly, less responsible persons are certain to exaggerate. Their obvious course as statesmen is either to talk about this miserable business privately, or not to talk about it at all." The London editor argued that neither Mellon, nor Churchill, was fully in the right. He invoked Hegel—"tragedy is the conflict not of right and wrong but of right and right"—and projected that the "justice of history" will render an impartial verdict that "will pronounce partly for both disputants, and partly against both."

To counter the vitriol that the Mellon-Churchill dispute had set off, Garvin wrote, "There are steady hands and decent hearts enough on both sides, let them work with might and main to stop Europe screaming at America and America sermonizing Europe." He held both sides responsible: "When Europe cries 'Shylock,' America cries 'Sponger.'"

"When reproaches begin," Garvin admonished, "and the usual exchange of insults follows, average human nature everywhere flames like naphtha, and there is a vile smell." He argued that cancellation would have been the best course but that since Britain had signed the Mellon-Baldwin agreement, he urged, "let's stick to it like men."[50]

Garvin had presented the debt issue from the perspectives of both Mellon and Churchill—and more objectively than had been done to date. He clearly meant to diffuse tensions. His effort resulted in the article being widely reprinted and referenced in papers in Britain, France, and the United States. It did not, however, stem the barrage of questions being raised about the debt settlements and the purpose of Mellon's vacation. Even at the Summer White House, lodged in the White Pine Camp, far north in New York's Adirondack Mountains, it was creating tension and having an effect.

"Mr. Coolidge's summer holiday has been troubled by reports of friction and agitation abroad regarding international debts," one correspondent reported, adding the announcement that "Secretary Mellon will depart from his original intention and confer with foreign statesmen before he returns home." The change in Mellon's directive from the president reflected the degree to which the Mellon-Churchill debate had impacted international relations in the few weeks since Garrard Winston had returned from meeting with European finance officials. Mellon and Rousseau would now have to find a way to adjust the vacation itinerary without compromising opportunities for relaxation and visits to the great art museums of Europe.[51]

Knowing the new directive would prompt European officials to request meetings with Mellon, Coolidge provided some political cover. At his next meeting with the press at his Adirondack camp, Coolidge explained first that the Treasury secretary had gone with his son on a motor trip in Europe and intended to visit his daughter in Rome. "Mr. Mellon," he continued, "doesn't possess, as Secretary of the Treasury, any authority to make negotiations with foreign governments. The only authority that he has in that respect is as Chairman of the Foreign Debt Commission." With the exception of a few small items, the president said, Mellon's authority in that connection had been exhausted, "so that it can be authoritatively stated that he is not in Europe on any government mission whatsoever." To put an end to the matter, Coolidge stated, "Rather, he has gone abroad to get away from government."[52]

❧

Meanwhile, in London, the question of the controversy between the British chancellor and the American Treasury secretary was raised in the House of Commons on August 4, before it adjourned for its summer recess. Austen Chamberlain rose to defend Churchill, who, he argued, had been right not to allow Mellon's misapprehension about war debts to prevail.

Chamberlain insisted that because the British government's proposal to cancel all debts and reparations had been rejected, "no British government would think it becoming to the dignity of this country, or compatible with our honour, to go cap in hand to those to whom they have undertaken obligations and ask to be excused. We make no complaint, and we will discharge our obligations, but at least we would like it to be known in what manner that money was borrowed and to what it was devoted."[53]

Garrard Winston and Ben Strong, however, had long felt that Churchill complained too often and too publicly. The undersecretary had recently confided to Strong on the matter, telling him: "I have seldom seen such persistent effort on the part of any European statesman to put this country in the wrong as Churchill's. He is gratuitous in his slur on our harsh treatment of our debtors." Strong had replied that, while he faulted Churchill for making the unprovoked and unforgiveable statement that ignited the Peabody controversy, he thought "our best policy is to keep our mouths shut and let the Winston Churchill's do the talking."[54]

In early August, several more influential voices came forward in calling for a cease-fire in the war of words between Churchill and Mellon. The editor of the *Economist*, Walter Layton, who had been Churchill's statistical officer at the Ministry of Munitions during the war, wrote of his hope "that the international bickering between England and America on the international debt question will cease." He argued that "Britain has nothing to gain, and there is a danger that we may lose a great deal of international goodwill, by carrying on the discussion and creating the quite false impression that we are trying by a side route to reopen the settlement reached in 1923."[55]

In *Time* magazine, an article titled "Churchill vs. Mellon" commented, "At this point, the debate, though showing every sign of being continued ad infinitum, passed into the limbo where hairs are split—often by honest, well-intentioned men."[56]

Walter Runciman, a prominent member of the Asquith government, stated that he could "not imagine anything more deplorable" than that the chancellor of the exchequer should be entering into a public controversy with the secretary of the American Treasury. "We were going to pay our debts," Runciman said. "If Mr. Mellon had given reasons why we should do so which were not in keeping with the historical records in this country, then let the chancellor of the Exchequer quietly point out to him the error of his ways. That he should hold him up in the Press to the opprobrium of all accurate-minded men was not likely to lead to better relations between this country and America."[57]

∽

Mellon had reached Rome by August 4. Thanks to Rousseau, he and the boys had enjoyed their drive through the Loire Valley undisturbed. They had been well-received everywhere they visited in what was somewhat of a sentimental return to the region for Mellon, who had last visited more than twenty years ago. But the reprieve had come to an end with his new directive from President Coolidge. Mellon now needed to interrupt his reunion with Ailsa and David.[58]

On August 5, Mellon paid a courtesy call on Giuseppe Volpi, who had represented Italy in its debt settlement negotiations. Later that day, he was received by Premier Benito Mussolini in his private apartment at the Chigi Palace, which was also Volpi's residence as minister of foreign affairs. The *New York Times* reported that Mussolini expressed "his personal gratification over the Mellon-Volpi agreement, which he said had been welcomed in Italy as being perfectly just to both sides and a typical expression of American fair-mindedness." The following day, Mellon had lunch with Mussolini at the Villa Torlonia, Mussolini's state residence on the Via Nomentana.[59]

Italy's undersecretary for foreign affairs told reporters that "Italy considers the debt settlement with the United States a closed matter with which we are satisfied." He added, "The Italian government and people feel for Mr. Mellon an enormous sympathy and gratitude." Italy had been given better terms than either Britain or France, based on the Debt Commission's "capacity to pay" principle. The efforts of Mellon and Rousseau succeeded in stemming the negative press commentary on war debts.[60]

Mellon had never visited Italy and was very eager to see the art galleries of the Vatican Museums. A private tour was arranged for the Mellon family on Sunday when the galleries were normally closed. The special privilege was probably granted as the result of efforts by Mellon's son-in-law, the vice counsel at the American embassy. Guided by the director of the museum, Mellon had the chance to view Michelangelo's frescos in the Sistine Chapel and Raphael's in the *Stanze di Raffaello*, virtually alone.[61]

During his weeklong visit to Rome, Mellon attempted to put the controversy with Churchill to rest. "The whole thing was most unfortunate," he told reporters, "especially as there was no call for it at all. My reply to Mr. Peabody was not intended for publication, but even then, I thought I was stating nothing but positive facts. However, it was most regrettable that it should have been published, and more regrettable still that it should have given rise to any controversy with Mr. Churchill."[62]

Mellon intended to make his opinion on the matter clear and final, telling reporters, "The matter is closed and of the past, so far as I am concerned."[63]

10

DINNER AT THE RITZ

B y the middle of August 1926, it seemed that Mellon's statement from Rome had at last ended the public row with Churchill.

"The debate which created so much international fury," announced George F. Authier, a veteran Washington correspondent, had "blown over." He wrote that Europe had awakened to the fact that, while "it might satisfy its spleen" by speaking against the United States, it was merely hurting itself. "This was especially true," he commented, "of England where Winston Churchill, chancellor of the exchequer, and the Rothermere Press made the mistake of violating the Englishman's sense of good international politics by attacking the United States vigorously. The Rothermere press references to the United States as 'Shylock' and 'U S-ury' were not relished here and there was a moment when the good relations between the two countries seemed about to be disturbed."

The syndicated correspondent also stated that "it is equally evident that the lid has been clamped down upon officials in this country who were inclined to become too vocal." This was a reference to both US Treasury and congressional officials. He added that Mellon had been credited in press reports as having put the matter to rest. He cautioned, however, that while the debt settlements seemed to have been brought about "in a fair way" and verified "the inviolability of international obligations . . . they may be only temporary for it is difficult to see how collections on this huge scale can continue for sixty-two years."[1]

Lord Rothermere had, in fact, ended his campaign a week earlier. He disavowed any responsibility, blaming the editor and staff of one of his newspapers for having "jumped in at the deep end of the recent discussion on inter-Allied debts and splashed about, saying that American war debt collection methods resembled the methods of Shylock." That, Rothermere claimed, was not his opinion. He believed that President Coolidge and Secretary Mellon were "quite incapable of suggesting or forcing a usurious settlement on any of the Allies of their country in the Great War." Nevertheless, he admitted that "Personally, I have never had any doubt about the complete unwisdom of the debt settlements." He added that he believed they would be revised within a few years, and "are, as at present constituted, an active contribution towards the destruction of international trade."[2]

Most notably though, Winston Churchill remained silent, even when two additional calls for the United States to cancel war debts made headlines.

The first had come on August 9, when Georges Clemenceau, the former French premier, had broken his six-year silence to protest US war debt policy, writing an open letter to President Coolidge stating that "divergences of opinion . . . threaten to have a serious effect on the future of the civilized world." He stated bluntly: "We are debtors. You are creditors. It seems this is regarded as purely a matter for the cashier's department." From his perspective, it was not. He framed his opposition as a question: "Must the myth of German reparations lead up to American cash collections?"[3]

Clemenceau was echoing the argument that Churchill had long advanced, yet still the British chancellor did not seize the opportunity to endorse the French statesman. Whether Churchill's silence influenced the reception of Clemenceau's letter or not, the French embassy in Washington disavowed it, the US Treasury Department disregarded it, and President Coolidge dismissed it.

Churchill held his tongue again when Newton D. Baker, the secretary of war in the Wilson administration, called for a mutual cancellation of all war debts. This was particularly significant because Baker had criticized the Mellon-Baldwin agreement for having resulted in a "magnificent disaster," an assessment with which no one would agree more than Churchill. Baker argued that the British settlement established an impossible precedent, pointing to the fact that none of the other debtor nations were even remotely able to settle on such terms. "We are obliged therefore to discriminate," he said, "and in order not to make the case against our treatment of England too awkward, we must appear hard-hearted and exacting of everybody else."[4]

But even such a kindred appeal did not rouse Churchill to comment.

∽

With all quiet across the English Channel, Mellon took Ailsa out for a row on Lake Geneva. They had left Rome in pursuit of a healthier climate for her to recover from a malady that her Italian doctors were unable to remedy. Her husband David had been greatly concerned, and when her father arrived, they held a "family enclave." It was decided that Ailsa and A. W. would go to Évian-les-Bains, a spa resort in France's Haute Savoie, while David waited in Rome for a leave of absence to be granted. On their way to France, they stopped for a few days in Geneva, before moving into luxurious suites at the Hôtel Royal on August 14. It had been built by the Évian Mineral Water Company and its grounds extended from the lakefront to mountain trails, made accessible by its special train. Perhaps it was the thermal springs and healing waters that restored Ailsa; she and her father were soon basking and boating in the Alpine summer sun.[5]

Mellon seemed to have chosen Évian-les-Bains on Parker Gilbert's recommendation. He and Louise were already there, benefitting from the restfulness of the lakeside retreat after Louise's recent surgery. Rousseau arrived with the boys soon after A. W. and Ailsa had settled in. Other friends, acquaintances, and associates followed. Reports reached Washington that the secretary had "fallen in love with Évian-les-Bains" and was spending long, leisurely hours rowing on the lake and hiking on the trails behind the hotel.[6]

The Royal Hôtel, in the spa resort town of Évian-les-Bains. *From a 1921 postcard.*

It was not only the healthful waters and fine dining that were being enjoyed at Évian, but also the great value available to the Americans and British due the fall of the franc. Like other French resorts, Évian had a grand casino, where gambling in francs seemed like play money to the well-heeled. A Paris newspaper reported that Évian-les-Bains was having a "most successful" summer season and that "the affluence has been more grand and greater than it had ever been before." Finding a room had become impossible without a reservation. The report also noted that there were few Germans there that season, "The society is French, American, and English."[7]

Ben Strong arrived by train during Mellon's first week at the Hôtel Royal. After their meeting in Dinard in late July, he had traveled with Mellon, Rousseau, and the boys as far as the city of Tours in the Loire Valley. Since then, Strong had been meeting with the top finance officials in Europe, including the new governor of France's central bank, Émile Moreau. Because of their concerns about the tenuous state of the French government and economy, Strong kept Mellon more informed than usual. The Fed governor had written three lengthy letters during the two weeks since they had last seen one another. Each of his letters expressed a growing apprehension about the US policy on war debts.

Strong had written in early August that he was now convinced that the future of the new Poincaré ministry would be "determined by the success or failure of efforts to secure ratification of the debt agreements by the Chamber." He was referring to the Churchill-Caillaux and the Mellon-Bérenger agreements. Strong urged Mellon to make a reassuring statement to allay fears of the United States commercializing the French debt, and to grant the safeguard clause. These were the two concessions that Churchill had made to the French, which Mellon and the debt commission had refused to grant. Strong's unexpected suggestion reflected the peril that the Mellon-Bérenger agreement faced in France's Chamber of Deputies. It also signaled to Mellon the depth of hostility his collection effort had engendered in France.[8]

In a six-page letter of August 10, Strong explained the effect of Allied loan repayments on American farmers. He argued that while 15 to 20 percent of

US farm production was exported, "the world is in fact today experiencing a real difficulty in paying for what it would otherwise buy from us." This, he said, was difficult to detect or appraise, "but it can safely be assumed that the many dollars required to pay loans reduce the amount available to buy our farm products." While cancellation of the debts "would be so unpopular politically as to be out of the question," Strong suggested "a moratorium . . . for a short period, say for three or at the outside not over five years, during which no interest would be required." The fact that Strong was making such a recommendation was startling, especially since the idea of granting a moratorium to a debtor was anathema to bankers. Experience teaches them that debtors are loathe to resume repayment once a creditor has released them from the responsibility, even temporarily. Better to find a way to keep the debt alive, as Mellon would say, than to absolve the debtor of the obligation even temporarily. Mellon surely understood that Strong would not make such a suggestion unless he felt it was the only feasible path for the American government to take.

The most shocking statement Strong made to Mellon, though, had to do with the safeguard provision that had been given to Germany. In the current Dawes Plan for German reparations, Strong reminded Mellon that the payments required to be paid by Germany to the Allies could "be suspended if capacity to pay is shown to be unequal to the burden." Neither the Mellon-Baldwin nor the Mellon-Bérenger agreement had such clauses. This meant, as the governor of the Federal Reserve Bank of New York put it, "We are now in the unfortunate position of extending greater leniency to the defeated enemy than we show to our victorious associates in the war."[9]

Once Strong arrived in Évian, he and Gilbert spent the next five days discussing that uncomfortable reality with Mellon. Soon there were reports that "three of America's leading financial authorities" were conferring there. Details emerged in the press about the conversations concerning "the immediate future in war debts stabilization" and the "untangling of the reparations muddle," along with observations that they were enjoying "the Hôtel Royal's celebrated cuisine, with its unrivaled wine cellars containing France's choicest vintages"—and its "eighteen-hole golf course."[10]

All of this was true.

Gilbert and Strong were not the only men who wanted to talk with the vacationing Treasury secretary. Mellon held court as visitors came and went, including Robert Horne, the former chancellor of the exchequer, who, reporters noted, "frequently motors over from Aix-les-Bains and lunches or dines with Mr. Mellon." Horne, like Parker Gilbert, had once been mentioned as a former suitor of Ailsa at various times before she married. Nevertheless, he had retained his influence with both Mellon and Baldwin after leaving office to pursue a business career in the City.[11]

Reporters could only get Mellon to say that his conferences with the procession of financiers "had no significance." Without any further statements from him, the Associated Press had little to report other than "the prominent Americans and French aristocrats, with whom the hotel is packed, are finding Mr. Mellon's confabs more and more interesting."

When Stanley Baldwin and his wife arrived in Aix-les-Bains on August 24, a Paris columnist could only report: "Nobody knows whether Prime Minister Baldwin, summering only a few miles from Mellon, will meet with him. It might be desirable for these summer neighbors to meet accidently during their country strolls and talk over America's relations with Europe."[12]

With Robert Horne motoring back and forth between Aix and Evian, they likely did.

∽

On Sunday evening, August 29, Andrew Mellon left Évian for Paris. Strong, Rousseau, and the boys were already there. Gilbert would stay on at the French spa resort where his wife and Ailsa were recovering. David Bruce would soon join them.[13]

By the time Rousseau met Mellon at the Gare de Lyon the following day, a plan to dodge reporters and photographers was in place. Using the Hôtel de Crillon trick again—with a $200-per-day suite reserved in Mellon's name—Rousseau whisked A. W. off, through a side door of the train station, to his own "handsome, old-fashioned apartment in the Quai Voltaire." This was reported by Henry Wales, the Paris correspondent for the *Chicago Tribune*, to whom Rousseau had given special access to Mellon that day. In his story, Wales also related that Mellon had strolled, smoking one of his cigars "with his straw hat pulled down over his eyes," over to Rue de la Paix and Place Vendôme, where he "bought some nifty pajamas, shirts, and scarves, and motored to a café near Versailles for luncheon." But that, and a brief interview, was as far as the access went.[14]

Mellon's luncheon that day was strictly private. After his shopping tour, he motored west from Paris, through the Bois de Boulogne and the suburbs, for about a dozen miles, to a chic but out-of-the-way café near Versailles. There, he and Ben Strong met up with one of President Coolidge's closest confidants, Dwight Morrow, who was also in Paris. Morrow wanted to talk with them about a highly sensitive dinner appointment in London the following week that would involve all three of them.[15]

While the Mellon-Churchill controversy had died down in the press, hostilities between the American and British Treasuries continued to rage. Several political insiders, both in Washington and London, feared further damage to Anglo-American relations. The idea of an off-the-record dinner was to give the two Treasury leaders the opportunity to settle their differences. Ideally, it would result in an announcement that they had come to an understanding, thereby putting an official end to their quarrel.

Although the Paris press focused on potential meetings between Mellon and Poincaré and other French officials, there was little to be accomplished in any of them. The French Chamber of Deputies would not meet again until October, and the French prime minister had repeatedly expressed his opposition to the ratification of the Mellon-Bérenger agreement. Coolidge, moreover, had made it clear that Mellon had no authority to make changes to the agreement. The Treasury secretary had reinforced this fact when he arrived, announcing "There is nothing I can say about the debt accord; that passed out of our hands and went before congress when Ambassador Bérenger and I signed it." Mellon could do little more in Paris than pay his respects and express pleasantries.[16]

He did so the following day. Mellon met with Aristide Briand, now the minister of foreign affairs, at the palatial ministry offices on the Quai d'Orsay, not far from Rousseau's apartment. The morning courtesy call lasted barely thirty minutes, during which the Treasury secretary had spent "a quarter of an hour viewing the Gobelin tapestries which decorated the salons of the Foreign Office," in which he had shown "a keen, artistic interest."[17]

Later that evening, Mellon and Rousseau motored to the Ministry of Finance at the Louvre Palace for his visit with Premier Poincaré. Questioned by reporters about whether he had come to discuss debts, Mellon told them: "The matter is now in the hands of the French government, and it would not be courteous to discuss it. I am merely paying my respects to the ministry." The meeting lasted eighteen minutes.[18]

French journalists were dismayed by Mellon's assertions that he had not come to discuss the debts, although they had to concede that the brevity of the visits seemed to support his claim. The American embassy had made it plain though in arranging the interviews "that it was unnecessary to prolong the visit by more than a quarter of an hour."[19]

Mellon allowed Rousseau to set up one more press interview before he left Paris, this one with the French journalist Marcel Pays, the editor of the Paris daily *Excelsior*. Ben Strong sat in on the interview which took place in Rousseau's apartment that he kept expressly for discrete rendezvous. "The setting," Pays wrote, "was one of those old town houses on the Ile Saint-Louis which retains a bit of the majesty of the seventeenth century. In the living room, with the high windows fanned by the green branches, and outside flowers were blooming, and birds were chirping."

The view out Rousseau's window also included the cathedral of Notre-Dame with its stained-glass windows and thirteenth-century flying buttresses. Pays described the moment when "Mellon leaned over the wrought-iron balcony, smiling, stretched out his hand in the direction of Notre-Dame, all petrified lace behind the moving foliage." He quoted the American visitor as saying: "The most beautiful site in the world. Such poetry, such history."

But any questions about the problems between the United States and France over the debt settlement were asked in vain. Mellon "preferred to talk, in detail, of all his amazing surprises during his journey through our beautiful country," Pays wrote.

Ben Strong however, less bothered by diplomatic propriety, posed a question of his own to Pays.

"The debts?" Strong asked Pays. "We no longer know exactly what you think of them yourselves. When you want good music, you hire good musicians. When you want good cuisine, you choose a *cordon bleu*. When you want a good financial plan, you turn to experts. You engaged experts. But what happened to their plan?" Strong was referring to an experts' plan commissioned by the French government to advise it on addressing the country's financial problems.

Pays had no answer for this. Mellon eased the silence by smiling and gesturing in a way that brushed aside the problems hanging in the air. "All that I can say," he murmured, "is my hope, my confidence, that between France and America the solution most consistent with the interests and traditional friendship of our two nations will soon emerge."[20]

᠆᠊᠎

It was not clear whether Mellon still believed that the most amiable solution was the ratification of the Mellon-Bérenger agreement. Mellon would not take lightly the counsel from Strong and Gilbert. Their recommendations, however, carried political impossibilities.

Strong's advice to have the US government extend more sympathy and support to France and the Allies by granting a three-to-five-year moratorium on debt repayment by the Allies, would mean that Mellon would have to persuade Coolidge to make a complete reversal of US policy and go against public opinion and the will of Congress.

To address Gilbert's concerns about the risk of Germany either refusing to pay, or being unable to pay, the escalating Dawes annuities would require Mellon and Coolidge to convince the Allies to lower their reparation demands from Germany. Without those payments, the Allies—with the exception of Britain—would not be able to repay their war debts to America. Gilbert had presented a scheme designed to shore up German finances by issuing railroad bonds, but that, too, would be highly controversial.

Mellon's two trusted colleagues had made a forceful case for a significant change in US policy on war debts. They, like many others, were frustrated in their efforts to facilitate the economic recovery of Europe and viewed war debts and reparations as impediments. Their frustrations boiled down to the realization of Germany's growing reliance on US loans to fuel the circular reparation-war debt payment system that the Dawes Plan had become.

Dwight Morrow, who had been a partner at J. P. Morgan and Company for a dozen years, shared his concern about a potential breakdown in the Dawes Plan, a fear also shared by most of his Morgan colleagues. Russell Leffingwell, the bank's best analytical mind, considered a breakdown "inevitable" because the plan rested on a fundamental ambiguity: it renewed French hopes of large reparations while offering to Germany the assurance that "these payments would not be exacted if inconvenient." The Morgan bank had led Wall Street in calling on Washington to cancel war debts for years, yet all the while it had continued to make profitable loans underpinning the Dawes Plan.[21]

President Coolidge, however, remained staunchly opposed to debt cancellation, as Morrow knew well. They had met as freshmen at Amherst College and had remained close. Morrow was also privy to the president's current thinking that the less said about war debts the better.

One member of Congress, in Paris at the time of Mellon's visit, had much to say publicly about war debts. "There is no sentiment in America for cancellation of the foreign debt," declared Democratic Senator Pat Harrison of Mississippi, who had just concluded a summer European tour. "Those Americans who exploit such a view are raising false hopes and delaying economic readjustment," he charged in a not-so-subtle reference to Newton Baker. Next, he took former premier Clemenceau to task for "the ungraciousness of some French statesmen in minimizing the part played by the United States in the World War." As far as the senator was concerned, "the cancellation of debts would be a gross betrayal" of the American taxpayer by the government. His opposition to granting leniency to the Allies had not changed in the year since the Belgian negotiations.[22]

Mellon had heard the case for US forbearance on war debts from Strong, Gilbert, and Morrow. Mellon had also heard the resolve of the president and Congress against leniency. He could easily deal with the financial issues, but acting on the political aspects of the situation was an entirely different matter.

American political observers wondered whether Mellon's thinking had evolved during his vacation on the continent in light of his conferences with Europe's heads of government and senior financial officials.

One columnist covering the Summer White House reported that several Republican leaders believed "there was a possibility that Mr. Mellon may be educated to see that Europe simply can't go on forever under the present staggering system of debt payments, all predicated upon the ability of Germany to pay them."[23]

Another commented that "there is a school of thought led by Secretary Mellon which would not hesitate to recommend a revision downward in the amount of all war debts the moment it became apparent that it was good business for the American people to permit further cancellation." He added, "the only question that has been unsettled is whether the amount of cancellation has been just."[24]

Irving Fisher of Yale University, one of the America's most respected economists, asked whether American statesmanship was up to the task of seizing "the present chance to relieve the treasuries of the world of this incubus of debts which, if they remain, may prove a cause of international trouble greater than those which led to the world war."[25]

His message was undoubtedly meant for Mellon's ears.

By the time Mellon left Paris on September 3 for London, he had made the requisite courtesy calls and been briefed on the American and British perspectives on the state of Europe's economic recovery by Strong, Gilbert, Morrow, Horne, and probably Baldwin. Thanks to Rousseau's efforts, Mellon had even received some favorable press, largely from US wire services. Headlines reflected that his visit had had a positive impact. FRANCE ENCOURAGED BY MELLON'S VISIT, was one; FRANCE IS BOOSTED BY MELLON VISIT another. More importantly, there was little mention of the Mellon-Churchill debt controversy.[26]

⁂

When Prime Minister Baldwin left London for Aix-les-Bains on vacation in late August, Churchill took charge of negotiations to end a coal lockout, then in its fourth month. Although a general strike had been called off by the Trades Union Congress after its first nine days in May, the miners felt betrayed. They refused to go back to work for lower wages and longer hours. Having been defeated in the general strike, they had little leverage over the owners, who quite reasonably refused to operate mines at a loss with the demand and price for coal so low. To prevent the shutdown of the coal industry the previous summer, Baldwin had granted a nine-month government subsidy to the mine owners in return for their pledge not to reduce wages. A royal commission, however, had since ruled against further subsidies.

When the subsidies expired in the spring and the general strike had begun, the Baldwin government had turned to Churchill. Railway and transportation workers had joined the miners in sympathy, as did many other tradesmen, including newspaper printers and typographers. The British cabinet decided that their negotiations with the miners and owners could not continue in the face of labor union efforts to silence the press. To fill the information gap between the government and the people, the cabinet decided to issue a government newspaper, with Churchill as its editor.

Churchill seized control of the national dialogue on the strike before the first issue of the *British Gazette* was issued. Speaking in the Commons, he told the members that the government viewed the strike as a threat to its ability to maintain "the life of the nation in essential services and public order," and therefore, there would be no compromise. Negotiations could only resume after the strike had ended.

Purchasers wait at a railroad coal depot in the East End of London during the 1926 coal stoppage. *From the* Illustrated London News, *1926.*

"The door is always open," Churchill assured. "We are prepared to take the utmost pains to reach a settlement in the most conciliatory spirit."[27]

Appropriating the offices and printing facility of the *Morning Press* on May 3, Churchill oversaw the production and distribution of the *British Gazette*, which was delivered largely by students, volunteers, air transport, and military escort. As circulation approached two million, the May 11 edition reported a key ruling that found that the unions not directly involved in the miners' dispute were striking illegally. This meant the miners would be on their own and daily life would return to normal free of the disruptions caused by the supportive unions. On May 13, the headline of the eighth and last edition of the *British Gazette* made its announcement: GENERAL STRIKE OFF. Churchill had masterfully mobilized British public opinion in support of the government.[28]

Edwin James, the *New York Times* correspondent in London, commented somewhat sarcastically that "every country may take a lesson from it."[29]

It was an extraordinary victory but not won without complaint and accusation. Charges that Churchill had been overbearing, biased, and unapologetically anti-union followed him into a review of the strike later that summer in the House of Commons. Labour members expressed their bitter disapproval of the *British Gazette*, and one intimated that a general strike might be tried again.

Churchill replied to the menacing recrimination, "I have no wish to make threats or to use language which would disturb the House and cause bad blood, but I must say this . . ."[30]

He paused to allow the expectations of the members to mount as they envisioned the venerated orator about to unleash "the thunderbolts of Zeus," as one of Churchill's biographers described the moment.

"Make your minds perfectly clear that if ever you let loose upon us again a general strike, we will loose upon you . . ."

He halted again, letting his bellow hang in the air.

". . . another *British Gazette*," he said, with a dramatic flourish, sitting down to roars of laughter from the full House.[31]

Churchill had effectively diffused political repercussions from the general strike in July. By the time Baldwin left on holiday at the end of August though, negotiations with the owners and miners had devolved into a waiting game as the two sides remained deadlocked.

On September 1, Churchill decided it was time to deploy his ultimate political weapon: dinner diplomacy. His plan was to invite the leaders of both sides, separately, and on different evenings, to Chartwell, where he would ply them with champagne and oysters while seeking to break the deadlock. This contravened his summer edict of economy—no champagne, no oysters, no holiday. It did not surprise Clemmie, who learned of the policy reversal while on holiday in Scotland with friends. She knew Winston believed, as one historian put it, that more could be achieved "at dinner parties and meals," than in "the more formal setting of a conference room."[32]

No one agreed more with this strategy than Andrew Mellon. He had used it productively on Baldwin and the British delegation in settling Britain's war debts to the United States.

∽

Mellon arrived in London around midnight on Friday, September 3. Rousseau had traveled with him as far as Boulogne-sur-Mer, where Mellon took the cross-channel ferry to Folkestone. There was no one at the train station in London to meet him except a representative of Claridge's Hotel and a few newspaper reporters. Mellon had not provided the American embassy with any details about his arrival. Churchill, however, knew that Mellon was now in London.[33]

By early the next morning, the two Treasury rivals had made indirect contact. A British Treasury official arrived in Claridge's lobby "to present the compliments of Winston Churchill" to Mr. Mellon.[34]

Speculation about a meeting between them followed quickly in the press. "The secret meeting," the *Manchester Guardian* declared on Monday, "that will no doubt take place in London between Mr. Mellon and Mr. Churchill ought to have its dramatic moments—and, let us hope, its profitable moments."[35]

Within another few hours, the press had specifics about the meeting to disclose: "Tomorrow is an important day on Mr. Mellon's calendar. He will meet Winston Churchill, Chancellor of the Exchequer. Although the Secretary's entourage insists that the call is entirely informal, it is expected here that the two Treasury heads will have a general talk on European finances and will iron out the recent differences of opinion regarding the purposes for which Great Britain borrowed money from the United States during the world war."[36]

They did meet on Tuesday, September 7, despite it being a very busy day for Churchill in the coal negotiations, but there were conflicting reports on exactly where and when the event took place. Some reports stated that Mellon had paid a courtesy call on Churchill at Whitehall, while others reported that Churchill had paid one at Mellon's hotel. All concurred, though, that the two had met.[37]

Neither Churchill, nor Mellon, had much to say publicly at this time. The *Evening Standard* complained: "Seeing Mr. Mellon . . . is rather harder than escaping from the Theban Sphinx. His hotel denies all knowledge of him. His secretary is invisible and undiscoverable. The telephone is answered by silence. And the one thing he will not grant is an interview."

Yet Mellon did acknowledge to the reporter privately, that he had paid a courtesy call on Churchill and, perhaps to appease him, also revealed that he had spent that morning at the National and Tate Galleries.[38]

While the coal dispute was the main topic of political discussions in London and the mining regions of Britain, the Mellon-Churchill dispute remained on the minds of journalists.

The *New York Herald Tribune* declared, "It was purely in the nature of a courtesy visit." The report commented that the recent controversy between them had made "the debt question" an unwelcome topic by officials. "The silence of Mr. Mellon and Winston Churchill on the subject to-day," it concluded, "is taken here as a confirmation of the general opinion that it is a 'dead issue.'"[39]

But not quite. Mellon told another reporter: "It must be obvious that when I see Mr. Churchill this week we will have a welcome and serviceable opportunity for going over several outstanding points existing between his department in Whitehall and mine in Washington. Matters arising from the war debts will form a subject of conversation which, from my point of view, may be unofficial and personal."[40]

By and large, however, the London papers seemed predisposed to avoiding the reopening of the Mellon-Churchill controversy. An American paper observed, "The English newspapers are now devoting almost no space to Mr. Mellon's visit and are satisfied to let the subject drop entirely."[41]

Montagu Norman had much to do with that. With the assistance of his friend, Ben Strong—and possibly Stanley Baldwin—Norman had successfully kept secret the eight o'clock dinner planned for Thursday evening, September 9, which had been organized as something of an intervention to put an end to the Mellon-Churchill dispute. The dinner had been the topic Mellon, Strong, and Morrow discussed in Paris. Many in British political circles felt, as Norman did, that their public war of words about the war debts had needlessly poisoned Anglo-American relations. Some also believed that the dispute was impeding the economic recovery of Europe by precluding more productive dialogues on the subject.

Churchill had consented to be the host for the dinner in honor of Mellon, as protocol required. Any advance publicity about it would only have revived talk of the bad blood between them.[42]

Held in a private room at the Ritz Hotel in Piccadilly, the dinner required a table for twelve. The group, in evening dress, proposed toasts and returned them.

There were three Americans at the table: Mellon, Strong, and Morrow. The rest were British. In addition to Norman and Churchill, the party included: Edward Peacock, a director of the Bank of England; Churchill's fellow cabinet member, Laming Worthington-Evans, the secretary of war; John Bradbury, a former Treasury official who was now a British delegate to the Reparations Commission; and Walter Layton, editor of the *Economist*, who publicly called for the international bickering about the war debts to cease in July. Also joining the party were two officials from HM Treasury, Warren Fisher, the permanent secretary, and Frederick Leith-Ross, deputy controller of finance. John Spencer-Churchill, Winston's brother and a partner in the brokerage firm of Vickers, da Costa, was also at the table that evening.[43]

Most of the dinner party guests had met recently with Norman in his office on Threadneedle Street, including Mellon, who had lunched with him earlier that day and on Monday.[44]

Everyone understood that neither Churchill, nor Mellon, had any authority to change the political reality of the Mellon-Baldwin agreement, no matter what would be said. The only outcome that could be realized by the dinner would be an agreement to put an end to the inflammatory rhetoric—"Shylock" and "Sponger"—and set an example of diplomatic statesmanship for the respective treasuries to follow.

Norman and the other guests knew that both men had had a politically charged summer.

Mellon's many hours of discussion with financial leaders had made him realize that while the war had been financed with real assets, which once they had been put onto the battlefield, became political debts. He now knew that the United States could not depend on the Allies to repay their loans according to the terms of the settlement agreements. To safeguard the finances of the United States, it would now rest on his ability to maintain the US Treasury's continued discipline in running budget surpluses and adhering to the debt reduction program.

Churchill had acquiesced in his campaign to force the United States to cancel war debts. The hard truth for Britain was that winning a war depended not only on managing military assets strategically, but financial ones as well. Mellon's very presence testified to the fact that the British Treasury had not managed its international credit well.

Neither man had much to gain from the dinner at the Ritz other than a bit of goodwill.

The evening ended at 10:30 P.M.

Remarkably, none of the dozen attendees said a word on the record afterward. Perhaps this was an indication that the feelings between Mellon

The architectural style of the Ritz Hotel, London, as seen in the Palm Court. *From the* Architectural Review, *May 1907.*

and Churchill had not been changed, or even that remarks had been made that were not well taken by one party or another.

All present agreed to refrain from further comment. The only report recorded about the dinner was that it had been cordial, but no name was attached to this sole assessment.

"It would be an extravagant expectation, no doubt," wrote a London columnist, "that the Government dinner last night to Mr. Mellon, the American Secretary to the Treasury, will have results corresponding to the mutual cordiality displayed. But the cordiality, at any rate was marked."[45]

The *New York Herald Tribune* correspondent in London reported, "It is understood that Mr. Mellon made a short talk in which he avoided any mention of political questions, confining himself to an expression of pleasure at his vacation visit to England." Another commented optimistically: "Mellon's principal achievement in London was the reestablishment of the entente cordial with Chancellor of the Exchequer Winston Churchill. It is expected Mellon's visit will end official recriminations between London and Washington over the debt question."[46]

John Maynard Keynes—who was not at the dinner and not interested in cordiality—published a pointed article the following day, stating that reparations and inter-Allied debts were being settled primarily by loans from the United States, not in goods. He argued, "America lends to Germany, Germany transfers the equivalent to the Allies, and the Allies pay it back to Washington—nothing really passes, and nobody is a penny the worse." He questioned "how long the game could go on." Keynes articulated Wall Street's worst fear, "The moment cancellation becomes unavoidable, a burning issue of practical politics will flame up and that moment will be when the circular flow of paper is impeded, and that artificial equilibrium is broken."[47]

In other words, the moment American investors stopped buying the Wall Street bonds that were underwriting the Dawes scheme, all would collapse.

11

A CEASE-FIRE

A s Mellon and the boys boarded the *Berengaria* to return to New York on the morning of the September 11, 1926, an American wire service commented that the American Treasury secretary was "leaving the debt situation ostensibly, exactly the way he found it."[1]

It did not mention that he had had no authority, nor intention, to do otherwise. With twelve debt agreements settled, and only the Mellon-Bérenger agreement with France unratified, his work on the debt commission had been largely completed before he left for his European vacation.

But if the foreign debt situation had not changed, Mellon's view of it had.

As he sailed back, his plan to reduce the national debt had taken on greater import. He realized that the attitudes he observed during the summer in Britain and France increased the risk of default thus putting one of the Coolidge administration's key policies in jeopardy. If the Allies did default on their loans, the US Treasury would still have to repay Americans who had purchased Liberty Bonds to fund them.

The default risk, coupled with the political risks surrounding the house of cards the United States had built on a foundation of borrowed money to fund German reparations—as well as the possibility of the cancellation of the war debts—made his efforts to institutionalize the practice of running budget surpluses to aggressively pay down the national debt even more critical. Mellon had explained this philosophy to Congress the previous year, stating: "This country is today exceedingly prosperous. It can afford to pay off its debts without undue burden on the taxpayers. Its history has always been prompt extinguishment of war debts. It is then ready for the next emergency when it comes. The time to repair your roof is in good weather. The time to pay your debts is when you can." Mellon was confident that President Coolidge would continue to see the reduction of the national debt as a top priority.[2]

With the United States enjoying great prosperity and with his other goals for the Treasury mostly achieved, Mellon had turned over much of the day-to-day responsibilities to his undersecretary, Garrard Winston. Yet, Mellon did keep one responsibility under his wing, the Federal Triangle project, which involved the design and construction of a complex of government buildings intended to accommodate the growing federal workforce in Washington. President Coolidge had inspired Congress to pass the requisite legislation, saying, "If our country wishes to compete with others, let it not be in the support of armaments, but in the making of a beautiful Capital City. Let it express the soul of America." No one agreed with that idea more than Mellon.[3]

Jurisdiction for the design of federal buildings resided in the Office of the Supervisory Architect, which was overseen by the Treasury Department. This essentially made Mellon the architect of the Federal Triangle. The role dovetailed conveniently with his plan to make an important gift to the nation—a national gallery of art in the nation's capital. While rumors about his retirement had been floated, Mellon had no intention of stepping down as Treasury secretary. He would need the authority of his position to make his bequest.[4]

As he crossed the Atlantic for home, Mellon found a large basket of peaches and grapes in his suite aboard the *Berengaria*. It had been sent by his London art dealer, Joseph Duveen. Mellon had spent much of his time in London with Duveen visiting London's National Gallery in Trafalgar Square and talking with Robert Witt, one of the museum's trustees. Earlier in his vacation, he had also seen inspiring art and architecture in Rome, both at the Vatican and in the city's classical ruins. In Paris, he toured the

Louvre and visited prominent art dealers' galleries on the Rue de la Paix and Place Vendôme. For the research-driven banker, the visits also allowed him to discuss matters of museum governance, operation, and display, with some of the world's best experts.[5]

"Dear Sir Joseph," Mellon wrote from aboard the ship to thank Duveen for the fine fruit, "We are having a good crossing, and I am enjoying the restfulness of it."[6]

Although he would miss Ailsa when he returned alone to the Dupont Circle apartment, he was pleased to have left her feeling happier and healthier than when he arrived. He had enjoyed showing Paul some of his favorite sites and observing his son's growing affinity for British art and culture. While Mellon had difficulty in expressing and understanding emotions, there was no doubt that taking vacations with his children was a great pleasure for him and a priority.

∽

Unknown to Mellon, a political storm had begun in Washington before he had returned. Influential members of Congress, both Democrats and Republicans, were calling for tax cuts rather than reductions in the national debt. It amounted to an attack on his management of the Treasury's finances.

Democrats argued that Mellon was paying down the national debt too quickly and that he was running large surpluses that were unfair to tax-payers. They objected to his aggressive twenty-year timetable for retiring the debt, proposing instead to stretch it out over thirty-two years. Speaking for his party, Senator Furnifold Simmons of North Carolina admitted that the additional twelve years would put "a part of the war burden on the next generation," but he justified the longer discharge period because it would facilitate an immediate tax reduction. "It is the clear duty of Congress to distribute this unneeded Treasury surplus and put a stop to this unnecessary taxation as soon as possible," the senator insisted.[7]

Simmons had been one of the critics of Mellon back in 1921, during the Senate Finance Committee hearings to consider the Treasury secretary's request for broad authority to settle war debts. At that time, he stated that, if his colleagues disagreed with Mellon, "they would be disposed to place some limitations upon his power." They had indeed disagreed with him, particularly with his suggestion that the United States should extend leniency in approaching the Allies' indebtedness. It had led them to limit his power by creating the five-member debt commission.[8]

Now the senator and his Democratic constituency were threatening Mellon's authority to systematically refund war bonds using the annual budget surpluses. They had been produced consecutively since the end of the war by both Democratic and Republican administrations, a discipline which so far had resulted in a 25 percent reduction of the national debt.

Worse still for Mellon, Martin Madden, the Republican chairman of the House Committee on Appropriations, had revived a proposal to prevent Treasury from applying the interest from the war debt settlement payments to pay down the national debt. That practice, in conjunction with running surpluses, were the two key components in Mellon's program to retire the national debt and pay off the Liberty Bonds. In taking aim at Mellon's use of the interest payments, Madden charged that the law did not sanction the use of war debt interest receipts for the retirement of bonds. He then called on Congress to halt the procedure.

When Mellon arrived back in Washington on September 17, he rejected a proposal to use the surpluses from prior years to cut taxes. He told reporters that he was "as anxious as others to cut taxes to the lowest safe limit, but we have got to look to future years." He argued that while the United States was enjoying unprecedent prosperity, past surpluses were not a sensible means to be used to reduce prospective tax revenues, especially since they had already been "applied toward reduction of the public debt."[9]

The challenges from Congress made it clear to Mellon that the political situation in the United States had changed for the worse over the summer. It had also changed in Europe, but not in America's favor. He had been advised during his vacation that the American policy on war debts must at

Mellon in his office at the Treasury, posed next to a portrait of Alexander Hamilton. *Credit: Granger.*

least be softened or economic disaster would ensue. Many in the suffering countries believed the decision was in his hands.

Frank Kent, the influential columnist for the *Baltimore Sun*, argued that Mellon should act. Reporting from Paris, Kent wrote that bankers there and in London had bluntly told Mellon that the debt settlements were unworkable and uncollectible—and they had urged him to lobby Coolidge and Congress for revisions. The columnist opined: "Whether what they said will have any real effect depends upon the sort of man Mellon really is. If, as some believe, he is just a tired old man who approves but does not originate policies, then there will be no effect. If, however, he is the able far-sighted, broad, dominant citizen others contend, the effect will be considerable."[10]

Mellon's success, however, had come from backing other men's efforts, not leading them. He had earned his celebrated reputation by surrounding himself with exceptional professionals and giving them broad authority and responsibility to act, while remaining behind the scenes with the financial wherewithal—not political capital—to achieve success. Mellon was not a politician; he was a businessman who did not like to operate in public view. It was not in his nature to confront the presidents under whom he was serving or legislatures that had already limited his authority.

On his return from abroad, Mellon reported to Coolidge that he had observed gradual improvements in economic conditions in Europe, but that nothing had come to his notice that "called for a recommendation of changes in the Administration's policy on war debts."[11]

Perhaps hoping to serve as America's conscience, Russell Leffingwell, the former Treasury official most familiar with wartime lending to the Allies, raised his voice once again. In a speech a few weeks after Mellon's report to the president, he warned that the issue of the debts going forward would not be based on the capacity to pay of the debtor—the core principle of US policy—"but upon the decision of the American people in agreement with the people of the rest of the civilized world upon the question whether one nation should be compelled to make such payments to another nation, friend or foe, from generation to generation." Leffingwell was asking, did Americans feel the settlements were fair?

He closed, asserting, "Great as the importance of the financial and economic aspects of indemnities and war debts may be, their political and sentimental importance is even greater." Mellon no doubt agreed with Leffingwell, but he would leave it to the politicians to change course.[12]

∽

In somewhat mysterious fashion, Andrew Mellon and Winston Churchill were drawn into another controversy in late October. It concerned tariffs and involved them only indirectly. A syndicate of over two hundred bankers and industrialists from sixteen countries published a "free trade manifesto" in newspapers, calling for the removal of European trade barriers. Their names were signed to the manifesto to demonstrate its broad support in international financial and manufacturing circles. The high-level plea argued that the trade barriers between European nations were blocking the continent's financial recovery, which still remained stalled, eight years after the end of the war.

Neither Mellon, nor Churchill, were signers. They had, however, purportedly endorsed the initiative, which contributed to its worldwide headlines. "Mr. Mellon," reported the *New York Times*, "discussed the manifesto in London with Winston Churchill, Chancellor of the Exchequer, who approved it. Once they had approved it," the *Times* added, "it was then easy to obtain signatures."[13]

This, however, was not true.

The mystery surrounding the manifesto, caused by its unusual release in the press, led financial reporters to suspect the governor of the Bank of England, Montagu Norman, as its originator. Who else could secure the endorsement of J. P. Morgan? And was it just coincidence that a three-dimensional model depicting geographical borders as tariff walls—essentially a visualization of the manifesto—happened to be on display in the lobby of Norman's bank on Threadneedle Street? The model had been conceived and built by Clive Morrison-Bell, a political economist, and Churchill's former parliamentary private secretary. The concept of "a

European free trade zone" was a bold idea at the time—and one shared enthusiastically by Norman, who had by now acquired what would be called a "reputation for economic and financial perspicacity."[14]

The day after news of the manifesto reached the United States, the *New York Times* reported that Mellon "never saw the plan until he read it in this morning's newspaper and that it was not even broached to him."[15]

Churchill made no statement, perhaps in keeping with the policy of silence adopted during the summer by the British government with respect to "all questions touching on Anglo-American relations." The cabinet had decided that the shortest way to reopen the discussion on the revision of the debt settlement was "to boycott discussion thereof altogether at this end, and since the debt question is fundamental to all Anglo-American relations, this self-denying ordinance extends more or less automatically to other issues."[16]

The manifesto's plea for tariff reduction was based on the signatories' view that the European debtors could not repay their war debts unless they were able to access the American market. They argued, "If we check their dealings, their power to pay their debts diminishes, and their power to purchase our goods is reduced."[17]

An editorial in the *Washington Post* interpreted the manifesto as a call for the cancellation of war debts. "The manifesto was designed to sway public sentiment in the United States in favor of tariff reduction," the editorial asserted, "on the pretense that it is the only means of collecting European debts," which was, it added, "a thesis maintained by foreign spokesmen for many months."

As evidence of this, the *Post* editorial quoted from an article in *The Times* of London that explained that this "work of popular education" was being done by students of politics and economics all over America, including "members of societies and associations of many sorts, professors, teachers and the like," who were writing "lucidly of the problem which lies within the three corners of the debts, the vast export of American capital, and the maintenance of a towering tariff wall." It further asserted: "A concerted plan is on foot to pave the way to a demand for cancellation of European debts. These debts are to be repudiated unless the United States reduces its tariff."[18]

There was in fact a campaign underway calling for the cancellation of the debts, which had been set in motion by professors, teachers, and students. The press in several counties had reported on it and some newspapers were encouraging it. The *New York Times* editorialized, "The international bankers spoke words of economic truth and soberness when they said that huge debts from one country to another can be paid only in goods." It went on to chide the *Post* "that the real conspirators in favor of a cancellation of the war debts are the politicians who shout that they will never consent to the slightest lowering of our tariff rates."[19]

The dialogue expanded on several fronts. Critics of the Coolidge administration's protectionist policy noted the contradiction between the high tariffs in the United States and the bankers' campaign for the removal of tariffs in Europe. They collectively pointed out, "It has been argued that lowering our tariff would enable Europe to pay her debt in goods."[20]

Reporters asked American signatories to the bankers' manifesto to explain why they supported high tariffs in the United States and no tariffs in Europe. They replied defensively, "It is only the European tariff that is bad. The American tariff is a different matter."[21]

After conferring with Coolidge, Mellon issued a statement on October 25, saying that the proposed removal of tariffs in Europe made common sense and that US policy should remain as it stands. In nine typewritten pages, he agreed with the manifesto's syndicate that Europe had economic problems that affected trade, and that much of it was due to the rearrangement of Europe since the war. The United States and Europe, he argued, "would only be comparable if we should consider each of the forty-eight states a separate nation, each having its own tariff, its own railroads, its own currency, and its own language." What the plea of the bankers sought to accomplish, he said, "is not a change in the world, but to bring about in Europe a condition similar to that in the United States. It is not a criticism of us but an emulation."

The "artificial barriers" hindering readjustment in Europe were not, in Mellon's analysis, a reason to change the present US policy, under which "foreign countries are able to sell the United States increasing quantities of the class of things the United States does not produce." He included figures showing that imports had increased greatly from prewar levels and noted, "it is a fallacy to assume that reduced import duties will enable this country to increase its purchases abroad, for the measuring stick is the nation's purchasing power and not the amount of duty assessed."

Mellon argued that the current US tariff policy protected American labor and the American standard of living. He cited figures showing that a laborer "gets six times more per hour in America than he does in France for the same kind of work." The Treasury secretary concluded by asking, "Can it be to the interest of the United States that equality be established by the removal of the protection of the tariff?"[22]

Mellon knew that few politicians or businessmen would disagree with his point about US prosperity. New industries and consumer markets were fueling rapid rates of economic growth and soaring corporate profits all over America. A rise in productivity of labor and capital, owing to advancements in the moving assembly line and expansion in the stock market, topped previous levels. More and more consumers could afford automobiles, spurring road construction and suburban housing developments. Widespread electrification now allowed many homes to incorporate washing machines, refrigerators, radios, and vacuum cleaners into daily life. The shorter workweek gave people more leisure time to enjoy the films of Charlie Chaplin and Clara Bow, the music of George Gershwin and Louis Armstrong, and popular dances like the Charleston and Foxtrot. Life was good in America—why change it?

The *Washington Post* called Mellon's statement a "double-barreled broadside leveled against those who misinterpret America's position, whether they be European statesmen or international bankers, and against the advocates of lowering the American tariff."[23]

∽

Mellon quieted the bankers on the tariff issue, but not the academics on war debts.

In late December, forty-two members of Columbia University's faculty issued a petition calling for an international conference to reconsider the whole issue of war debts and reparations. They were petitioning for a revision, not cancellation, of all settlements since Versailles. In making their argument, the professors condemned the administration's policy both economically and morally. Their objection had to do with the capacity-to-pay formula, which they contended was unjust, especially in light of the great sacrifices made by the Allies before the United States entered the war. The academics opened a third front of criticism directed at Mellon. They had taken a position in between Congress—which opposed cancellation or leniency of any kind—and the European powers pressing for outright cancellation.

All three—Cancellationists, Hardliners, and now the Revisionists—stood in opposition to Mellon's efforts to strike a fair balance between each of the debtor nations and the United States.

Columbia's president, Nicholas Murray Butler, not only endorsed his faculty's petition, but circulated it to wire services and foreign correspondents. The Associated Press distributed the 1,500-word story in the United States, where it ran in hundreds of papers. It was also published widely in British newspapers, and in some, at considerable length.

The *Manchester Guardian* ran it in full. *The Times* of London reported that it "promises to influence profoundly American public opinion about inter-Allied war debts and reparations, not only because of its intrinsic force, but also because of the prestige of its authors." Many British papers quoted *The Times*'s statement, professing: "In our judgment the war debts are unsound. They have created and are fostering a deep sense of grievance against the United States."[24]

In France, the Columbia appeal was also widely covered. *La Liberté*, a Paris evening paper, commented: "The manifesto of the American professors shows that we would be wrong to hurry into ratification of the Bérenger agreement. American financiers and industrial leaders have already warned their government against demanding from Europe money that does not exist."[25]

President Coolidge did not ask Mellon to reply.

Instead, he told reporters at a scheduled news conference on December 21 that he had not read the Columbia petition with "any great care," but felt it should be ignored, going as far as to say, "I doubt if a statement such as has been given out will be helpful to the situation at the present time."[26]

The dismissive statement from the president seemed to put an end to Columbia's efforts to influence the war-debt controversy. Or rather, it did until the spring of 1927, when President John Grier Hibben of Princeton University and 116 members of its faculty wrote to Coolidge in support of the plea made by their Columbia colleagues "for a reconsideration of the settlement of Allied Debts." The educators argued: "The enlightened opinion of the country calls for a revision of the debt settlements with our former Allies . . . we do not desire to impose tremendous burdens of taxation for the next two generations on friendly countries who are struggling to regain their strength at the very time when we are amassing a national fortune." Empathetic to those burdens, they further scolded, "To divorce the financial provisions of the loans from the moral situation in which they were asked for and given is to invent an unreal economic abstraction."[27]

Both institutions had awarded honorary degrees to Mellon only a few years earlier. This time he replied.

In a stern and censorious press release, he admonished the university critics for ignoring the will of the American people as expressed through their chosen representatives in Congress, which had been overwhelmingly "opposed to more lenient terms" in the settlements.

The Treasury secretary asserted that the settlement terms demonstrated the great consideration given to each debtor. He wrote that he knew of "no fairer formula than capacity to pay," which had been generously applied.

Neither the Columbians, nor the Princetonians, had requested information from the Treasury Department or interviews with its officials. Mellon chided them for not doing their homework: "The training of these gentlemen . . . would have led me to believe that they would have conceived it to be their first duty to present a dispassionate analysis of the facts based on original study rather than to submit their conclusions unsupported by facts."

Mellon stressed the administration's opposition to reopening the settlements, which he argued would be a "step backward." His reply went on for another six pages of typeset copy detailing the rationale for collecting the debts, the legislative history of the agreements, and the settlement details. His statement was full of precise figures and pointed out again that no faculty member of either Columbia or Princeton "saw fit" to examine the "data available at the Treasury department" or to interview any of the officials who negotiated the settlements.

In addition to the contentious tone of his communique, Mellon made both an inaccurate and highly inflammatory statement in denying the academic's contention that the Allies were suffering from the burden of the settlements. He wrote, "Now, all of our principal debtors are already receiving from Germany more than enough to pay their debts to the United States." This, however, was not true of America's largest debtor—Great Britain. German reparations alone were not covering Britain's debt payments to the United States. It was also provocative in having linked war debts with reparations, something the administration, and the debt commission in particular, had resolutely avoided.[28]

Mellon's antagonistic reply to Hibben ignited a firestorm, including an immediate rebuttal from the Princeton president. He issued a statement on March 17, criticizing Mellon for his inconsistency. He reminded the Treasury secretary that the debt commission had asserted in 1925 that the issues of war debts owed to the United States and reparations were "separate problems." This, he pointed out, contradicted the argument Mellon had just made to him. It had indeed. Whether Mellon's frustration with the criticism coming from all corners was responsible for the gaffe, or a lack of attention on his part to the reply when he signed it, is not clear. But Hibben had both called out the Treasury secretary and put a major inconsistency in US policy on war debts in the spotlight.

The university president also charged that using reparations to pay war debts went against the purpose of reparations, which were "designed originally to repair damages of the war." He denounced the practice, arguing, "The nations which suffered cannot use the reparations for the repair of their own destroyed property but must pass it on immediately to their ally in the war, the United States."

In its front-page article on Hibben's follow-up statement, the *New York Times* included an excerpt from an editorial in the *Daily Princetonian* supporting the faculty initiative. The editor of the article charged that the demands the United States was making of its Allies added an element of danger: "The fact is that we do not need the money and we are paying for it a price of extortion and ill-will so great that no extraordinary psychic power is necessary to foresee the possibility of another war, which would cost us every penny that we have been able to squeeze and then five times or so as much again." As far as the Revisionists in academia were concerned, the US government was not acting as either a fair or honest creditor.[29]

Fleet Street reporters in London concurred.

The financial columnist of *The Times* insisted that Mellon's calculations "cannot pass unchallenged" and stated, "We are not receiving, and are not likely to receive, more from all our European debtors than we have to pay the United States." According to his figures, "in the financial year ending with this month, we shall have paid again more than £33,000,000 to America and will have received from Germany and the other European debtors little more than £20,000,000."[30]

The British government's policy of silence, though, remained in force. The *Manchester Guardian* attempted to get a reaction from Churchill on March 19 but could only report, "Since the famous Churchill-Mellon controversy on the subject of debts, the Treasury takes the line that Mellon's views are known and that they do not call for further comment."[31]

A few days later, Churchill was questioned about Mellon's misstatement in the House of Commons. He responded, "As soon as I saw the newspaper report, I asked the Foreign Office to make inquiries in order that we many know exactly what happened." Figures he cited in the Commons that day largely confirmed those published by *The Times*. Churchill further added that "in accordance with the policy outlined in the Balfour

Note," the government would "make a proportional abatement to its debtor if the receipts from reparations and war debts exceeded the payments to the United States."

In answering another question on the matter, Churchill—most diplomatically—replied that "he did not think we ought to assume Mr. Mellon's statements are misleading until the report is received of what was said."[32]

Six weeks later, on May 2, 1927, the British ambassador, Sir Esmé Howard, delivered an official note on behalf of his government to US Secretary of State Frank B. Kellogg. The note stated that Mellon's response to President Hibben of Princeton University "does not correspond with the facts as known by His Majesty's Government," and that "public opinion in both countries should have a fair opportunity of judging the position."[33]

The London correspondent of the *Philadelphia Inquirer* explained, "In this latest phase of the war debt controversy, Great Britain not only tells Secretary Mellon that he is all wrong, but also points out how in its opinion he came to be mistaken."[34]

The fact that the note was sent by the Foreign Office, and not from the British Treasury to the US Treasury, gave it the force of a state paper between the two countries, which particularly irked Kellogg.

Even though Churchill had announced in March that an inquiry would be made, a formal reply sent through diplomatic channels was unexpected. The London bureau of the Associated Press reported, "News that the note had been sent caused surprise in London, as there was no intimation of its existence until word was received that Sir Esme Howard, the British ambassador, had delivered it to the American State Department." The note, however, was "understood to be the outcome of the controversy over the war debt between the American Secretary of the Treasury, Andrew W. Mellon, and the British Chancellor of the Exchequer, Winston Churchill."[35]

The State Department suspected that the British note had been based on a twelve-page memorandum written by Churchill. After confirming that it had, the American diplomats decided not to disclose the fact publicly.[36]

The London correspondent of the *New York Times* did not hold back though, stating categorically that the note was "prepared by the British

Secretary of the Treasury," and was "more than a simple quarrel about figures between Winston Churchill and Secretary Mellon." It was intended, he wrote, "over and above that, as an attack on the American debt policy and another plea for reconsideration of the international indebtedness which the great war left to a weakened world."[37]

Kellogg responded to the new quarrel in a terse note. He stated that the United States "regards the correspondence between Mr. Mellon and Mr. Hibben as a purely domestic discussion and does not desire to engage in any formal diplomatic exchanges on the subject."[38]

The secretary of state was angry that diplomatic channels were being used to stir up anti-American political publicity. He informed the British embassy "that Mr. Winston Churchill could appeal to the press any time he saw fit; that he had not been backward about doing it heretofore and I did not understand why he did not do that now unless he wished to use the note as a means for getting publicity."[39]

Kellogg's statement that the British note was not a matter for further diplomatic discussion was also viewed in Whitehall as undiplomatic. It was also mocked in the British press.

To make matters worse, Mellon released another long statement on May 5, citing a "typographical error" in his response to Hibben, which had inadvertently omitted the words *except Great Britain*. He also explained the discrepancy in the figures as due to differences in which the two countries defined terms. Unfortunately, it was a long, complicated, and difficult document, packed with figures that did little to diffuse the issue or to repair the damage.

The Washington-based correspondent of *The Times* reported that the Mellon-Hibben incident had caused the American government "some annoyance, as it reopens a controversy which the Coolidge Administration in general, and the Treasury Department in particular, desperately desires to avoid." He also called for a correction, saying, "It is generally admitted . . . that if Mr. Mellon's letter to Mr. Hibben left in Great Britain or in any other part of Europe the impression that, in spite of the principle laid down in the Balfour Note the British Treasury was receiving 'more than enough' to pay the United States, some rectification was desirable."[40]

On the afternoon of May 5, Churchill was asked in the House of Commons if he was "aware that Mr. Mellon has repeated the statement that we are receiving more from Allied countries than we are paying to the United States, and that these statements have done great harm to our interests in France and Italy?"

Churchill replied, "Both by speech in this House and by formal Note, we have placed our view of these transactions on record. I am quite sure there is no step which it is in our power to take other than the steps we have taken."

Another member queried, "Has the government denial received wide publicity in the United States press?"

"I think all these matters do obtain great publicity," Churchill replied, "and from some points of view, that publicity is regrettable. But I do not see how in the circumstances that have arisen we could have avoided taking the steps we have taken."

Churchill was also asked whether he would "see that publicity is given throughout Europe to our reply to Mr. Mellon?"

"I think it will obtain a full measure of publicity," Churchill replied. "We cannot do more that state publicly the views we have. Other views may be stated in contradiction of them, but public opinion will judge, both inside this House, and outside."[41]

Churchill had conducted himself as a model statesman; Mellon clearly had not.

The London correspondent for the *Manchester Guardian* reported, "All that the British Government set itself to do was to state clearly the simple facts about inter-Governmental indebtedness and to show that, far from the British Treasury ever receiving more than she has to pay, Great Britain is saddled with a mass of unpaid debt, which, as Mr. Bonar Law said, will reduce the standard of British life for three generations." This argued not only that Mellon was wrong, but that Baldwin had made a bad bargain in agreeing to such harsh terms. It was a bitter assessment.[42]

Others felt the same way.

"The British note is unanswerable and unanswered," said the *Westminster Gazette*. "Mr. Mellon under a clever smoke screen beats a retreat."[43]

The London correspondent for the *Baltimore Sun* reported that "the whole British public is solidly behind the Government's presentation of the British case," and that there was no doubt whatsoever that Bonar Law's opinion of the war debt settlement "is the view held by all shades of British opinion."[44]

Mellon's blunder had reawakened British resentment of the United States. It also refocused international press coverage on war debts. "The Anglo-American war debt controversy has reached a high pitch of acrimony in the British press," the Associated Press reported from London. "British newspapers in streaming headlines and terse outspoken editorials employ more of a tone of indignation at the American attitude on the war debts, rather than of regret that the question is again disturbing Anglo-American relations."[45]

∽

As 1927 drew to a close, so too did the continuing war of words between Andrew Mellon and Winston Churchill. They had stuck to their guns but ceased firing.

Mellon resisted the calls to reopen the debt settlements and quietly let British diplomats know of his plan to extinguish the national debt by 1940, after which "the Allied debts would then be remitted to them." His work, as far as debt collection went, was done. The five-year term of the World War Foreign Debt Commission had expired on February 7, 1927. Of the thirteen countries with which it had made settlements, only the French agreement had yet to be ratified. From the perspective of satisfying the terms set by Congress, it had been largely successful. Ninety-seven percent of the principal amount of foreign indebtedness to the United States, or $9.8 billion, had been refunded. Using interest rates well below the 4.25 percent set by Congress, the commission effectively

Clementine and Winston Churchill outside 11 Downing Street, on April 15, 1929. *Credit: Alamy.*

canceled 43 percent of the Allies' total indebtedness. Most of the settlements provided for deferred or postponed interest payments in the early years. The concessions, however, had been made in such a way as to deliberately obscure them. This had prevented the United States from getting credit for its benevolence, just as Leffingwell had feared it would.[46]

In leading Britain's effort to make settlements, Churchill had finalized agreements with six of the eight countries to which it had loaned money to fight the war. The other two, Belgium and Russia, were resolved through reparations and repudiation, respectively. When the issue of Britain's debt settlement with the United States came up in the House of Commons in November, Churchill ended the discussion, saying, "No useful purpose would be served by further official action in the matter."[47]

Through the lens of the percentage of the total debt settled, Mellon refunded 66 percent compared to Churchill's 37 percent.[48]

In later reflecting on Churchill's negotiations with the French and Italians, longtime British Treasury official Frederick Leith-Ross commented, "We found out afterwards that in both cases their governments had authorized their representatives to offer substantially more" than what he had accepted.

Leith-Ross said of Churchill, "Winston had too generous a heart to be a hard debt-collector."[49]

12

PRINCE'S GATE

W hen a courtesy call brought Andrew Mellon and Winston Churchill together again, two years later, on October 18, 1929, the leadership of both the American and British governments had changed.

Calvin Coolidge had surprised the world by choosing not to run for reelection, paving the way for Herbert Hoover to win the presidency in 1928. Coolidge's commerce secretary ran on a message of continued prosperity. A representative campaign advertisement exclaimed, ELECT HOOVER AND INSURE PROSPERITY. The simple message worked; Hoover won in a third Republican presidential landslide.[1]

A year earlier, the humorist Will Rogers had predicted it, quipping to aspiring Democrats, "You can't lick this Prosperity thing; even the fellow that hasn't got any is all excited over the idea."[2]

Hoover's ties to the legacy of economic success left by the Harding and Coolidge administrations drove Americans seeking to sustain their financial well-being to vote for him overwhelmingly.

Despite the frosty relationship that had developed over the years between the president-elect and Mellon, Hoover understood the political advantage the respected Treasury secretary would add to his cabinet and retained him. For his part, Mellon was only too pleased to stay on. The finances of the government were in good order—government spending had been reduced by almost 10 percent and the national debt by a third since he took office—and he could continue work on the Federal Triangle project as well as his planned gift to the nation of a national art museum, while a new undersecretary, Ogden Mills, handled routine Treasury business.[3]

Less than three months after President Hoover took office, the Conservative government of Stanley Baldwin won the British general election by a slim majority of the popular vote. The affable prime minister decided, however, to resign and give Labour leader Ramsay MacDonald another chance at solving Britain's problems. Baldwin remained a member of Parliament and was reported to be as cheerfully nonchalant as ever. Asked what he might cast about for in the future, he told reporters that he planned to take up tennis and had "bought a second-hand tennis racket from a friend."[4]

Winston Churchill also kept his seat in Parliament, but his exit from the Baldwin Cabinet put a new strain on his personal finances. He had lost both his government residence at 11 Downing Street and his ministerial salary. Needing to increase his income, Churchill decided to take a break from Whitehall politics and make a grand tour of North America to promote his new book, the fifth volume of *The World Crisis*, titled *The Aftermath*. The tour promised to be lucrative because his New York literary agent had arranged for Churchill to write serialized articles for the *Daily Telegraph* and *Collier's* about his experiences and observations during the tour.[5]

Frederick Leith-Ross remembered Winston once telling him "with a schoolboyish grin," that he particularly enjoyed writing for American magazines. "You don't know what a savour there is," he said, "in dictating at a dollar a word."[6]

The lecture tour was also an expedition of sorts. Over the course of three months, Churchill traveled west across Canada from Quebec City to Victoria, British Columbia, and then east from California to New York, stopping in major cities along the way to make speeches.

He was a sought-after personality in both Canada and the United States, and toured with an entourage that included his son, Randolph, now eighteen; his brother, Jack; and Johnny, Jack's twenty-year old son.

After arriving in Quebec on August 9, they set off by train for the westbound leg of the tour. Traveling in a private railway car provided by the Canadian Pacific Railroad, Winston described it to Clemmie as "a wonderful habitation," with "large cabins with big double beds and private bath rooms." He also wrote of the "fine parlour with an observation room at the end and a large dining room which I use as the office, and in which I am now dictating." The vice president of the railroad had also lent Winston his stenographer for the trip.[7]

Churchill was well received in speech after speech, particularly in Vancouver on September 4. "Waves of applause" and cheers greeted him from an audience of more than a thousand packing the theater. There was no mistaking Churchill as he took to the stage—"his shining pate, his cutaway coat, wing collar and cravat marked him the personality still called Britain's 'busy young man.'" With a smile, the British "statesman, author, soldier, and splendid adventurer of life and politics," proudly proclaimed his faith in the British Empire which "captured the imagination of his hearers."[8]

Churchill spoke on many of the same topics as he had in his prior speeches, but on this evening, he also commented on war debts.

The topic was back in the news because of a rescue plan to save the circular payment system of loans, reparations, and war debts, created by the Dawes Plan. Germany's increasing difficulty in making reparations payments had set off fears that the roundabout system might implode and trigger an international financial crisis. Keeping the system in operation depended on the United States. Its government, however, continued to eschew any connection between reparations and war debts. To maintain its policy, American officials once again turned to an expert from the private sector. They tasked Owen Young, the president of General Electric and a member of the 1924 Dawes committee, with developing a plan to reduce German obligations but still allow the defeated power to pay the Allies enough to make their war debt payments to the United States.

As Churchill was making his way to Vancouver, the Young Plan was adopted, despite strong opposition from the new British Labour chancellor, Philip Snowden. In his speech that evening, Churchill praised his successor for opposing the plan. Like many in Europe, they both had hoped the Dawes Plan would break down, and thereby create an opportunity for a complete reconsideration of war debts and reparations. Churchill suggested that the concessions secured in exchange for Britain's acceptance of the Young Plan presented an opportunity for Britain "to seek a release from the self-denying limitations of the Balfour Note." This, he argued, would "carry general relief to the British taxpayer."[9]

This was a stunning statement given Churchill's past conception of, and dogged insistence on, the British government's adherence to the policy expressed in the Balfour Note, and its design had been to trumpet British financial superiority, not to provide relief to the British taxpayer. Churchill's about face, however, passed largely without comment.

As they traveled west of Calgary, Churchill was captivated by the scenic beauty of the Pacific Rockies and called for a temporary halt in the lecture tour. He described the region to Clemmie as "twenty Switzerlands rolled into one." On the terrace of the majestic Banff Springs Hotel at the foot of Sulphur Mountain, he set up his easel to paint the view of Bow Valley. By this time, Churchill had achieved some acclaim as a painter. He had won an amateur contest in 1925, judged no less by Joseph Duveen, Mellon's art dealer, and Kenneth Clark, the future director of London's National Gallery of Art. The third judge of the contest, Oswald Birley, had already painted a portrait of Mellon and would later paint one of Churchill.

After a two-night stay, the Churchill party left the "castle in the wilderness," for a three-day, three-hundred-mile motorcar tour through a trio of the Rocky Mountain National Parks—Kootenay, Yoho, and Banff. He painted landscapes of the idyllic Emerald Lake, which he reported to Clemmie was "more turquoise or jade than emerald" in color, and the "truly enchanting" Lake Louise.[10]

The natural beauty of America also ensorcelled Churchill. He described the Redwood Highway as "an aisle in the cathedral of trees." He marveled that "men look like ants and motor-cars look like beetles" up against the massive trunks of the redwoods. In addition to "nature's panorama in California," as Churchill put it, the glamor of Hollywood continued to dazzle the British entourage. "A carnival in fairyland," Churchill wrote of it in an article for the *Daily Telegraph*, after touring the sets and studios of what he dubbed the "Peter Pan Township of the Films."[11]

When Churchill reached New York City in early October, he dined with the rescuer of the Dawes Plan, Owen Young. They no doubt discussed the formidable challenge Young and his committee of experts had faced in preserving the discrete obligations each nation had pledged to others, or as one historian put it, reconciling "Allied demands for money with German reluctance to pay, while protecting America's position on war debts." Churchill would have been unsympathetic on the latter part of the effort. Despite their differences, Young recorded that the evening had been "marvelously entertaining."[12]

One of the purposes of the American leg of the tour was to meet with "the leaders of its fortunes," and Churchill visited with many of them, including William Randolph Hearst, Louis B. Mayer, and Charles Schwab. The prominent New York banker Otto Kahn, also an art collector, hosted a dinner for Churchill at his Upper East Side mansion, which was adorned with Old Master paintings by Bellini, Rembrandt, and Hals.[13]

Churchill was impressed by the American spirit, particularly its qualities of industry, resilience, and ingenuity. One institution especially astounded him—the stock market. He reported that "workmen of every class, including chauffeurs, train conductors, railwaymen, and waiters," dabbled in it. "The housemaid," he wrote, "who makes your bed is a stockholder on margin." As he observed more and more of the new world, Churchill could not resist "the utterly novel" speculative machine. By the time he reached Washington on October 18, he had invested all of his earnings from his North American tour into the US market.[14]

In the nation's capital for just one day, Churchill made two brief, but high-level appearances.

The British embassy in Washington had arranged an appointment for him to meet with President Hoover around noon. Ronald Ian Campbell, the chargé d'affaires substituting for the British ambassador, who was away on a visit to the West Indies, presented Churchill—formally clad in black silk top hat, bow tie, and carrying a Malacca silver-knobbed walking stick—to the American president. The courtesy call was intentionally brief. Not only did Churchill view Hoover as the most anti-British member of the debt commission, but Hoover did not want to enhance Churchill's stature in any way. The president had just entertained Britain's new prime minister, Ramsay MacDonald, during the previous week, in the hope of improving Anglo-American relations, and Churchill was a highly visible member of the opposition to the MacDonald government.[15]

After the brief White House visit, Campbell hosted a luncheon in honor of Churchill at his townhouse on Jefferson Place, a few blocks north of the White House. Among the "small group of distinguished men assembled" to salute the renowned author and former British chancellor were several members of the Hoover Cabinet, including Andrew Mellon.[16]

The lunch had not been announced to the press in advance, likely owing to the uncertainty of Churchill's travel schedule, but it did find its way into the society pages of the Washington papers. Neither political commentators, nor financial reporters, however, took an interest in the fact that the two Treasury titans, who had so bitterly debated war debts for years, were meeting face to face for the first time on American soil. That an official diplomatic event in Washington involving Mellon and Churchill went largely unreported, reflected the fact that they were no longer viewed as principals in the politics of international finance.

In virtually every speech Churchill had made during his tour, he had called for Anglo-American cooperation and friendship. That, it seemed, did not extend to Mellon, as there was no indication of any friendly interaction between the former treasury adversaries during his visit to Washington.

Typically, Mellon invited visiting dignitaries and colleagues to his Dupont Circle apartment, where they could be entertained in grand style and view his highly regarded art collection. In Churchill's case, however, it seems that no invitation was extended, though it may be possible that Churchill's tight schedule might not have allowed him to accept one. The former British chancellor had squeezed his Washington visit in between two back-to-back dinners in New York that had arisen somewhat opportunistically.

Whatever the circumstances, Churchill hurried off after lunch to catch the three o'clock train to New York in order to arrive on time for a dinner party being hosted by Mrs. William Randolph Hearst in his honor. The guests included the Astors, Vanderbilts, and Condé Nasts.

While the tour of more than six thousand miles boosted Churchill's popularity, the financial gain that he sought to acquire from it eluded him. When he sailed for home on October 28, the novice British investor had lost every cent he earned during his tour in the rapid succession of Wall Street losses that had played out over his last days in the United States.[17]

He left for England, however, without rancor, and only with a new appreciation, and perhaps a growing conviction of the need for Anglo-American understanding.

"No one can say the public was not warned," he wrote of the stock market debacle in an article for the *Daily Telegraph* published after his return. He pointed to the cautionary efforts that had been made, "Many times have the Federal Reserve authorities denounced speculation and raised the rate to check it."

Nor did Churchill blame Mellon. Instead, he reminded his readers of the Treasury secretary's warnings to prove his point that alarms had been sounded before the crash.

"Repeatedly Mr. Mellon declared the position unsafe, and counseled investments in bonds," he wrote magnanimously.[18]

⁜

The 1929 stock market crash laid bare Germany's dependence on borrowing from US banks to remain solvent. It also revealed that the American payment system for reparations and war debts, as Leffingwell had said of it, amounted to little more than a house of cards, and one that Keynes had assured would ultimately break down. Despite their faltering economies,

Germany and the Allies continued to meet their obligations until the spring of 1931.[19]

Financial conditions in Germany then worsened precipitously, alarming US officials that the crisis would not only impact reparation payments but might also trigger another financial panic in the United States.

On June 5, Heinrich Brüning, the chancellor of Germany's Weimar Republic, issued a manifesto declaring that the Young Plan was unworkable. He asserted that "the limit of privations that we can impose on the nation has been reached." The assumptions upon which the Young Plan was based, he said, "had proved erroneous." Most disturbing to the European countries that were receiving German reparations—particularly France—was Brüning's conclusion that "the economic and financial situation of the Reich, which is menaced in the extreme, inevitably compels the relief of Germany from the intolerable reparation obligations."[20]

That same day, Hoover was advised by Thomas Lamont of J. P. Morgan and Company to declare "a holiday of international governmental debt payments." Jack Morgan had called the idea "a life-saver for the world." The debt holiday was also in America's interest, Lamont argued, as US banks held much of Germany's short-term debt, which would be adversely affected if German banks failed. If the United States did not act, there could be a financial crash in Europe that would prolong the Depression in America for years to come. But it was Parker Gilbert, now at the Morgan bank, who perhaps exerted the most influence on Hoover. He urged the president to take immediate action.[21]

Hoover promptly called Mellon, Secretary of State Henry Stimson, and Treasury Undersecretary Mills to the White House. The president proposed to them that the United States "should postpone all collections on allied debts for one year in consideration of all the Allies making similar postponements of reparations and all claims during the same period."

Stimson was all for it. Mellon was not and stated "his unqualified disapproval." Mills echoed Mellon's disapproval and warned that the proposed moratorium would require congressional approval because "it would break down the debt structure." He added, given that Congress was not in session, it would necessitate convening a special session.

Mellon was leaving for a European vacation the following day. Hoover urged him "to make independent inquiries there." In Hoover's account of the moment, he wrote, "I was . . . relieved to be able to deal directly with Mr. Mills, who would be acting Secretary of the Treasury and had a younger and more vigorous mind than Mr. Mellon." Afterward, Hoover told Stimson that he was leaving Mellon "to find out for himself" about the dire economic conditions in Germany and the threat posed to the United States, during his European vacation. He added that "he thought it would be a great shock to him."[22]

It was, in fact, a shock to Mellon.

Immediately after arriving in London on June 16, Mellon had meetings with Prime Minister MacDonald and Montagu Norman, who laid out the impending and disastrous circumstances facing Europe.

"There is no doubt," wrote London's *Daily Mirror*, "that the frequent secret conversations" between Mellon, MacDonald, and Norman "have been largely concerned with the acute financial position of Germany." The report went on to say that it was well known "that the political situation in Germany is exceedingly acute, and unless a financial improvement takes place by the autumn, the Hitler Party, the principal point of whose programme is the repudiation of war debts, may gain control of affairs."[23]

Mellon reported back to Hoover and Stimson on June 18 by cable. "I am convinced," he wrote, "while making allowance for the extremely pessimistic attitude of the authorities here, that the situation is very grave and has possibilities of serious consequences." He added: "My personal judgment, in view of this situation, is that the President would be justified in initiating some proposal under our war debt agreements, toward a postponement of payments. The French, without payment from Germany, will undoubtedly refuse to continue payments under their agreement." Mellon believed the other debtor countries would refuse as well. He suggested a postponement of "at least two years," but he was concerned that the French "may not be in a frame of mind to cooperate," since they had not been consulted in advance.[24]

Two days later, Hoover issued a statement to the press, announcing "the postponement during one year of all payments on inter-governmental debts and reparations," subject to confirmation by Congress. This pause would begin on July 1, but only if similar action was taken by the other "important creditor powers." This meant that the Allied nations would have to agree to postpone further receipt of German reparations. By making the debt remission from the United States conditional on the Allies making reparation concessions, Hoover had made the very connection between war debts and reparations that US policy had assiduously avoided.

"The purpose of this action," Hoover's statement continued, "is to give the forthcoming year to the economic recovery of the world to help free the recuperative forces already in motion in the United States from retarding influence from abroad. The world-wide depression has affected the countries of Europe more severely than our own . . . the fabric of inter-governmental debts, supportable in normal times, weighs heavily in the midst of this depression."

Hoover recorded that he was subsequently in "hourly touch" with US officials in London, Paris, and Berlin by "transatlantic telephone," and that they were "in similar close touch with one another." It was the first time, he noted, "that such extensive use had been made of the telephone" by government officials. Hoover added, "the telephone afforded far better understanding" and allowed "much quicker contact than was possible with the slow coding and decoding of formally phrased cables."[25]

It turned out that Mellon was right about the French government. It was furious that it had not been consulted by the Hoover administration and therefore was not disposed to cooperate with it.

On June 22, Hoover asked Stimson to contact Mellon, who had left London to meet his son in Cambridge, where they were both receiving degrees from the university, the senior Mellon's being honorary. Hoover wanted Mellon to go to Paris to smooth tensions. Mellon was reluctant to further interrupt his vacation as Paul, Ailsa, and David were expecting to travel with him to the South of France. A. W. had rented a villa in Cap Ferrat, just east of Nice on the Côte d'Azur, for the months of July and August.[26]

In short order though, Teddy Rousseau received a call, and three days later, Mellon arrived in Paris. He was met by Rousseau on the platform of the Gare du Nord and a group of reporters and photographers. Suddenly, a Frenchman of medium height and a high forehead moved quickly through the crowd and approached the American Treasury secretary.

"Are you glad to be in Paris, Mr. Mellon?" he asked in English.

Mellon stopped and then, to everyone's surprise, smiled. "Monsieur Lacour-Gayet," he answered enthusiastically, "we are here!"

All who heard the remark laughed, according to the *New York Times* correspondent, as this was an unexpected bon mot from the usually diffident Treasury secretary. Mellon knew his history and was echoing the famous statement, "Lafayette, we are here!" made during the war by an American colonel in General John J. Pershing's command after the American Expeditionary Forces arrived in France.[27]

Lacour-Gayet had been in Washington as the financial attaché of the French embassy during the 1926 negotiation of the Mellon-Bérenger agreement and was now an official of the Banque de France. The Mellon-Bérenger agreement had been the last of the debt settlements to be ratified and was the only one signed by President Hoover.

Ironically, Mellon was now in France at Hoover's bequest, to stop payments on that agreement and all others made by his debt commission, knowing that it was likely that no further debt payments would ever be made on any of them.

Mellon soon realized that Stimson had not only mishandled the related diplomatic aspects of the moratorium, but that he had also grossly under-reported the level of French hostility toward it. The German ambassador to France articulated the French attitude best: "France sees what she regards as her absolutely sacred right to her unconditional reparations claim placed in question. In terms of opinion, moreover, France feels the American action to be an unheard-of presumption and an unprecedented encroachment on French rights." He wrote further, "Still greater is the bitterness over an ultimatum-like demand from America . . . that no consideration will be given to counter-proposals."[28]

Over eleven days of highly contentious negotiations between Paris and Washington, Hoover's seventy-six-year-old Treasury secretary prevailed.

Mellon initialed Hoover's Franco-American moratorium agreement on July 6, 1931.

In December, when Congress passed that moratorium, it did so only by including a clause prohibiting the cancellation of war debts. Little did the legislators realize that their own action gave rise to their predecessors' worst fears—the United States was now facing a united European front of debtors.

"The outlook for revision of the debts by consent of Congress," British ambassador Ronald Lindsay wrote home to the Foreign Office, "is about as bleak as it could be."[29]

∽

On February 9, 1932, while on another lecture tour to the United States promoting Anglo-American economic cooperation, Winston Churchill made surprising headlines. The *New York Times* reported that the former British chancellor OPPOSES VOIDING WAR DEBT.

"Great Britain and the United State are the greatest creditor nations," Churchill asserted in an address to the Economic Club at New York City's Hotel Astor. "We cannot afford to countenance repudiation, still less encourage a situation in which it will occur."

If Parker Gilbert wasn't in shock from the statement as he sat among more than 1,500 others in the audience, he soon had another opportunity to be astounded when Churchill "defended the United States against the European charge of 'blood sucker.'" Churchill pointed out that far from extracting from Europe any great amounts in payments, the United States "had actually poured billions of dollars into European countries since the war." Churchill had "characterized as illusory any hope of future collection of international debts . . . but at the same time rejected the idea of repudiation of debts by European nations."[30]

Gilbert undoubtedly appreciated the irony of the moment, not just because of his own experience with Churchill in executing US policy on war debts and reparations, but because he knew that Mellon, who had officially tendered his resignation as treasury secretary the previous day, would be equally, if not more stunned.

Mellon's achievements in settling Allied wartime indebtedness, paying down the national debt, and reducing taxes had all been obliterated by the depression. Worse, he had become a political target, as the Hoover moratorium did little to contain the world's economic crisis, which continued on its devastating course. In the United States, unemployment continued to spread; tens of thousands lost their homes to foreclosure, Congress stalled the Federal Triangle project, and the US government booked a deficit of almost $3 billion. As Mellon's biographer summed up the moment, "Second now only to Hoover in the nation's list of loathed leaders was Andrew Mellon."[31]

Hoover could hardly afford the political liability of his discredited treasury secretary, and in a mutually beneficial act of grace, offered Mellon a dignified exit, the post of ambassador to Great Britain.

When the announcement of Mellon's appointment was made, the Washington correspondent for the United Press wrote, "The selection of Mellon for the London post removes from the cabinet one of its most picturesque and mysterious figures and gives the court of St. James such an American ambassador as it probably never has seen before." He included a rare portrait of the everyday Mellon: "Washington will miss the familiar bent little figure, with sunken eyes and gray hair and moustache, walking briskly to and from the massive treasury building, disregarding traffic signals, jaywalking across busy streets in the middle of a block, smoking long slim cigars."

Mellon had told the correspondent: "the purpose of life is to be occupied and serve in the most useful capacity, provided it is an honest endeavor. The question is to find where one can give the most service. My main pleasure in work is being able to accomplish results . . . I have been very happy in my work as secretary of the treasury."[32]

When Churchill arrived in Washington as part of his lecture tour on February 11, the closest he and Mellon came to one another was in a society column. Their respective Treasury experiences had ended, not in greatness, but in disappointment and diminished stature. Neither reached out to commiserate or to shake hands. They remained as cool to one another as ever, despite the fact that they no longer commanded any standing in the international debate over war debts.

∽

From the moment Mellon presented his credentials as ambassador to King George V on April 9 and lunched with Their Majesties at Windsor Castle, his daily life became a heady whirl of top hats and toasts. Edward, the Prince of Wales, welcomed him at his first social dinner event, saying, "Your appointment is a great gesture on the part of the American people. It is a gesture that cannot fail to strengthen our mutual faith and to give us heart to tackle the problems that beset us."

Mellon returned the sentiment of Anglo-American friendship, saying, "In helping the world over its present difficulties, Great Britain and America are equipped to play together a role of inestimable value." All then raised glasses of champagne to the king of England and the president of the United States.[33]

The American ambassador's residence in London, at 14 Prince's Gate, was a five-story terrace house overlooking Hyde Park in Westminster. Jack Morgan had donated the property to the US government in 1920, during the Wilson administration. After a long period of renovation and refurnishing, Ambassador Alanson Houghton took up occupancy in 1927. On May 29, Houghton had hosted his first overnight guest, Charles Lindbergh, who was brought there after landing his plane at Croydon Aerodrome eight days after his epic nonstop flight from New York to Le Bourget, the airfield near Paris.[34]

When Mellon took up residence at Number 14, he was joined by Ailsa and David, who left their home in New York to join A. W. and help him with the many attendant social obligations. In readying for the events that the Mellons would host, Ailsa assisted with the refurnishing of the residence, which previously had mostly bare walls and bland decor. They decided to ship more than forty paintings from her father's art collection

The majestic portrait of the *Marchesa Balbi*, painted by Sir Anthony van Dyck, circa 1623, was one of more than forty paintings from Mellon's art collection that were shipped from Washington to hang in the American ambassador's residence at 14 Prince's Gate. *Courtesy of the National Gallery of Art, Washington, DC.*

across the Atlantic to display at the embassy. Ailsa had the library paneled in oak expressly for the Rembrandts and Van Dycks. One of the latter was Mellon's favorite, the stunning life-size portrait of *Marchesa Balbi*. Her likeness was placed such that it was the first canvas to greet guests from her stately perch on the stair landing.[35]

Mellon "took great pride in the grace with which his daughter presided over the embassy residence," remembered David Finley, his former Treasury assistant and personal secretary. Finley had accompanied Mellon to London to continue to write his speeches and work on Mellon's plan for a national gallery of art in Washington. The long-serving aide recorded that he and Mellon visited London's National Gallery frequently, not only to admire the paintings, but to study how they were displayed.[36]

Another associate of Mellon later wrote, "It was his Anglophilia which, outside his business, molded his life; and it was the National Gallery in Trafalgar Square which always retained for him the ideal museum and the model" for Washington. Mellon fashioned Prince's Gate as the first iteration of his grand plan for an American National Gallery of Art.[37]

The Mellons took up life in London with pleasure and enjoyed the many privileges of the diplomatic post. As it was customary for women aspiring to be accepted into British high society, Ailsa and Margaret Finley, the wife of Mellon's loyal assistant, were presented to the king and queen at Buckingham Palace at the first Court of the season.

During the following week, the Mellons hosted Amelia Earhart overnight at the embassy after she became the first woman to fly nonstop across the Atlantic. Ailsa took her on a shopping expedition for clothes in the West End the next day, as the acclaimed aviator had arrived in nothing but her flight suit.

On the Fourth of July, they threw open the doors of Prince's Gate to hundreds of guests for an Independence Day party, at which "the exquisite taste" of the new décor and the "the wonderful pictures" from his collection were noted.[38]

The issues of war debts and reparations, however, followed Mellon from Washington to Westminster.

Andrew Mellon congratulating Amelia Earhart, the first woman to make a nonstop, solo flight across the Atlantic, on May 22, 1932. *Credit: Associated Press.*

When he first arrived, a London correspondent suggested that "Europe regarded him as a special ambassador on war debts and reparations." Mellon replied, "I had not considered myself so," and asked, "Who invented that?" He went on to say, "I have no special instructions to deal with financial matters."[39]

War debts had long ceased being topical and the Hoover administration did not want Mellon to be involved in a continuing dialogue. Mellon was happy to comply, but he did not resist the opportunity on July 12 to see Winston Churchill debate in the House of Commons against the MacDonald government's strategy to cancel all German reparation obligations.

With German reparations paused and the Allies' debt payments to the United States coming due, on top of the most recent demonstration of American intransigence by Congress against cancellation, MacDonald had taken the lead in bringing together the European powers of Britain, France, Belgium, and Italy to attend a conference in Lausanne, Switzerland, for the purpose of resolving the issue once and for all. They reached an agreement on Germany's obligations, already cut to $10 billion by the Young Plan, to be canceled altogether. Proud of his success, the prime minister declared that this was not a new page in history, nor the end of a chapter, but a whole new book. What was not disclosed immediately was that the agreement included the condition that both of the creditor governments—Britain and the United States—needed to agree to cancel all war debts owed to them, otherwise the agreement would be void.[40]

Churchill learned of this condition by reading *The Times* on the morning of July 11. Its Paris correspondent wrote that "Lausanne is recognized to be only the first step in the much larger task of coming to an agreement with the United States." This irked Churchill, as did the "warm welcome" MacDonald received for his great victory in Lausanne. Churchill also learned that MacDonald had decided not to attend the House of Commons that day but instead planned to open debate on the Lausanne Conference the following day.[41]

Fired up, Churchill began the day's debate without him in the Commons that afternoon. He quickly brought up the Lausanne agreement, while acknowledging "there is to be debate tomorrow." He would not touch upon it today, he said, were it not for the fact that it required immediate clarification. "The public, as far as I can see," he judged, "is completely bewildered as to what has taken place."

"If the settlement at Lausanne is conditioned upon settlement of our debt to the United States," he continued, "we cannot say Europe is saved. We can only say Europe is saved subject to ratification." This brought laughter in the Commons. An emboldened Churchill added, "I want to know what is the purport of all this fanfare and trumpeting and proclaiming round the world that a new era has begun, that a new book has been opened."[42]

The next day's papers set up the debate to come. The *Daily Telegraph* commented that the mysteriousness of Lausanne was too great for Churchill to resist rolling out his "heavy artillery," and that he was "in better rhetorical form than he has been of late, and he soon had the House laughing heartily with him." It was a "mischievous speech," the paper said, and "has given Mr. MacDonald something to answer tomorrow."[43]

The *Manchester Guardian* noted that Churchill had "spoken with scornful relish." One provincial paper referred to his "impish delight in stirring up trouble" and another noted that for the MacDonald and Churchill match coming up later that day, "there has been a great demand for seats in the public galleries."[44]

Obtaining a seat was not a problem for the American ambassador.

৩

On the afternoon of July 12, when Prime Minister MacDonald arrived for the debate on the Lausanne agreement, the House of Commons was crowded and hot. Every seat on the floor was occupied, and some members had to sit in the side galleries. Several made fans of their papers, and it was noted that Lady Astor, the female MP, had removed her hat.[45]

MacDonald was greeted with prolonged cheers as he entered. He opened quickly with a light jab at his critic of the day before. "Perhaps I ought to begin by offering an apology," he said, looking at Churchill on the opposite bench, "to my right honourable friend, the Member for Epping, for not having been present when he started the debate yesterday. He had given me no notice of his intention or, I can assure him, I should have been in my place."[46]

Not only was the floor of the House full, but the upper galleries were also packed. According to the London correspondent of the *Liverpool Daily Post*, "Few failed to notice the presence of Mr. Mellon, the American ambassador, who, leaning forward and supporting his chin on his hands, and his hands on the rail at a point nearly over the clock, listened intently to the Prime Minister."[47]

Those like Mellon, who were expecting a spirited debate between Mac-Donald and Churchill, were disappointed however, as Churchill—having made his points the day before—was given the opportunity to ask but a few, brief questions. Most of their exchange consisted of a back-and-forth on the secrecy surrounding the disclosure of the condition that the Allies would cancel reparations only if the United States canceled war debts.

The prime minister finished the exchange, turning one last time to Churchill to say, "I hope especially that those who have voices which carry across the Atlantic will not use those voices to make it more difficult for America to understand the European situation." MacDonald then tried to correct the notion that the Allies had "designed to present something in the nature of an ultimatum to the United States."

This may have been addressed to Mellon in the gallery and, more broadly, to the American government. "I wish to make it absolutely clear that all Lausanne did was to straighten out the internal difficulties of Europe."[48]

The American ambassador made no comment afterward. Hoover and Congress would later make it clear that the United States would not agree to the cancellation of the Allies' indebtedness, thereby invalidating the Lausanne agreement, and leaving the Allies to face default if they did not make payments on their war debts to the United States.

No one noted whether there was any interaction between Mellon and Churchill that afternoon, but the former rivals knew that they would be seeing one another later that evening.

∽

The occasion was a dinner celebration of the bicentennial of George Washington's birth, held in the Grand Hall of the Victoria Hotel. Hosted by the Pilgrim's Society, whose charter was to promote goodwill between the United States and Great Britain, Mellon and Churchill found themselves together yet again at an event promoting Anglo-American friendship. Nearly a decade had passed since their first meeting at the Westminster Abbey ceremony celebrating the same theme.

Filling the hall were almost three hundred men suited in evening dress, many of the British wearing ceremonial ribands of honor and medals and socializing at their assigned tables. The banquet seating arrangement accommodated ten around each table. Press representatives sat together at one of their own in center of the room. In addition to the many British and American diplomatic personnel, there were several men from the arts familiar to both Churchill and Mellon. Sir Joseph Duveen was one. Another, Philip de László, the Hungarian portraitist, had painted Churchill's son, Randolph, and Mellon's daughter, Ailsa.

Seated next to one another at the head table, Mellon and Churchill raised glasses of Pol Roger champagne in toasting the king of England and the president of the United States. Other fine wines were served during the five-course dinner that began with turtle soup and ended with vanilla ice cream.

Over the years, their association had never been friendly, and it had undoubtedly been a vexing and disappointing experience for both men. Their inability to come to an understanding on war debts caused them to miss opportunities to join forces and work cooperatively. Had they been able to find common ground on the question of what governments owed to one another, the rise in resentment might not have escalated on their watches. The unanswered question not only compromised Anglo-American relations and their respective national economies, but also their personal ambitions during their tenure as treasury chiefs.

After-dinner speeches were broadcast by radio in Britain and to the United States. Mellon had not been asked to make one. Ironically,

Winston Churchill and Andrew Mellon at the Pilgrim Society dinner in London to celebrate the bicentennial of George Washington's birth on July 12, 1932. *Credit: Associated Press.*

the two featured speakers were men who had waged fierce campaigns against his efforts to collect war debts—Winston Churchill and Nicholas Murray Butler, president of Columbia University.

Churchill began by saluting George Washington and the long relationship between Britain and America. He also touched on past troubles that had been overcome by a unity of shared values. In speaking of the present day, Churchill acknowledged that "the economic crisis in which the world is gripped still holds its full intensity." Many in the hall had likely experienced it in some way.

But Churchill, whenever in front of an audience, always found a way to inspire and entertain. "Of course," he said, "in this workday world there must be disputes and differences, there must be competing commercial interests, there must be some tiresome arguments over money matters . . ."

He paused, long enough for his words to sink in and for the hall to erupt in laughter. Mellon may have enjoyed the moment too.

The great orator continued, "But be assured that none of those quarrels will disturb the onward march of Anglo-American friendship."[49]

A photograph of the two former Treasury titans endures from that evening on what would be their last meeting. They stand side by side, not as friends, but in an obligatory pose as formal as the white ties and waistcoats they were wearing.

The looks on their faces tell the story; debt had taken its toll.

EPILOGUE

B y the time Andrew Mellon resigned as ambassador to Great Britain in March 1933, as was the custom upon the inauguration of a new president, Alexander Hamilton's founding principles of American government finance—balanced budgets and disciplined debt reduction—had been supplanted by habitual deficit financing.[1]

Herbert Hoover, who instituted a moratorium on the collection of war debts during the Great Depression, had lost his bid for a second term in the 1932 election. The new administration of President Franklin Roosevelt launched its own effort to collect the outstanding war debts owed to the United States upon taking office.

Later in 1933, Germany canceled reparations payments, renounced the Treaty of Versailles, and withdrew from the League of Nations, to pursue the rearmament of its military. Winston Churchill was among those who perceived the actions as a threat. With German indemnities repudiated, the Allies' resentment toward the United States intensified over its refusal to discharge war debt obligations.

In 1934, US congressional opposition to the cancellation or revision of war debts hardened further. Legislation was enacted that required wartime debtors to make installment payments in full or be considered in default. The law also prohibited nations in default from accessing capital in the United States.

Great Britain, France, Belgium, and Italy defaulted over the next few months.[2]

That same year, the Roosevelt administration charged Andrew Mellon with tax evasion. The prosecution claimed that Mellon had not, in fact, donated his art collection to the government, nor did he have any intent to do so—which made the charitable deductions that he took on his tax returns fraudulent. At trial, the jury found otherwise and exonerated him.[3]

With congressional approval, President Roosevelt accepted Mellon's gift to the nation in December of 1936. It included his art collection, a museum building under construction on the National Mall that he had commissioned, and a sustaining endowment. Mellon died eight months later. The National Gallery of Art opened in Washington, DC, in 1941.

With the Allies fighting German aggression once again, Congress enacted the Lend-Lease Act that same year to supply food, oil, and munitions as aid, rather than financing another war on credit. The Roosevelt administration developed the policy following discussions with Prime Minister Winston Churchill and his cabinet. Roosevelt persuaded Congress to pass the legislation, arguing that it was vital to national security. Inspired by the indominable spirit of Churchill, the United States and the Allies went on to defeat Germany.

On a visit to Washington, DC, in 1943, Clementine Churchill visited the National Gallery of Art; her husband did not.

Winston Churchill was the first person to be made an honorary citizen of the United States. In conferring the award in 1963, President John F. Kennedy said of him: "He mobilized the English language and sent it into battle. The incandescent quality of his words illuminated the courage of his countrymen."[4]

Ailsa Mellon Bruce made a mark in her own right as a benefactor of medical research, art education, and academic scholarship. She and her brother Paul funded the East Building expansion of the National Gallery of Art on a site that had been set aside by their father for such a purpose.

In 1985, the United States became a debtor nation for the first time since the Wilson administration. The reversion was due in large part to a dependence on foreign countries to finance American budget deficits through the purchase of US Treasury securities.[5]

Germany joined France, Belgium, Italy, Britain, and twenty-two other countries to establish the European Union in 1993 for the purpose of promoting peace, political cooperation, and economic integration, based on a long-held desire to make war as unthinkable as impossible.[6]

A bronze bust of Winston Churchill was dedicated in the US Capitol during a 2013 ceremony in Statuary Hall. It stands in the House Rotunda on the building's first floor.[7]

Hamilton, the 2015 musical adaptation of the life story of the first US secretary of the Treasury, broke box office records and won a Pulitzer Prize for Drama. Its phenomenal success, however, did not inspire a return to his financial principles. Regulators, agencies, and monitors repeatedly warn about the risk that the "loose" fiscal policy of the United States poses for the global economy—specifically overspending and a ballooning national debt, some $35 trillion as of July 2024.[8]

"We want our leaders to save the day," sang the company in *Hamilton*, "but we don't get a say in what they trade away."[9]

ACKNOWLEDGMENTS

The telling of this story was made possible by Gary Griffith, the best journalist I know. After disconfirming my research findings over three consecutive evenings, he encouraged me to press on. As the years passed in putting the story together, he cheered every discovery, worked with me side by side, and responded to all dead ends and disappointments by telling me to dig deeper.

One of the earliest deep digs led to the Churchill Archives Centre at Churchill College in Cambridge. I am grateful to Dr. Allen Packwood, the director, and his staff, for their unfailing support in responding to my many requests, especially to the first one confirming that the Mellon-Churchill relationship had been largely overlooked by historians. He generously mentioned my research to Lee Pollock, the executive director of the International Churchill Society, who offered not only his enthusiastic encouragement, but a grant from the society to put the story down on paper. I then became a beneficiary of Lee's ability to move mountains and received an appointment to George Washington University as a visiting scholar, complete with interlibrary loan privileges, which are so vital to independent scholars.

My appreciation for the help I received during the early research goes to the many archivists and librarians who refused to let the COVID-19 pandemic thwart access to their collections. Margaret Dakin at Amherst

College and Shirlene Newman at the District of Columbia Public Library made it possible for me to study Dwight Morrow's papers through an inventive interlibrary loan collaboration between their institutions. Shireen Zainab found her way into Columbia University's Rare Book and Manuscript Library to dig through the Nicholas Murray Butler Papers to get the seating chart and menu for the George Washington Bicentennial Dinner. Archivists at the Library of Congress, especially Amber Paranick; Tab Lewis at the National Archives; Craig Wright at the Hoover Presidential Library; and the Manuscript and Archives staff at Yale University Library, all found ways to continue to provide assistance even when their institutions were closed. I owe a special thank you to Andrew Young and Kim Carter, the exceptional librarians at the US Department of the Treasury, who replied to each "just-one-more question" with their inspiring expertise and unflagging cheerfulness.

In Britain, I am grateful to the resourceful staffs at several libraries and archives, particularly the National Archives at Kew, the British Library, the Bank of England, and Parliamentary Archives. Many thanks to John Wells, senior archivist, at Cambridge University Library, who provided a key insight on an official British government log kept in the Baldwin Papers. Whenever it seemed impossible to find a critical document, Simon Fowler came to the rescue with his considerable expertise in locating papers in both public and private collections. I greatly appreciated a grant from the Jennie Churchill Fund for a subscription to the Churchill Online Archives. I am also grateful to Gordon Wise and Lily Kovacs at Curtis Brown, which represents the Churchill Estate, for permission to include Churchill's 1921 painting *Cairo from the Pyramids with the Artist Painting*.

The idea that the paper I wrote for the International Churchill Society should be turned into a book was first suggested by the late Bruce Cole, the renown renaissance scholar and chairman of the National Endowment of the Humanities. It was seconded by two of his friends who are stars in the literary world—Michael Shelden, who advised that papers are good, but books are best, and Amity Shlaes, who encouraged me to go forward and contribute to the historical record. George Hall, professor of economics at Brandeis University, not only gave me a master class on the history of the US national debt and put Mellon's management of it into context, but he also encouraged me to read Kenneth Garbade's definitive work on the US Treasury during the period. Sir David Cannadine, author, historian, and professor provided key insights on both Andrew Mellon and Winston Churchill that shaped my thinking. Eric Hilt, professor of economics at Wellesley College, took time to provide counsel and encouragement when he had none to spare, but he did so anyway.

How lucky can a researcher get?

It turns out, even luckier. Cita Stelzer, another literary luminary, happened to zoom into a discussion of my research organized and hosted by the dynamic Jason Reash, the current executive director of the International Churchill Society. Cita urged her publisher, Claiborne Hancock, the founder of Pegasus Books, to take a look at a book proposal I had just completed using the outstanding online resources offered by Jane Friedman. I am particularly grateful to Cita for her wise counsel and steadfast encouragement, but even more, for her friendship which grew out of our many chats.

This book has many friends. Dearest of all, Alexandra Huebner and Catherine Thompson, whose faith in me has long made all the difference, and David and Mary Ann Marshall, who believed in this story from the beginning. Diane Colasanto thoughtfully introduced me to her friend, the bestselling author Lynne Olson, who provided expert advice. Cartographer Morgan Kraft made the custom maps and Ava Coibion lent her skillful eye to several early drafts. Brittany Rassbeharry at PARS International, the agent for content from the *New York Times*, went the extra mile to make it possible to include the stunning *NYT* full-page graphic. At Pegasus, support from Claiborne Hancock, Jessica Case, and Maria Fernandez never waned, despite my many rookie mistakes. Molly Slattery inspired me to read one of her favorite books at a key moment. I am forever grateful to Nicholas Gleysteen, Janet Diederichs, Rick Pivirotto, Deborah Ann Cernauskas, Leigh Hough, Molly Kihara, Barbara Sideman, Vickie Dorgan, John Bierbusse, Marsha Barnes, and Ted Peck for their warm hands of friendship, which I treasure. I am truly fortunate to have the love and support of my sister-in-law, Barbara Walker, who has also cheered this project on from day one.

My appreciation begins and ends with Gary, my partner, husband, and North Star, who agreed to invite Mellon and Churchill into our home for a stay that ended up lasting several years.

A NOTE ON SOURCES

Much of the research for this book is based on newspaper reports of the period. A 1926 article in the *New York Times*, datelined London, was the original inspiration for the story of *Mellon vs. Churchill*. It reported: "Winston Churchill, Chancellor of the Exchequer, entertained Mr. Mellon at dinner tonight at the Ritz."

That news item sparked countless questions, many of which could only be answered by piecing together other reports and articles published in newspapers far and wide. They became a critical source for this book to document events, reference speeches, and capture images. Most of the articles were recorded by journalists who were eyewitnesses to the events, often following them as foreign correspondents with the ability to personally interview the principals in the stories they were writing.

Many of the articles used here were syndicated reports, printed in hundreds of subscribing newspapers, in which local editors would write the headlines for them. In selecting the articles to be referenced in the notes, headlines that added meaning or summarized the reports most accurately, have been chosen when possible. These articles were found and accessed primarily through the following newspaper databases:

The British Newspaper Archive
Chronicling America (Library of Congress)
The Economist Archives
Gallica (Bibliotèque Nationale de France)
Newspapers.com
TimesMachine (*New York Times*)

ProQuest (through the Washington, DC Public Library)
The Times Archive (*The Times* of London)

The following archival collections were also consulted:

Baldwin Papers, University Library, Cambridge
Basil P. Blackett Papers, British Library, London
Calvin Coolidge Papers, Calvin Coolidge Presidential Foundation,
Plymouth, Vermont
Duveen Brothers Records, Getty Archives, Los Angeles, California
David E. Finley Papers, Library of Congress, Washington, DC
Charles S. Hamlin Papers, Library of Congress, Washington, DC
Burton J. Hendrick Papers, Yale University, New Haven, Connecticut
Herbert Hoover Papers, Herbert Hoover Presidential Library, West
Branch, Iowa
Edward M. House, Yale University, New Haven, Connecticut
Philander C. Knox Papers, Library of Congress, Washington, DC
Russell C. Leffingwell Papers, Yale University, New Haven,
Connecticut
Dwight D. Morrow Papers, Amherst College Library, Amherst,
Massachusetts
Papers of Montagu Norman, Bank of England Archives, London
Papers of Benjamin Strong, Jr., Federal Reserve Archives, St. Louis,
Missouri

Newspapers and archival information provided historical accounts, anecdotes,
and insights that helped to tell the story, building on the foundation laid by the
books and articles listed in the bibliography.

NOTES AND REFERENCES

The references below are intended to be used in conjunction with the archival sources previously cited and with those in the bibliography.

Unless otherwise stated, Churchill's speeches are to be found in the eight-volume *Winston S. Churchill: His Complete Speeches, 1897–1963* (New York: Chelsea House, 1974), edited by Robert Rhodes James. Cited as *Complete Speeches*.

CAB   Cabinet Papers, British National Archives, Kew

CHAR   Chartwell Papers, Churchill Archives Centre at Churchill College, Cambridge

CV   *Companion Volumes* to the official biography of Winston S. Churchill by Martin Gilbert

DCC   Combined Annual Report of the World War Foreign Debt Commission, Washington, DC

DCM   Minutes of the World War Foreign Debt Commission, Washington, DC

DOCS   *The Churchill Documents*

FO   Foreign Office Papers, National Archives, Public Records Office, Kew

FRUS   Papers Relating to the Foreign Relations of the United States, Washington, DC

Hansard   House of Commons Parliamentary Debates

NARA   US National Archives, Washington, DC

OB   The official biography of Winston S. Churchill by Martin Gilbert

PA   Parliamentary Archives, House of Lords, London

Senate   *Refunding of Obligations of Foreign Governments*, Washington, DC

TAR   Annual Report of the Secretary of the Treasury, Washington, DC

TV   Treaty of Versailles, Washington, D.C.

Introduction

1   See Self, *Debt Controversy*, 15–33; Adam Tooze, *The Deluge: The Great War, America and the Remaking of the Global Order, 1916–1931* (New York: Viking, 2014), 78; Kathleen Burk, *Britain, America and the Sinews of War* (Boston: George Allen and Unwin, 1985), 79, 92, 93; and Hew Strachan, *The First World War: To Arms* (New York: Oxford University Press, 2001), 967–77.

2   John Keegan, *The First World War* (New York: Alfred A. Knopf, 1999), 353; John H. Morrow Jr., *The Great War: An Imperial History* (London: Routledge, 2004), 203. See also Admiral Reinhard Scheer, *Germany's High Sea Fleet in the World War* (London: Cassells and Company, 1920), 224–25; and Trevor Wilson, *The Myriad Faces of War: Britain and the Great War, 1914–1918* (Cambridge: Polity Press, 1986), 427–29.

3   A. Scott Berg, *Wilson* (New York: G. P. Putnam's Sons, 2013), 436; Arthur S. Link, *Woodrow Wilson and the Progressive Era, 1910–1917* (New York: Harper and Brothers, 1954), 242–43; Woodrow Wilson, HR1, 65th Cong., 1st sess., *Congressional Record*, 118–20 (April 2, 1917). See also John Chambers, *To Raise an Army: The Draft Comes to Modern America* (New York: Free Press, 1987), 186; and Morrow, *The Great War*, 68, 129.

4   Arthur S. Link, ed., *The Papers of Woodrow Wilson* (Princeton, NJ: Princeton University Press, 1992), 37:384; Arthur S. Link, ed., *The Papers of Woodrow Wilson* (Princeton, NJ: Princeton University Press, 1992), 38:613–14.

5   See Cannadine, *Mellon*, 56, 252–58. The official biography of Andrew Mellon. See also W. L. Mellon, *Judge*, 294–95, 327–29, 358–59, 375–78; J. R. Mellon, *Founder of a Fortune*, 387; and Murray, *Mellon*, 20–22. A Hamilton portrait would not only hang in Mellon's office at the Treasury but another in his Dupont Circle bedroom.

6   Violet Bonham Carter, *Winston Churchill: An Intimate Portrait* (New York: Harcourt, Brace & World, 1965), 333. See also Gilbert, *Churchill: A Life*, 361–73; Roberts, *Churchill*, 244–53; Shelden, *Young Titan*, 1–12, 306–24; and Soames, *Letters*, 6.

7   See Kathleen Burk, "The Diplomacy of Finance: British Missions to the United States 1914–1918," *Historical Journal*, June 1979, 351–72; Strachan, *First World War*, 989–92: Balfour, *Autobiography*, 237–38; and Lloyd George, *Memoirs*, 3:1677–78.

8   Quoted in Charles Seymour, *The Intimate Papers of Colonel House* (Boston: Houghton Mifflin Company, 1928), 3:38, 50.

9   "Emergency Bond Issue," HR3, 65th Cong., 1st sess., *Congressional Serial Set*, 7252 (April 11, 1917).

10   "$400,000,000 Loan Monthly to Allies," *New York Sun*, April 27, 1917, 5.

11   "200,000,000 Loan to Great Britain," *Commercial and Financial Chronicle*, April 28, 1917, 1651; "Long War Ahead Financiers Say," *Washington Herald*, April 26, 1917, 1. See also "Treasury Certificates of Indebtedness Oversubscribed," *Commercial and Financial Chronicle*, April 28, 1917, 1651; and "200,000,000 Loan on British Note," *New York Times*, April 26, 1917, 1.

12   "No Entanglements for U.S.—Balfour," *Washington Times*, April 25, 1917, 3.

13   "No Entanglements."

14   W. L. Mellon, *Judge*, 449.

15   "City and Financial World," *Gloucester Citizen* (England), April 28, 1917, 4, 5.

16   See Woodrow Wilson to Edward House, July 21, 1917, Edward M. House Papers, MS 466, Yale University, New Haven, Connecticut.

17   Kennedy, *Over Here*, 106.

18   "Liberty Loan A Patriotic War Weapon," *Burlington Free Press & Times* (VT), June 7, 1917, 8; "'To Avoid Bombs, Buy Bonds' Message To Be Dropped from Planes," *South Bend News-Times* (IN), June 2, 1917, 1. See also William G. McAdoo, *Crowded Years* (Boston: Houghton Mifflin Company, 1932), 378–410; Labert St. Clair, *The Story of the Liberty Bonds* (Washington, DC: James William Bryan Press, 1919); and Eric Hilt and Wendy M. Rahn, "Financial Asset Ownership and Political Partisanship: Liberty Bonds and Republican Electoral Success in the 1920s," Working Paper 24719, *National Bureau of Economic Research*, June 2018.

19   See Cannadine, *Mellon*, 253; and Kennedy, *Over Here*, 102.

20   See Tooze, *Deluge*, 204–08.

21   February 19, 1919, CAB 23/9.

22   The symbol, M, refers to German gold marks, the German currency cited in the Treaty of Versailles. In 1923, a new currency not backed by gold was introduced, the Rentenmark (RM), followed in 1924 by the Reichsmark (RM) in 1924; Treaty of Versailles, Articles 231, 235, 2:138–39.

23   Kennedy, *Over Here*, 125.

24   Philander C. Knox, *Constitution of League of Nations: Speech of Hon. Philander Knox, March 1, 1919* (Washington, DC, Government Printing Office, 1919), 33.

25   Mellon's support of the League opposition was not widely known until the publication of George Harvey, *Henry Clay Frick: The Man* (Washington, DC: Beard Books, 1928), 324–30. See also Clinton W. Gilbert, "The Paradox of Andrew Mellon," *Current History*, July 1931,

295–97; Cannadine, *Mellon*, 267; Stone, *The Irreconcilables*, 81, 95, 145; and Allan Nevins, "Andrew Mellon," in *Dictionary of American Biography* (New York: Charles Scribner's Sons, 1958), 22, sup 2: 446–52; and Harvey, *Frick*, 327.

26   *Knox, Speech, March 1, 1919*, 33; Philander C. Knox, *Treaty of Versailles: Speech of Hon. Philander Knox, August 29, 1919* (Washington, DC: Government Printing Office, 1919), 34.

27   See Harvey, *Frick*, 324–30; Gilbert, *Paradox*, 295–97; Cannadine, *Mellon*, 267, Stone, *Irreconcilables*, 81, 95, 145; and Nevins, *Andrew Mellon*, 446–52.

28   See Arthur S. Link, *Woodrow Wilson: A Brief Biography* (Cleveland: World Publishing Company, 1963),163, 166–68; and John Cooper Milton, Jr., *Breaking the Heart of the World: Woodrow Wilson and the Fight for the League of Nations* (Cambridge: Cambridge University Press, 2001), 266–69, 330.

29   "Treaty's Fate Rests With President," *Baltimore Sun*, November 21, 1919, 1; Albert W. Fox, "All Attempts at Compromise Meet with Failure," *Washington Post*, November 20, 1919, 1.

30   "Glad Tidings!" *New York Evening World*, November 20, 1919, 30; "Three International Lawyers Discuss Treaty Defeat," *Washington Times*, November 20, 1919, 2.

31   Edwin L. James, "Paris Resentful Over Senate Action," *New York Times*, November 23, 1919, 1, 2; "Anxious Moments," *Western Times* (Exeter, England), November 21, 1919, 6.

32   Winston Churchill, "Will America Fail Us?" *Illustrated Sunday Herald* (London), November 30, 1919. The Churchill Archives has a typescript copy. See also Kay Halle, ed., *Winston Churchill on America and Britain* (New York: Walker and Company, 1970), 203–10.

33   Robert L. Merritt, "Woodrow Wilson and the 'Great Solemn Referendum,' 1920," *Review of Politics*, 27, no. 1 (January 1965): 78.

34   Quoted in Kennedy, *Over Here*, 248. See also R. K. Murray, *Harding Era*, 81–85.

35   "Harding Makes Sharp Attack on Democrats," *Baltimore Sun*, October 26, 1920, 1; R. K. Murray, *Harding Era, 66*. See also Wesley M. Bagby, *The Road to Normalcy: The Presidential Campaign and Election of 1920* (Baltimore: Johns Hopkins Press, 1962), 159; Kennedy, *Over Here*, 100–106.

1: Mr. Mellon Goes to Washington

1   "Washington News by Henning," *New York Daily News*, November 10, 1920, 22. See also, "Lowden Harding Choice for Treasury Secretary,"

Minneapolis Morning Tribune, November 11, 1920, 4; and "Weeks Mentioned for Treasury Head," *Wall Street Journal*, November 30, 1920, 3.

2   "Harding Ship Off Coast of Mexico," *Evening Star* (Washington, DC), November 21, 1920, 3.

3   See "Knox Arrives for Inspection of Hospitals," *Pittsburgh Gazette Times*, November 30, 1920, 1; and "Knox Not in Ill Health," *New York Times*, December 3, 1920, 2.

4   See Franklin Toker, *Pittsburgh: An Urban Portrait* (Pittsburgh: University of Pittsburgh Press, 1986), 265; and Walter C. Kidney, *Landmark Architecture: Pittsburgh and Allegheny County* (Pittsburgh: Pittsburgh History and Landmarks Foundation, 1985), 276; and Bureau of the Census, *Fourteenth Census of the United States*, January 25, 1920, Pittsburgh, PA, Ward 14, Sheets 12B, 13A. See also Cannadine, *Mellon*, 259–61.

5   See Cannadine, *Mellon*, 268.

6   Mellon memorandum to R. B. Harris, June 6, 1934, Ray Baker Harris Collection, Ohio Historical Society.

7   See Lawrence L. Murray, "Andrew Mellon: The Reluctant Candidate," *Pennsylvania Magazine of History and Biography*, October 1973, 97: 522; L. L. Murray, *Mellon*, 30–36; Cannadine, *Mellon*, 253, 268; Kennedy, *Over Here*, 102; and Hays, *Memoirs*, 270.

8   *Speeches of Warren G. Harding of Ohio* (New York: Republican National Committee, 1920), 95; Albert W. Fox, "Ovation for Harding as Congress Convenes," *Washington Post*, December 7, 1920, 1, 2.

9   Hays, *Memoirs*, 270.

10   See "Will Represent Senate," *Evening Star* (Washington, DC), December 9, 1920, 1; "Will Hays Appoints Inauguration Head," *Kenosha News* (WI), December 16, 1920, 1; and Evalyn McLean with Boyden Sparkes, *Father Struck It Rich* (Boston: Little, Brown & Co., 1936), 250.

11   See Lucius Beebe, *Mansion on Rails: The Folklore of the Private Railway Car* (Berkeley, CA: Howell-North, 1959).

12   Quoted in Cannadine, *Mellon*, 270; P. Mellon, *Reflections*, 103.

13   Hays, *Memoirs*, 270.

14   Harry N. Price, "League Has No Part in Harding's Policy, Senator Knox Thinks," *Washington Post*, December 31, 1920, 1; Robert Ginter, "A. W. Mellon, Local Banker, Considered for Cabinet," *Pittsburgh Gazette*, December 31, 1920, 1, 3.

15   Per Mellon's January 1, 1920 diary entry, cited in Cannadine, *Mellon*, 268; W. L. Mellon, *Judge*, 396.

16   "Penrose Declares Mellon Excellently Fitted for Post of Treasury
      Secretary," *Pittsburgh Post*, January 1, 1921, 1.

17   W. L. Mellon, *Judge*, 396; Per an undated letter from Ailsa Mellon to her
      father, Andrew Mellon, believed to have been written in late 1920 or early
      1921, cited in Cannadine, *Mellon*, 268. See also W. L. Mellon, *Judge*, 398.

18   "Banker Gives Dates in Divorce Case," *Washington Herald*, February 17,
      1912, 1.

19   P. Mellon, *Reflections*, 96–7.

20   Quoted in Cannadine, *Mellon*, 271.

21   "Mellon Surveys Work at Treasury," *Washington Post*, March 1, 1921,
      1; and "Mellon Pays A Visit to Treasury," *New York Times*, March 1,
      1921, 15.

22   Eye Witness (pseudonym), "Andrew W. Mellon," *New York Daily
      News*, March 24, 1921, 29; "Cabinet Members Like School Boys
      After First White House Meeting," *Baltimore Sun*, March 9, 1921, 2;
      and Remarks made by David Houston recorded by Charles Hamlin,
      March 4, 1921, *Papers of Charles S. Hamlin*, Library of Congress,
      Washington, DC.

23   Edward G. Lowry, *Washington Close-Ups: Intimate Views of Some Public
      Figures* (Boston: Houghton Mifflin Company, 1921), 155.

24   William Atherton Du Puy, "Andrew Mellon, Keeper of Nation's
      Pocketbook," *Sunday Globe Magazine* (Boston), May 22, 1921, 14.

25   L. L. Murray, *Reluctant*, 526.

26   See Edwin L. James, "Viviani is Coming to Plead With Us," *New York
      Times*, March 6, 1921, 1.

27   See R. K. Murray, *Harding*, 124.

28   W. L. Mellon, *Judge*, 450.

29   "Cabinet Decides Allied Loans Are Not To Be Waived," *New York
      Herald*, April 2, 1921, 1, 2; "Denby Studies Navy," *Washington Herald*,
      March 27, 1921, 38.

30   "Harding Arranges Press Conference," *New York Times*, March 23,
      1921, 17; and J. F. Essary, *Covering Washington Government:
      Government Reflected in the Public Press*, 1822–1926 (Boston: Houghton
      Mifflin Company, 1927), 89–90.

31   See "U.S. To Stand with Allies on German Reparation Demands,"
      Commercial and Financial Chronicle, April 9, 1921, 1468–69; "Harding
      Insists Germany Must Pay Debt in Full," *San Francisco Examiner*,
      April 2, 1921, 1; and Arthur Sears Henning, "Dashes German
      Hopes," *Los Angeles Times*, April 2, 1921, 2, 3.

32   J. F. Essary, "U.S. Will Keep Firm Attitude to Germany," *Baltimore
      Sun*, April 2, 1921, 1; and "Cabinet Upholds Demand of Allies

That Germany Pay," *New York Times*, April 2, 1921, 1; and "Cabinet Decides Allied Loans Are Not To Be Waived," *New York Herald*, April 2, 1921, 1, 2.

33 TAR, 1921, 40.

34 Senate, *Refunding*, June 29, 1921, 4–5.

35 "Mellon Bill Faces Fight in Congress," *Los Angeles Times*, June 25, 1921, 1.

36 "Democrats Attack Refunding Plan," *New York Times*, June 25, 1921, 15.

37 "Revolt Brewing in Congress over War Debt Bill." *Houston Post*, June 25, 1921, 1.

38 "U.S. and the Allies' Debt," *Western Daily Press* (Bristol, England), February 8, 1921, 8.

39 Senate, *Refunding*, July 14, 1921, 50–52; See "Britain A Year Ago Proposed That We Cancel All Debts," *New York Times*, July 15, 1921, 1.

40 "Wilson Told Britain Debts Must Be Paid," *New York Times*, July 19, 1921, 13.

41 Wilson's rejection of Lloyd George's proposed cancellation was carried by the Associated Press to hundreds of US papers. Reuters distributed its version to British papers, and Agence Havas to the French. See, for example: "Mr. Wilson's Refusal to Lloyd George," *Daily Herald* (London), July 19, 1921, 1; "Wilson Note Refusing to Cancel England's Debt Is Made Public" *Great Falls Tribune* (MT), July 19, 1921, 1; and "Les Etats-Unis et les dettes interalliées," *Le Matin* (Paris), July 19, 1921, 3; See Woodrow Wilson to David Lloyd George, November 3, 1920, in Arthur S. Link, ed., *The Papers of Woodrow Wilson* (Princeton, NJ: Princeton University Press, 1992), 66:307; and Moulton and Pasvolsky, *War Debts*, 65–70.

42 TAR, 1920, 59.

43 Senate, *Refunding*, July 20, 1921, 99.

44 R. K. Murray, *Harding*, 129.

45 Senate, *Refunding*, July 28, 1921, 182.

46 "Mellon Gets Free Hand in Funding Allied Debt," *Baltimore Sun*, July 29, 1921, 2.

2: Churchill in the Highlands

1 The *Esperia* was part of the Italian steamship Sitmar Line, (Societa Italiana di Servizi Marittimi). It reached Naples from Alexandria on April 3. See "Mr. Churchill at Naples," *Leicester Mercury* (England), April 4, 1921, 4.

2 Gilbert, OB, 4: 527–33.

3 Quoted in Janet Wallach, *Desert Queen: The Extraordinary Life of Gertrude Bell* (New York: Doubleday, 1996), 300; Thompson,

Assignment Churchill, 18. It may also be possible that Lawrence wanted the hundred-plus Arab observers facing the group to know that Churchill was the kind of man who would not submit to a moment of personal humiliation, but instead would find a way to remount and charge off triumphantly. Lawrence knew camels better than any other British subject of his time. He had personally selected Churchill's camel that day and may have had a hand in "adjusting" the wooden saddle such that Churchill would fall while the camel was low to the ground, posing little risk of serious injury to his friend. According to Thompson, Lawrence joked at the time: "It was only to be expected you know, Winston. The old camel blew himself out when he heard that he was to have the honor of carrying such a great man, but when he saw the way that you ride, he decided that he must have been misinformed. He deflated himself and the saddle girth slipped round, throwing you." While the others flanking Churchill hid their laughter, the real audience for the premature dismount may have been the observers who questioned Lawrence's alliance with the new colonial secretary, a renowned guardian of the British Empire; *Palestine Weekly*, cited in Gilbert, OB, 4:556; Wallach, *Desert*, 300.

4   Churchill, *Painting*, 32; see also "Winston Falls from A Camel," *Port-Glasgow Express* (Scotland), March 23, 1921, 2.

5   Thompson, *Assignment Churchill*, 20; Stafford, *Oblivion or Glory*, 116; In a 1935 note to his book, *Seven Pillars of Wisdom*, Lawrence wrote that Churchill "made straight all the tangle" of British-Arabian relations in 1921. "So we were quit of war-time Eastern adventure, with clean hands, but three years too late." See T. E. Lawrence, *Seven Pillars of Wisdom* (London: Jonathan Cape, 1935), 283n.

6   "Out of the Limelight," *Daily Record* (Glasgow), March 21 , 1921, 8; "'Winston's' Newest Job," *Daily Mirror* (London), March 20, 1921, 6.

7   "U.S. Warning to Germany: Reparations Must Be Paid, Allied Debts an Asset," *The Times* (London), April 4, 1921, 10.

8   Gilbert, OB, 4:581.

9   "International Affairs," June 8, 1921, *Complete Speeches*, 3:3092-94

10   Lord Curzon to Winston Churchill, June 13, 1921, CV, IV, part 3: 1503.

11   Winston S. Churchill, "Cabinet Memorandum," July 23, 1921, in CV, IV, part 3: 1563. The United States had limited experience in participating in international conferences, let alone hosting one. While primarily a European practice, they served as a means for nations to reach binding agreements on portentous issues. The most recent such conference had taken place in early May when the Allied Supreme

Council met at 10 Downing Street to quantify the amount of German reparations. By the close of the conference, the Council, made up of representatives from Great Britain, France, Italy, Belgium, and Japan, forced Germany to agree to the settled-upon sum by threatening military action and occupation of the defeated power's vital industrial Ruhr region.

12   "U.S. Expects Jap 'Yes' on Parley Today," *Washington Herald*, July 26, 1921, 1.

13   "Disarm or Pay Up, Borah Tells Europe," *New York Times*, July 26, 1921, 2.

14   "Disarm or Pay Up;" "Debt as a Club: Senator Borah's Way to Disarmament," *Pall Mall Gazette* (London), July 26, 1921, 4; "Navies of Great Powers Compared: The Race for Superiority," *Sheffield Daily Telegraph*, January 10, 1921, 5; and "America's Big Programme," *Nottingham Evening Post*, January 10, 1921, 1.

15   "Navy Estimates," August 3, 1921, *Complete Speeches*, 3:3125–3127.

16   "Millions to Spend on Warships," *Daily News* (London), August 4, 1921, 3; "Economy Farce: Outlay on Four Capital Ships to Proceed," *Westminster Gazette* (London), August 4, 1921, 2; George Harvey to Charles Evan Hughes, (telegram) August 4, 1921, in FRUS, 1921: 1, 51; "Curieuse preface à la conference du désarmement," *Le Matin* (Paris), August 4, 1921, 1.

17   "No Financial Conference," *Manchester Evening News*, August 16, 1921, 2.

18   Stafford, *Oblivion or Glory*, 205.

19   Sir George Ritchie to Winston Churchill, June 17, 1921, July 2, 1921, and August 5, 1921, CHAR 5/24.

20   Soames, *Letters*, 241.

21   Bendor's nickname came from one of his grandfather's racehorses, which was named Bend Or, derived from the Grosvenor family's ancient heraldic shield, which had a diagonal stripe of gold (*or* in French) on an azure field. The thoroughbred won the 1880 Derby Stakes at Epsom, when the grandson was fifteen months old. The handsome child's auburn hair was said to be the same shade as the famous stallion, and, as one of his biographers states, "the name stuck, and for the rest of his life he was known as this, even to strangers." See Leslie Field, *Bendor: The Golden Duke of Westminster* (London: Weidenfeld & Nicolson, 1983), 14–15.

22   Field, *Bendor*, 154.

23   Richard M. Langworth, "Churchill's Character: Sense of Duty," *Churchill Project Newsletter*, June 27, 2016; Soames, *Letters*, xvii.

24   "Duke's Private Train," *Belfast Telegraph*, September 13, 1921, 7.

25   Soames, *Letters*, 241–42.

26   Gilbert, *Churchill: A Life*, 440; "Staffordshire Day by Day," *Evening Sentinel* (Staffordshire, England), May 27, 1915, 4.

27   Soames, *Letters*, 241.

28   "Men and Women of Today: Private Cinema Parties," *Courier* (Dundee), August 2, 1921, 8; Soames, *Letters*, 241; Gilbert, *Churchill: A Life*, 440.

29   Soames, *Letters*, 241–42.

30   "Mr. Churchill to Speak," *Belfast Telegraph*, September 19, 1921, 3.

31   "Reply to Sinn Fein Despatched," *Yorkshire Post* (Leeds, England), September 8, 1921, 7; "Historic Day at Inverness," *Courier* (Dundee), September 8, 1921, 5.

32   "Thirty-Two People in Dundee Court," *Evening Telegraph* (Dundee), September 9, 1921, 6; "Sequel to Dundee Disturbances: 19 Persons Remitted to Sheriff," *Courier* (Dundee), September 13, 1921, 7.

33   Winston Churchill to Sir Laming Worthington-Evans, September 16, 1921, CHAR 5/24.

34   "The Gairloch House Party," *Scotsman* (Aberdeen), September 21, 1921, 6.

35   See "From Gairloch to Dundee," *Courier* (Dundee), September 23, 1921, 4.

36   "From Gairloch," *Courier* (Dundee), September 23, 1921, 4; "Mr. Churchill at Dundee," *Northern Whig* (Belfast), September 23, 1921, 5; "Mr. Churchill in Dundee," *Courier* (Dundee), September 24, 1921, 7; and "Mr. Churchill at Dundee," *Aberdeen Press and Journal* (Scotland), September 23, 1921, 4.

37   "Mr. Churchill and the Problem," *Northern Whig* (Belfast), September 24, 1921, 5; and "Mr. Churchill in Dundee," *Belfast News-Letter*, September 24, 1921, 5.

38   "Queue for Mr. Churchill's Meeting," *Courier* (Dundee), September 26, 1921, 3.

39   "The Churchill Meeting," *Evening Telegraph* (Dundee) September 26, 1921, 2; "Churchill's Plan to Stabilize Trade," *Courier* (Dundee), September 26, 1921, 5; "Mr. Churchill on Causes of Bad Trade," *Western Daily Press* (Bristol, England), September 26, 1921, 5.

40   "Constituency Address," September 24, 1921, *Complete Speeches*, 3:3134–3140.

41   "Mr. Churchill at Dundee," *Scotsman* (Aberdeen), September 26, 1921, 7; and "Pooling of War Debts," *Courier* (Dundee) September 10, 1921, 4.

42   "Cancel the Allied War Debts," *Courier* (Dundee), September 28, 1921, 4; "Our Debts to America," *Belfast News-Letter*, September 28, 1921, 4.

43   "Want Finance Kept Out of Conference," *New York Times*, September 29, 1921, 15.

44   "Within Call of Inverness," *Yorkshire Post* (Leeds, England), September 9, 1921, 7; Arthur S. Draper, "British Prepare to Decide Arms Council Policy," *New York Tribune*, September 18, 1921, 1, 4.

45   See, for example, Roland Quinault, "Churchill and Democracy," *Transactions of the Royal Historical Society*, 11 (2001): 201–20; and Richard M. Langworth, *Winston Churchill, Myth and Reality: What He Actually Did and Said* (Jefferson, NC: McFarland & Company, 2017), 25–30.

46   Winston Churchill, "The Unemployment Situation," September 28, 1921, CHAR 22/7.

3: The Balfour Note

1   G. Martin Moeller, Jr., *AIA Guide to the Architecture of Washington, D.C.* (Baltimore: Johns Hopkins University Press, 2005), 255. The architect of 1785 Massachusetts Avenue was Jules Henri de Sibour, a Parisien who studied at the École des Beaux-Arts.

2   M. E. Hennessy, "National Leaders in the Spotlight," *Boston Globe*, February 3, 1922, 12.

3   Grace Graham Wilson (1870-1953), wife of Cornelius Vanderbilt III; "President and Mrs. Harding to Be Guests at Dinner," *Evening Star* (Washington, DC), January 15, 1922, 4; "Vice President and Mrs. Coolidge Honored," *Washington Herald*, January 25, 1922, 6; Society News, *Evening Star* (Washington, DC), January 18, 1922, 8; "Pinchots Entertain," *Washington Times*, January 10, 1922, 18.

4   "Society News," *Washington Times*, January 13, 1922, 8; "Cabinet Wives Hostesses for Second of 'At Homes,'" *Washington Herald*, January 15, 1922, 17.

5   "Society News," *Washington Post*, December 18, 1921, 36.

6   World War Foreign Debt Commission Act, February 9, 1922, 67th Congress, Public Law 67-139, U.S. Statutes At Large 42: 363.

7   Leffingwell, "Treasury Methods," 25.

8   Skidelsky, *John Maynard Keynes*, 207–8; Keynes, *Consequences of the Peace*, 275, 280.

9   Austen Chamberlain to R. C. Leffingwell, February 9, 1920, Senate, *Refunding*, July 14, 1921, 50.

10   Leffingwell, "Analysis," 110, 114; Leffingwell, "Treasury Methods," 25.

11   R. C. Leffingwell, "Allied Debts as a Factor in Europe's Recovery," *Baltimore Sun*, May 20, 1922, 9; Leffingwell, "Analysis," 110–11.

12   Leffingwell, "War Debts," 37–39.

13   In fact, Daniel Manning, the thirty-seventh US secretary of the
        Treasury, 1885–1887, was genial, well-liked, and remembered as
        having started out as a "roystering young politician." See "Secretary
        Manning," *Burlington Free Press & Times* (VT), January 31, 1887, 7.
14   DCM, April 18, 1922, 2.
15   The Secretary of State (Hughes) to the American ambassadors in
        Paris, Brussels, Prague, Helsingfors, London, Budapest, Rome,
        Warsaw, Bucharest, and Belgrade, April 21, 1922, FRUS, 1:399.
16   Self, *Debt Controversy*, 35.
17   Moulton and Pasvolsky, *War Debts*, 60.
18   Basil Blackett to Austen Chamberlain, February 2, 1920, CAB
        24/97/86.
19   Blackett, CAB 24/97/86.
20   Quoted in Self, *Debt Controversy*, 27; George Curzon memorandum,
        April 17, 1920, CAB 24/103.
21   Winston Churchill memorandum, April 23, 1920, CAB 24/104/57.
22   M. P. A. Hankey to David Lloyd George, May 19, 1920, PA, Papers
        of David Lloyd George, LG/F/24/2/36.
23   The role of Winston Churchill in framing the Balfour Note has long
        been suspected, but complicated by its official attribution to Balfour,
        and subsequently by Lloyd George's claim in 1932, that it was "drafted
        by me." In Lloyd George's recounting of the conception, drafting,
        and discussion of Balfour Note, Churchill is not mentioned. See his
        polemic: Lloyd George, *Truth about Reparations and War Debts*, 111.
24   June 16, 1922, CAB 23/30/13.
25   April 23, 1920, CAB 24/104/57; June 16, 1922, CAB 23/30/13.
26   Elizabeth Johnson, ed. *The Collected Writings of John Maynard Keynes*,
        vol. 16 (Cambridge: Cambridge University Press for the Royal
        Economic Society, 2013), 187. See also Burk, *Sinews*, 45.
27   June 30, 1922, CAB 23/30/14; TV, 2: 148. Wm. Roger Louis,
        Great Britain and Germany's Lost Colonies 1914–1919 (Oxford:
        Oxford University Press, 1967), 9–13; G. Gareth Jones, "The British
        Government and the Oil Companies 1912–1924: The Search for an
        Oil Policy," *Historical Journal* 20, no. 3 (September 1977): 668–69.
28   Secretary of state to the ambassador in Great Britain (Harvey), June 15,
        1922, *FRUS*, 1922 1:402.
29   See Wesley M. Bagby, "The 'Smoke Filled Room' and the Nomination
        of Warren G. Harding," *Mississippi Valley Historical Review* 41, no. 4
        (March 1955): 662.
30   "London Adopts Harvey Goggles," *New York Daily News*, August 5,
        1923, 35.

31 "Anglo-American Amity," *Gloucester Citizen* (England), June 20, 1922, 3.

32 "Pilgrim's Banquet to Chief Justice Taft," *Daily Telegraph* (London), June 20, 1922, 7.

33 "Tafts Are Guests at Dinner to King," *New York Times*, June 25, 1922, 16. The heavy police presence was due in part to the assassination of Sir Henry Wilson, the British field marshal, two days earlier, by the Irish Republican Army, only a block away from Harvey's residence. See "Sir Henry Wilson Shot Dead," *Evening Standard* (London) June 22, 1922, 1.

34 "Tafts Are Guests," and "King and Queen at Harvey Dinner for Justice Taft," *New York Herald*, June 25, 1922, 15.

35 Henry F. Pringle, *The Life and Times of William Howard Taft*, (New York: Farrar & Rinehart, 1939), 2:1004.

36 "King and Queen at Harvey Dinner for Justice Taft," *New York Herald*, June 25, 1922, 15; "Tafts Are Guests," 16.

37 "Taft Tells London What 1776 Meant," *New York Herald*, July 5, 1922, 10.

38 "Londoner's Diary," *Evening Standard* (London), July 5, 1922, 4.

39 Henry Wales, "Yankees in London Observe Natal Day," *Sioux City Journal* (IA), July 5, 1922, 1; "Americans Observe Fourth in England," *Hartford Courant*, July 5, 1922, 4.

40 Frank R. Kent, "Increased Prestige Gained by Harvey in Great Britain," *Baltimore Sun*, July 6, 1922, 1, 9; "Londoner's Diary," *Evening Standard* (London), July 5, 1922, 4.

41 Edward Grigg, "Note of a Conversation at 10 Downing Street," July 5, 1922, CAB 23/36/13.

42 Edward Grigg to David Lloyd George, July 6, 1922, Papers of David Lloyd George; PA Dayer, "British War Debts," 589.

43 July 7, 1922, CAB 23/30/16.

44 Edward Grigg to Arthur Balfour, July 8, 1922, CAB 23/36/13. See also Edward Grigg to David Lloyd George, July 6, 1922 and July 8, 1922, PA Papers of David Lloyd George, LG/F/86/2/4 and LG/F/86/2/5.

45 Basil Blackett to Chancellor of the Exchequer, "British Debts to the United States," July 12, 1922, PA, Papers of David Lloyd George, LG/F/86/2/8.

46 "World Finance Genius," *Daily Telegraph* (London), August 16, 1935, 2.

47 Basil Blackett, July 12, 1922, LG/F/86/2/8.

48 "Lord Balfour's Note on Inter-Allied Debts," *Federal Reserve Bulletin*, September 1922, 1047–48.

49 July 25, 1922, CAB 23/30/20.

50 Middlemas, *Baldwin*, 133.

51 July 25, 1922, CAB 23/30/20.

52   "Official View on Debts," *Gazette* (Montreal), August 1, 1922, 1.
53   "France Holds Debt Note Means Reparations Stand," *New York Herald*, August 3, 1922, 4.
54   "French Press Views," *Liverpool Post and Mercury*, August 4, 1922, 7.
55   "Most Criticism Adverse," *Transcript-Telegram* (Holyoke, MA), August 3, 1922, 3; "America Resents the Balfour Note," *Guardian* (Manchester), August 4, 1922. 7; "Londoner's Diary," *Evening Standard* (London), August 2, 1922, 4.
56   "Uncle Sam as a Grasping Creditor," *Philadelphia Inquirer*, August 4, 1922, 12. See also "The Interallied Debts," *Cincinnati Enquirer*, August 5, 1922, 4; "Britain Calls on Allies to Pay Her What She Owes Us," *New York Times*, August 2, 1922, 1; Henry Wales, "Uncle Sam Blamed, Balfour Sends Hot Note," *Kansas City Times*, August 2, 1922, 1; Middlemas, *Baldwin*, 133–34.
57   "France Holds Debt Note Means Reparations Stand," *New York Herald*, August 3, 1922, 4; "French Press Views," *Liverpool Post and Mercury*, August 4, 1922, 7.
58   "Britain Is Solvent," *Evening Standard* (London), August 2, 1922, 1.
59   "Britain," *Evening Standard* (London), August 2, 1922.
60   "Washington's View of Lord Balfour's Note," *Daily Telegraph* (London), August 4, 1922, 9.
61   Austen Chamberlain, February 22, 1921, Hansard 138, columns 761–62.
62   R. C. Leffingwell, "Allied Debts as a Factor in Europe's Recovery," *Baltimore Sun*, May 20, 1922, 9; Leffingwell, "Analysis," 111.
63   Gilbert to Mellon, August 17, 1922, "Fiscal Relationship of the United States & Foreign Countries, 1917–1941," NARA, RG 39, 50.
64   W. L. Mellon, *Judge*, 447–48.
65   "Parliament," *Daily Telegraph* (London), August 4, 1922, 6.
66   Robert Horne, August 3, 1922, Hansard 157, column 1744; "Parliament"; "The Reparations Debate," *The Times* (London), August 4, 1922, 15.
67   FRUS, 1922, 1:410.
68   Royal J. Schmidt, *Versailles and the Ruhr: Seedbed of World War II* (The Hague: Martinus Nijhoff, 1968), 10–11.
69   "Britain Not Asked to Pay for Allies," *New York Times*, August 25, 1922, 11.
70   Montagu Norman to Benjamin Strong, November 27, 1922, Papers of Benjamin Strong, Jr.

4: The Mellon-Baldwin Agreement

1   "A Londoners Diary," *Evening Standard* (London), October 9, 1922, 4.

2   R. J. Q. Adams, *Bonar Law* (Stanford, CA: Stanford University Press, 1999), 320.

3   Ball, *Baldwin*, 3; Lord Beaverbrook, (Max Aitken), *The Decline and Fall of Lloyd George* (New York: Duell, Sloan and Pearce, 1963), 190.

4   Arthur Windham Baldwin, *My Father: The True Story* (London: George Allen & Unwin, Ltd., 1955), 115.

5   Adams, *Bonar Law*, 322.

6   "The Near East: Pronouncement by Mr. Bonar Law," *The Times* (London), October 7, 1922, 11.

7   "A Fateful Hour," *The Times* (London), October 7, 1922, 11.

8   Adams, *Bonar Law*, 321.

9   Adams, *Bonar Law*, 320–21.

10   Williamson and Baldwin, *Baldwin Papers*, 74–5.

11   "Mr. Bonar Law's Position," *Evening Standard* (London), October 18, 1922, 1.

12   Middlemas and Barnes, *Baldwin*, 123.

13   Adams, *Bonar Law*, 327.

14   "Official Report of Carlton Club Meeting: Mr. Bonar Law," *Daily Telegraph* (London), October 20, 1922, 8.

15   "Political Crisis Follows Carlton Club Drama," *Evening Standard* (London), October 19, 1921, 1; "The King and the Crisis," *Evening Standard* (London), October 19, 1921, 1.

16   Williamson and Baldwin, *Baldwin Papers*, 76.

17   Middlemas, *Baldwin*, 124.

18   "Governments Majority: 87 Over All Parties," *Daily Telegraph* (London), November 17, 1922, 11.

19   "Dundee's Verdict: Mr. Churchill's Ordeal," *Daily Telegraph* (London), November 17, 1922, 11.

20   "Special Interview with Chancellor," *Evening Standard* (London), December 27, 1922, 1.

21   "British Debt Mission Sails for America," *Pittsburgh Post*, December 28, 1922, 7.

22   "Baldwin for Easier British Debt Terms," *New York Herald*, December 28, 1922, 2; "British Mission to United States," *Daily Telegraph* (London), December 28, 1922, 7; "Chancellor Leaves for U.S.," *Evening Standard* (London), December 27, 1922, 1.

23   "Special Interview with Chancellor," *Evening Standard* (London) December 27, 1922, 2. A New York report from London mentions the carriage and says that Norman "has a reputation of . . . shunning speeches, interviews, and every type of publicity." See "Baldwin Embarks, Hopeful

over Debt," *New York Times*, December 28, 1922, 3. Norman's reputation for privacy was more recently regaled in Ahamed, *Lords of Finance*, 1.

24   "Special Interview," *Evening Standard* (London), December 27, 1922, 1. See also "Shy Governor of the Bank," *Evening Standard* (London), December 19, 1922, 3.

25   David Church, "Baldwin on Way to U.S. Ready for Discussions," *Pittsburgh Press*, December 27, 1922, 1, 10.

26   Grigg, *Prejudice*, 98.

27   Merchant ships were divided into "three classes, viz. liners, other merchant ships, and fishing boats" and were to be distributed to the Allied governments on the basis of "ton-for-ton" and "class-for-class" of the ships or boats lost. TV, 2:35, 148.

28   "White Star Buys the *Bismarck*," *Daily Mail* (Hull) February 12, 1921, 4; "World's Largest Liner: The *Majestic* Arrives at Southampton," *Liverpool Post and Mercury*, April 11, 1922, 9.

29   "*Majestic* Starts on Maiden Voyage," *Liverpool Post and Mercury*, May 11, 1922, 8; "*Majestic* Is Due in N.Y. This Week," *Philadelphia Inquirer*, May 14,1922, 43; "*Majestic*, World's Largest Ship, Here," *New York Herald*, May 17, 1922, 26; "World's Greatest Ship, the *Majestic*, on Maiden Trip," May 17, 1922, 1.

30   "Through the Storm: More Stories of Terrific Weather," *Western Daily Press* (Bristol, England), December 28, 1922, 8; "Shipping Intelligence," *Daily Telegraph* (London), December 28, 1922, 3.

31   David Magarshack, *Stanislavsky: A Life* (London: Faber and Faber, 1986), 360.

32   "More Gales," *The Times* (London), December 28, 1922, 8; "Rough Weather in the Atlantic," *The Guardian* (Manchester), December 30, 1922, 6.

33   "Wild Weather in the Atlantic," *Evening Despatch* (Birmingham, England), December 30, 1922, 1.

34   See Grigg, *Prejudice*, 98; Boyle, *Montague Norman*, 154.

35   Montagu Norman to Benjamin Strong, October 31, 1922, Papers of Benjamin Strong, Jr.

36   "The Mission to America: Mr. Baldwin and his Colleague," *The Times* (London), December 27, 1922, 10.

37   "Commission's Arrival Delayed: The April Visit of Mr. Norman," *The Times* (London), January 3, 1923, 8.

38   "The Mission to America: Mr. Baldwin and his Colleague," *The Times* (London), December 27, 1922, 10.

39   "Backhaus Back in London," *The Guardian* (Manchester), October 4, 1922, 13.

40   Williamson and Baldwin, *Baldwin Papers*, 79. See also Montgomery Hyde, *Baldwin: The Unexpected Prime Minister* (London: Hart-Davis, 1973), 126–27.

41   "History of the Anglo-American Debt Negotiations and Settlement, 1914–1928," undated, Baldwin MSS 233, Cambridge University Library, part 2, section 31, 128.

42   "Text of Harding's Letter to Senator Lodge on the Borah Proposal and the Allied Debt," *New York Times*, December 29, 1922, 1.

43   "President Harding's Suggestion," *The Times* (London), December 30, 1922, 9.

44   "History Debt Negotiations" part 3, section 33, 1.

45   Benjamin Strong to Basil Blackett, January 8, 1923, Papers of Benjamin Strong, Jr.

46   "A Seasick Comer," *Liverpool Echo*, January 2, 1922, 4.

47   Magarshack, *Stanislavsky*, 362; "U.S. Cutter Lands Debt Commission Delayed in Storm," *Evening Star* (Washington, DC), January 4, 1923, 2; "'Day by Day Coué,' Makes a Big Hit," *Boston Globe*, January 5, 1923, 1, 12.

48   "British Envoys See Hope for Debt Plan," *New York Times*, January 5, 1922, 1, 2; "British Debt Mission Lands in U.S.," *Guardian* (Manchester), January 5, 1923, 7; "Baldwin Wants to Make Deal That Will Satisfy All," *Montreal Gazette*, January 5, 1923, 2.

49   "British Envoys." Norman's answer referenced the New Testament gospel usually quoted as Matthew 7:9.

50   The US Debt Funding Commissioners: Andrew Mellon, Treasury Secretary, and chairman of the commission; Charles Evans Hughes, secretary of state; Herbert Hoover, commerce secretary; Senator Reed Smoot; and Representative Theodore Burton. The members of the British delegation: Stanley Baldwin, chancellor of the exchequer and head of the British delegation; Montagu Norman, governor of the Bank of England; Ernest Rowe-Dutton, HM Treasury official; and Loring Christie, Canadian Department of External Affairs. Also present at the commission meetings: Eliot Wadsworth, assistant secretary of the US Treasury; and P. J. Grigg, private secretary to Baldwin. See DCM, 30-31; "England Wants Fair Settlement of Debts," *Wall Street Journal*, January 9, 1923, 4; "Cheque to America for 11,300,000," *Liverpool Post and Mercury*, October 12, 1923, 7.

51   "British to Pay All, Ask a Square Deal, Debt Board Is Told," *New York Times*, January 9, 1923, 3.

52   "History, Debt Negotiations," part 2, section 31, 120–122.

53   "Easier Debt Terms Favored by Harding," *New York Times*, January 10, 1923, 3.

54   "History, Debt Negotiations," part 3, section 33, 5; "British Debt
      to U.S.," *The Times* (London), January 10, 1923, 11; and "Spotted
      Prosperity," *The Times* (London), January 10, 1923, 10.
55   DCM, January 10, 1923, 33.
56   Montgomery H. Hyde, *Baldwin: The Unexpected Prime Minister*
      (London: Hart-David MacGibbon, 1973), 128.
57   The 187 million dollar annual payment included terms for funding
      a sinking fund. Originally crafted in Britain, sinking funds were
      introduced in the United States by Alexander Hamilton, the first
      secretary of the Treasury. Such a fund can be thought of as a savings
      account to hold money being set aside to pay off a specific debt.
      Typically, regular deposits are made into the sinking fund to assure
      payments on the interest and principal of an outstanding debt can
      be made. This reduces the risk of the debtor not having the ability to
      make future payments. Hamilton used sinking funds to reduce the
      national debt and enhance American credit internationally.
58   "History, Debt Negotiations," part 3, section 33, 6–7, 9.
59   Washington Telegram No. 14, Stanley Baldwin to Andrew Bonar
      Law, January 14, 1923, CAB 24/158/18.
60   DCM, January 12, 1924, 34.
61   "History, Debt Negotiations," part 3, section 33, 10–11; Washington
      Telegram No. 14, Stanley Baldwin to Andrew Bonar Law, January 14,
      1923, CAB 24/158/18.
62   "History, Debt Negotiations," part 3, section 33, 12.
63   DCM, January 16, 1924, 35.
64   "British Debt to U.S.," *The Times* (London), January 17, 1923, 10.
65   "History, Debt Negotiations," part 3, section 33, 15.
66   "History, Debt Negotiations," part 3, section 33, 16–17.
67   "The American Offer," *The Guardian* (Manchester), January 19, 1923,
      6; see also "British Debt Parley Fails," *Detroit Free Press*, January 19,
      1923, 1; "London Grieved by Failure of Debt Funding Trip," *Daily
      Palo Alto Times* (CA), January 19, 1923 1; "Deadlock on Debt," *Daily
      News* (London), January 19, 1923, 1; "American Debt Deadlock,"
      Daily Herald (London), January 19, 1923, 3.
68   "History, Debt Negotiations," part 3, section 33, 17.
69   "History, Debt Negotiations," part 3, section 34, 13. Foreign Office
      Telegrams, Andrew Bonar Law to Stanley Baldwin, January 12–13,
      1923, CAB 24/158/16; "British to Pay All, Ask a Square Deal, Debt
      Board Is Told," *New York Times*, January 9, 1923, 1, 3.
70   Grigg, *Prejudice*, 102. See also "Coincidences," *Wall Street Journal*,
      January 19, 1923, 1.

71   "History, Debt Negotiations," part 3, section 34, 20.

72   "Debt Situation Is Delicate, Says Baldwin, Sailing," *Brooklyn Daily Eagle*, January 21, 1923, 5.

73   Danelski and Tulchin, *Hughes*, 206.

74   John Evelyn Wrench, *Geoffrey Dawson and Our Times* (London: Hutchinson & Co., 1955), 215.

75   Randolph Churchill, *Lord Derby of Lancashire: The Official Life of Edward, Seventeenth Earl of Derby* (London: Heineman, 1959), 496.

76   "The American Debt: Arguments Against Acceptance," *The Times* (London), January 27, 1923, 6; quoted in Wrench, *Geoffrey Dawson*, 215.

77   Adams, *Bonar Law*, 351.

78   "The American Debt: Arguments Against Acceptance," *The Times* (London), January 27, 1923, 6.

79   "Mr. Baldwin on His Task," *Weekly Dispatch* (London), January 28, 1823, 9.

80   "Congress Blamed for British War Debt Pact Hold Up," *Lancaster Intelligencer* (PA), January 27, 1923, 1.

81   "Congress Blamed," 1.

82   "U.S.A. and War Debts," *Evening Express* (Liverpool), January 27, 1923, 1.

83   "Offered Debt Rate under 4 Per Cent," *New York Times*, January 28, 1923, 3; see also "U.S. Plan Is Revealed," *Washington Star*, January 27, 1923, 1.

84   "Senator Demands Baldwin Apologize," *New York Times*, January 29, 1923, 3; "Baldwin Spills the Beans," *Washington Star*, January 27, 1923, 6: "An Indiscreet Chancellor," *New York Times*, January 29, 1923, 14.

85   The quote came from F. A. Lawrenson, an employee of Union Carbide Corporation and a member of the New York Advertising Club. The story was distributed by Central News, a British syndicate, and was published in papers in Great Britain and the United States as early as Sunday, January 28. See "America Eager to Search British Pockets," *Sunday Sun* (Newcastle) January 28, 1923, 1; and "Britain Dissatisfied with U.S. Offer to Reduce Debt ¼ P.C.," *Philadelphia Inquirer*, January 28, 1923, 1. See also "Mr. Bonar Law: Reported Statement on Debt," *Weekly Standard* (London), January 28, 1923, 1, which includes the attribution to Central News.

86   Adams, *Bonar Law*, 348.

87   "The Debt to America," *The Times* (London), January 29, 1923, 11.

88   "To Debate Baldwin Report To-Morrow," *Victoria Daily Times* (British Columbia), January 29, 1923, 1, 3. See also "British Press Urges Accepting on Debt," *New York Times*, January 29, 1923, 1, 2.

89   Middlemas and Barnes, *Baldwin*, 144.

90   Lord Derby diary entry, quoted in Adams, *Bonar Law*, 350.

91   R. S. Churchill, *Lord Derby*, 495.

92   R. S. Churchill, *Lord Derby*, 497; "Cabinet Accepts U.S. Debt Offer," *Evening Standard* (London), January 31, 1923, 1; "The British Debt to America," *Guardian* (Manchester), February 1, 1923, 6. "Cabinet Accepts the U.S. Debt Terms," *Daily Telegraph* (London), February 1, 1923, 11. See also "British Accept Terms with Unexpected Speed," *Boston Globe*, February 1, 1923, 2.

93   Robert Blake, "Baldwin and the Right," in John Raymond, *The Baldwin Age* (London: Eyre & Spottiswoode, 1960), 40.

94   "Sees Need of a Long Rest," *Nebraska State Journal* (Lincoln), March 6, 1923, 1.

95   "The Debt Settlement," *New York Times*, February 17, 1923, 12.

96   Quoted in Sir Henry Clay, *Lord Norman* (London: Macmillan, 1957), 178–79.

5: Westminster Abbey

1   CV, IV, part 3: 2124.

2   Soames, *A Daughter's Tale*, 7, 8.

3   See Behrend, *Luxury Trains*, 89. He writes, "The smart set immediately christened it the *Blue Train*," and being seen on it "was an essential part of the snobbish social round."

4   DOCS, 11:22–3.

5   "Notes on Current Events: Mr. Churchill," *Derby Daily Telegraph* (England), January 27, 1923, 2.

6   "Notes on Current." London papers and the Press Association also contacted Churchill and printed his response. See, for example, "Mr. Churchill's Denials," *Evening Standard* (London), January 26, 1923, 8.

7   Montgomery-Massingberd and Watkin, *The London Ritz*, 43, 47.

8   DOCS, 11:23–6.

9   "Mr. Churchill's Book: 'The Times' Articles," *The Times* (London), February 6, 1923, 10.

10   "Mimic Battles and Mimosa," *Sunday Pictorial* (London), January 28, 1923, 12.

11   Soames, *Painter*, 56.

12   DOCS, 11:42–43.

13   Edward, Prince of Wales to Winston S. Churchill, April 12, 1923, in Gilbert, DOCS, 11:43.

14   "The World Crisis: Mr. Churchill's Own Story," *The Observer* (London), April 15, 1923, 12.

15   Cannadine, *Westminster Abbey*, 332; "Royal Wedding," *Daily Telegraph* (London), April 21, 1923, 9; "A Gala Week," *Sunday Pictorial* (London), April 22, 1923, 6.

16   "A Wonderful Wedding," *Western Daily Press* (Bristol, England), April 27, 1923, 7.

17   "Real Socialist Menace: Mr. Churchill's Warning," *The Times* (London), May 5, 1923, 6.

18   "Real Socialist."

19   "London Letter," *Midland Daily Telegraph* (Coventry, England), May 5, 1923, 2; "Mr. Churchill's Re-Entry," *Daily Mail* (Hull), May 5, 1923, 2.

20   Williamson and Baldwin, *Baldwin Papers*, 82–83.

21   "Mr. Baldwin as Prime Minister," *Daily Telegraph* (London), May 23, 1923, 11.

22   "Londoner's Diary," *Evening Standard* (London), May 26, 1923, 4.

23   George Allardice Riddell, *Lord Riddell's Intimate Diary of the Peace Conference and After, 1918–1923* (New York: Reynal & Hitchcock, 1934), 409.

24   "Insists Churchill Will Join Tories," *New York Times*, June 3, 1923, 122; "Men and Affairs: Winston and Toryism," *Birmingham Gazette* (England), January 6, 1923, 4.

25   Soames, *Letters*, 229.

26   See "Echoes from Town," *Nottingham Evening Post*, May 21, 1923, 3, which refers to "the Embassy Club, the smartest of the town's dinner and dance clubs;" also, "Modern Ballroom Deportment," *Evening Sentinel* (Staffordshire, England), June 28, 1923, which refers to "the Embassy Club, perhaps the most exclusive dance club in London"; also "Where to Dine and Dance: Derby Night and Every Night," *Daily Telegraph* (London), June 6, 1923, 7, stating, "The popularity of Ciro's Club and the Embassy Club remains undiminished, and nightly at these exclusive haunts many of the leaders of London society are to be seen dining and dancing."

27   "Dances: Mrs. Cornelius Vanderbilt," *Daily Telegraph* (London), July 3, 1923, 13.

28   "Mr. Walter H. Page: A Proposed Memorial," *The Times* (London), January 25, 1923, 11.

29   "A Memorial to Mr. Page," *The Times* (London), January 25, 1923, 11.

30   James Russell Lowell, a poet, editor, and diplomat, had been the American ambassador to the Court of St. James's from 1880 to 1885. He was honored in 1893 with a plaque and two stained glass windows near the Chapter House. The first American to be permanently memorialized in Westminster Abbey was the poet Henry Wadsworth Longfellow, he of *Paul Revere's Ride*.

31   Rodwell, *The Chapter House*, 7. The Chapter House vestibule had both
      a plaque and a stained-glass window that had Lowell's life and work
      portrayed, with angels holding the arms of Britain and the United
      States, installed in 1893.

32   "British Empire: From the Inside," *Time*, April 14, 1923.

33   "The Cabinet: A Champion Sails," *Time*, July 2, 1923.

34   "Tablet to Page Is Unveiled at Abbey by Grey," *New York Tribune*,
      July 4, 1923, 9.

35   Walter Hines Page Honored in Abbey," *New York Times*, July 4, 1923, 12.

36   "Lord Grey's Tribute to W. H. Page," *The Times* (London), July 4,
      1923, 16.

37   "A Great Ambassador," *Daily Telegraph* (London), July 4, 1923, 8; "The
      Page Memorial Service in Westminster Abbey," *Landmark* 5, no. 8
      (August 1923): 495.

38   Naphtali, "In Westminster Abbey," *International Interpreter* (New
      York), August 4, 1923, 572; "Lord Grey's Tribute to W. H. Page,"
      The Times (London), July 4, 1923, 16; "Walter Hines Page Honored in
      Abbey, *New York Times*, July 4, 1923, 12.

39   DOCS, 11:26.

40   "House of Commons: The American Debt," *The Guardian*
      (Manchester), July 5, 1923, 11.

41   Frederic William Wile, "Washington Observations," *Evening Star*
      (Washington, DC), August 1, 1923, 6. The MP quoted is Thomas
      Power O'Connor.

42   "House of Commons: The American Debt," *The Guardian*
      (Manchester), July 5, 1923, 11.

43   "House of Commons."

44   "Britain Gives $4,000,000,000 on War Loans," *Evening News*
      (Harrisburg, PA), July 6, 1923, 13; "Complete Last Act in Debt
      Refunding," *Des Moines Register*, July 6, 1923, 3; "U.S. Reveals
      Contract on British Debt," *San Francisco Examiner*, July 10, 1923, 2.

45   "Garden Party at No. 10," *The Guardian* (Manchester), July 6, 1923, 5;
      "London Letter," *Western Daily Press* (Bristol, England), July 6, 1923, 5.

46   Duveen to Mellon, May 7, 1923, Duveen Brothers Records, Getty
      Archives; Duveen Brothers (London) to Duveen Brothers (New York),
      July 20, 1923, Duveen Brothers Records, Getty Archives.

47   "Stern Path of Economy: Mr. Baldwin's Speech to Bankers," *The
      Times* (London), July 25, 1923, 14; "Britain's Achievement in Debt
      Reduction," *Daily Telegraph* (London), July 25, 1923, 12.

48   "Royal Garden Party: Dress and Guests," *Daily Telegraph* (London),
      July 27, 1923, 9; *Evening Star* (Washington, DC), July 30, 1923, 8.

49   "Mellon in Paris; Curzon Presses French to Reply," *Pittsburgh Press*, July 28, 1923, 1.

50   See "Paris Sees Mellon on Debt Mission," *Evening Star* (Washington, DC), July 29, 1923, 1.

51   "Mellon Motors to Devastated Regions," *Pittsburgh Press*, August 1, 1923, 7; "Paris Eager to Hear of Harding," *Vancouver Sun*, August 1, 1923, 9; "Mellon Will See Poincare Friday, May Talk Debts," *Chicago Tribune*, August 2, 1923, 2.

52   "That Changed Political Aspect," *Evening Star* (Washington, DC), August 4, 1923.

53   Fuess, *Calvin Coolidge*, 309; Shlaes, *Coolidge*, 257.

54   Shales, *Coolidge*, 256.

55   Edwin W. Gableman, "Views of Coolidge Given," *Cincinnati Enquirer*, August 15, 1923, 1, 3.

56   "Coolidge Adopts Harding Policies, Home and Abroad," *New York Times*, August 15, 1923, 1.

57   "Mellon Will Stay at Treasury Post, He Tells Coolidge," *Philadelphia Inquirer*, August 21, 1923, 1.

6: The Rise of the Rivalry

1   Russell Leffingwell to Parker Gilbert, February 8, 1923, Correspondence between the United States and Other Nations, 1918–1941, Great Britain, Loans Made by the United States, Funding, NARA, Record Group 39.

2   "A Wise Decision," *The Times* (London), February 1, 1923, 11.

3   "A Nasty Corner Turned," *The Guardian* (Manchester), February 1, 1923, 6.

4   David B. Lawrence, "America Silent as Europe Sinks," *Birmingham News* (AL), August 14, 1923, 2.

5   "Why Did He Do It," *Stockport County Borough Express* (England), November 29, 1923, 9.

6   "Why Did He Do It."

7   "President Takes Firm Stand in Message," *Evening Star* (Washington, DC), December 6, 1923,1.

8   R. G. Hawtrey, *Currency and Credit* (London: Longmans, Green and Co., 1928), 264; Frank D. Graham, *Exchange, Prices and Production in Hyper-Inflation: Germany, 1920-1923* (Princeton, NJ: Princeton University Press, 1930), 4, 11; and Egon Larson, *Weimar Eyewitness* (London: Bachman and Turner, 1976), 56.

9   "Americans to Join in Investigation of German Finances," *New York Times*, December 12, 1923, 1, 2. For more on the use of

business-government cooperation to resolve complex political issues, see Michael J. Hogan, *Informal Entente* (Columbia: University of Missouri Press, 1977), and Leffler, *Elusive Quest*.

10   "Mr. Baldwin Still at Downing Street," *The Guardian* (Manchester), December 11, 1923, 8.

11   "Mr. Baldwin's Exit," *Evening Standard* (London), January 22, 1924, 4.

12   "Dawes Advises Allies to First Cure Germany," *Philadelphia Inquirer*, January 15, 1924, 1, 4; Schuker, *End of French Predominance*, 28.

13   Kathleen Burk, "The House of Morgan in Financial Diplomacy, 1920-1930," in McKercher, *Anglo-American Relations*, 144.

14   "Owen Young Will Get World's Biggest Job," *Commercial Appeal* (Memphis), August 24, 1924, 3.

15   Costigliola, *Awkward Dominion*, 123.

16   O. D. Tolischus, "Gilbert Assumes Duties as Dawes Plan Executive," *Buffalo Courier* (NY), November 1, 1924, 1.

17   "Mr. Baldwin's Task," *The People* (London), November 9, 1924, 8.

18   "Churchill Chancellor," *Western Daily Press* (Bristol, England), November 7, 1924, 10. "Mr. Churchill Chancellor of the Exchequer," *The Guardian* (Manchester), November 7, 1924, 9; "A Strong Team," *The Guardian* (Manchester), November 7, 1924, 9.

19   "Cut Down, Cut Down!" *Sunday Mirror* (London), November 9, 1924, 6. Lough, *Champagne*, 155.

20   "The New Cabinet: Transfer of Seals," *Daily Telegraph* (London), November 8, 1924, 9.

21   "The President's Message," *Evening Star* (Washington, DC), December 3, 1924, 6; see "Coolidge Saves $1700 Traveling to Chicago in Public Pullman," *St. Louis Globe-Democrat*, December 4, 1924, 1.

22   "Coolidge Message Stresses Economy; World Court," *New York Times*, December 4, 1924, 1, 8.

23   Coolidge's sophisticated statement on war debts would be reduced to the phrase "Well, they hired the money, didn't they?" and go on to characterize his attitude on war debts, despite no one to date being able to quote Coolidge actually saying it. See Fuess, *Calvin Coolidge*, 333n19.

24   "L'Amérique maintient ses créances sur les Alliés," *Paris Soir*, December 4, 1924, 1; "M. Coolidge s'oppse a l'annulation des dettes interalliées," *Le Matin* (Paris), December 4, 1924, 3; "French and British Interpret Coolidge Message Differently," *Baltimore Sun*, December 4, 1924, 2.

25   "Allied Debts to the United States," *Daily Telegraph* (London), December 4, 1924, 11; "French and British Interpret Coolidge Message Differently," *Baltimore Sun*, December 4, 1924, 2.

26   DOCS, 11:284.

27   DOCS, 11:292–93; "Mr. Churchill in His New Role," *Birmingham Post* (England), December 1, 1924, 10.

28   See "Mr. Churchill in His New Role," *Birmingham Post* (England), December 1, 1924, 10.

29   "Inter-Allied War Debts," December 10, 1924, *Complete Speeches*, 4:3506–3510.

30   DOCS, 11:299.

31   "Inter-Allied War Debts," 3506–10.

32   DOCS, 11:299.

33   "Churchill Statement: Obvious and Logical," *Boston Globe*, December 11, 1924, 19.

7: Best Intentions

1   Hamilton attended King's College, which was renamed Columbia after the American Revolution. The dinner honored the 150th anniversary of Hamilton's matriculation. See Chernow, *Alexander Hamilton*, 31; Gene R. Hawes, "The Men from Morningside," in *A History of Columbia College on Morningside* (New York: Columbia University Press, 1954), 254.

2   Alexander Hamilton, "On Public Credit," January 9, 1790, in *Reports of the Treasury of the United States* (Washington, DC: Department of the Treasury, 1928), 1:3–4; Chernow, *Alexander Hamilton*, 297, 480; Mellon, *Taxation*, 25; Garbade, *Birth of a Market*, 153.

3   "Mellon Ranked with Hamilton at Dinner Honoring Both," *Pittsburgh Gazette*, December 5, 1924, 2; "Mellon Hailed Here as Second Hamilton," *New York Times*, December 5, 1924, 3.

4   Quoted in Cannadine, *Mellon*, 310.

5   "Mellon Ranked."

6   "Mellon Ranked."

7   "War Debts Omitted as French Liability," *Philadelphia Inquirer*, December 28, 1924, 2.

8   FRUS, 1925, 1:898–908; "Demand That France Pay Her Debt to U.S. Made in Congress," *New York Times*, December 30, 1924, 1.

9   "Demand that France Pay Her Debt."

10   Charles S. Groves, "French Debt Attitude Scored in Congress," *Boston Globe*, December 30, 1924, 7.

11   Groves, "French Debt."

12   Edwin L. James, "French Note Asks 10-Year Moratorium and 80 Years to Pay," *New York Times*, January 3, 1925, 1.

13   J. F. Essary, "France Sending Debt Proposal to Washington," *Baltimore Sun*, January 3, 1925, 1.

14   "British Watching Franco-American Debt Discussions," *Los Angeles Times*, January 3, 1925, 1; "La Vigne de Naboth," *La Liberté* (Paris), January 3, 1925, 1; James, "French Note," FRUS, 1925, 1:929.

15   James, "French Note."

16   See *Commercial and Financial Chronicle*, January 17, 1925, 242; "What the Allied Chancellors Decided," *Daily Herald* (London), January 15, 1925, 1.

17   DOCS, 11: 280, 324.

18   "Mr. Churchill Makes Reparations Pact with U.S," *Sunday Mirror* (London), January 11, 1925, 3; *Commercial and Financial Chronicle*, January 17, 1925, 243.

19   See "Mr. Churchill's Diplomacy," *The Guardian* (Manchester), January 13, 1925, 8; "The Paris Negotiations," *Economist*, January 10, 1925, 52; "Mr. Churchill," *Daily Mirror* (London), January 15, 1925, 3; "Mr. Churchill on U.S. Participation," *Daily Telegraph* (London), January 15, 1925, 9; quoted in *Commercial and Financial Chronicle*, January 17, 1923, 243.

20   DOCS, 11: 341.

21   "Allied Finance Pact Signed at Conference: Tributes to Churchill," *Evening Dispatch* (Birmingham, England), January 14, 1925, 1.

22   FRUS, 1925, 1:143.

23   Benjamin D. Rhodes, "The United States and the War Debt Question, 1917-1934," (PhD diss., University of Colorado, 1965), 145; see also Leffler, *Elusive Quest*, 127–29, who calls this policy "the loan embargo."

24   FRUS, 1925, 1:114, 116, 119.

25   DCC, August 10, 1925, 167.

26   Schuker, *American Foreign Policy*, 295.

27   DCM, August 14, 1925, 85.

28   "Miscellaneous Mentions," *Time*, June 6, 1925, 5; "Secretary of Treasury Mellon and His Daughter on Vacation," *St. Louis Star and Times*, September 7, 1925, 4.

29   "Planes to Keep Mellon Posted on Vacation," *Minneapolis Daily Star*, July 2, 1925, 9; "Mellon to Keep Informed on Debt," *Daily Messenger* (Canandaigua, NY), July 2, 1925, 1; "Overnight Air Mail Delivery Unites Chicago and New York in Useful 8-Hour Service," *Democrat and Chronical* (Rochester, NY), July 3, 1925, 1; and William D. Tipton, "With the Flyers," *Baltimore Sun*, June 22, 1925, 13.

30   "Herrick Will Be Guest," *New York Times*, August 17, 1925, 15; "National Affairs: Miscellaneous Mentions," *Time*, June 8, 1925, 5.

31   David Lawrence, "3 Master Minds Hold Conference in Quaint Plymouth," *Rutland Daily Herald* (VT), August 18, 1925, 1.

32   John Edwin Nevin, "Accord is Expected Today," *Washington Post*, August 18, 1925, 1. "President Decides Belgian Debt Terms; Expects Agreement," *New York Times*, August 18, 1925, 1.

33   "Belgians Sign Debt Funding Terms," *New York Times*, August 19, 1925, 1; "Debt Impasse Ends," *Baltimore Sun*, August 18, 1925, 1.

34   "Anti-Wilson Group Opposes Belgian Deal," *New York Times*, August 23, 1925, 1.

35   T. R. Ybarra, "British Fix Terms on France's Debt, Contingent on Ours," *New York Times*, August 27, 1925, 1.

8: Rough Passages

1   "Debt Agreements Assailed in Senate," *Baltimore Sun*, December 16, 1925, 1.

2   "Storm in Senate Over Move to Act on Debt Compacts, *New York Times*, December 17, 1925, 1.

3   "Debt Agreements."

4   "Foreign Debts Cause Heated Senate Debate," *Baltimore Sun*, December 17, 1925, 1.

5   "Debt Agreements."

6   "Foreign Debts Cause"; "War Debt Policy Scored in Senate," *Boston Globe*, December 17, 1925, 1,4.

7   "Accept Debt Terms or Receive Nothing," *New York Times*, January 5, 1926, 1.

8   "Mellon Backs Debt Pacts," *Evening Journal* (Wilmington, DE), January 5, 1926, 13.

9   "Experts on Italian Settlement," *The Guardian* (Manchester), January 29, 1926. 7.

10   "The Italian Debt Settlement," *The Guardian* (Manchester), February 3, 1926, 9.

11   "Lord Bradbury and the French Debt," *Daily Telegraph* (London), August 25, 1925, 9.

12   "A Transparent Manoeuvre," *The Guardian* (Manchester), August 29, 1925, 11.

13   "Press Comment on the French Debt Agreement," *New York Times*, August 29, 1925, 4.

14   "Our Stand on Debt Worries British," *New York Times*, August 30, 1925, 6; Edwin L. James, "French Now Press for a Debt Accord on British Terms," *New York Times*, August 29, 1925, 1.

15   "French Outlook on Debt Payment," *The Guardian* (Manchester), January 29, 1926, 7.

16   "France's War Debt," *Daily Telegraph* (London), February 1, 1926, 10.

17   "French Debt Settlements," *New York Times*, February 4, 1926, 22.

18   G. Gould Lincoln, "Tax Plan Called Millionaires' Bill," *Evening Star* (Washington, DC), February 3, 1926. 4.

19   Andrew Mellon to Calvin Coolidge, February 10, 1926, DCC, 237-39.

20   "President Defends Italian Settlement," *New York Times*, February 20, 1926, 2: "Coolidge Leaves Bed to See Newspapermen," *New York Times*, February 20, 1926, 2.

21   "Coolidge Wants Action on the Italian Debt," *New York Times*, February 24, 1926, 19.

22   "Mellon Forecasts Debt Deal Approval," *New York Times*, March 7, 1926, 19.

23   "British Crisis Linked With Return to Gold," *Baltimore Sun*, August 17, 1925, 7; "Britain Pays Us This Year $160,000," *Boston Globe*, February 17, 1926, 2.

24   See Lough, *Champagne*, 168; "The Sheikhs of St. Stephen's," *The Guardian* (Manchester), March 31, 1926; "Sunshine Group of M.P.s," *Evening Standard* (London), March 30, 1926, 4.

25   DOCS, 11:641, 667.

26   "Inter-Allied War Debts," March 24, 1926, *Complete Speeches*, 4:3893–94; "Debt Tangle Is Blamed on US in Commons," *Baltimore Sun*, March 25, 1926, 1.

27   "Inter-Allied War Debts," 3892.

28   "Economy Bill," April 15, 1926, *Complete Speeches*, 4:3899–3900.

29   "A Londoner's Diary," *Evening Standard* (London), March 25, 1926, 6.

30   "War Remarks Draw Fire," *Baltimore Sun*, March 31, 1926, 2.

31   "No Cant, Mr. Churchill," *Baltimore Sun*, March 26, 1926, 12.

32   "Sense Dictated War Debt Pacts, Assets Mellon," *Philadelphia Inquirer*, March 25, 1926, 1, 6.

33   "Mr. Churchill and War Debt Payments," *Daily Telegraph* (London), March 26, 1926, 11; "Slave Who Pays," *Evening Standard* (London), March 25, 1926, 6.

34   Ratification of the Italian debt settlement had taken three days to get through the House of Representatives, and three months to get through the Senate. "Italian Debt Pact Ratified 54 to 33," *Washington Herald*, April 22, 1926, 1; "Last War Debt Pact Approved," *Los Angeles Times*, April 29, 1926, 3; "Czech Debt Is Ratified by Senate," *Cincinnati Enquirer*, April 29, 1926, 3; "Thirteen Nations Pledge to Pay US," *New York Times*, May 3, 1926, 4.

35   Churchill's announcement belied the reality that the ink on the
        provisional agreement governing the payment had not dried. Adding
        to the uncertainty, the provisional agreement had been struck with
        Raoul Péret, the fourth French finance minister to serve since the
        Churchill-Caillaux settlement was negotiated in August, 1925. The
        Mellon-Bérenger agreement set an average interest rate of 1.64 percent.
        The below-market rate effectively canceled over half of France's total
        indebtedness while at the same time allowed the United States to claim
        the principal would be repaid in full. Mellon, held firm, though, on
        two concessions granted by Churchill in his settlement with France, no
        safeguard clause or payment moratorium.

9: Andrew Mellon's Summer Vacation

1   "After-Luncheon Settlement," *Birmingham Gazette* (England), July 13,
        1926, 1.
2   See "Value of Franc Is Based upon Debt Payments," *Hamilton Spectator*
        (Ontario), July 6, 1926, 1.
3   See "French Official's Talks with Mr. Churchill," *The Guardian*
        (Manchester), July 8, 1926, 12; "Britain and France," *Devon and Exeter
        Daily* (England), July 9, 1926, 16; "Caillaux Signs for Paris; Gets
        London Credits," *Chicago Tribune*, July 13, 1926, 1.
4   See "Had to Sign," *Producer's News* (Plentywood, MT), July 16,1926,
        1; "M. Caillaux's Flying Visit to London," *Newcastle Daily Chronicle*,
        July 12, 1926, 1.
5   See, for example, "Churchill to the Aid of Caillaux," *Daily Herald*
        (London), July 10, 1926, 3; "French Debt to Britain," *The Observer*
        (London), July 11, 1926, 16.
6   "Anglo-French Relations," *Taunton Courier* (England), July 7, 1926, 8.
7   "French Funding Debt," *Liverpool Daily Post*, July 10, 1926, 1;
        "Caillaux to Fly to London," *Sunday Mercury* (London), July 11, 1926, 1.
8   Edwin L. James, "Maimed and Blind Lead Paris Parade to Protest on
        Debt," *New York Times*, July 12, 1926, 1, 5.
9   "Caillaux Here in Good Spirits," *Evening Standard* (London), July 12,
        1926, 9.
10   "Caillaux Here."
11   See "British Give France Concessions on Debt She Wants from US,"
        New York Times, July 13, 1926, 1; "French Debt Change Now up to
        Congress," *New York Times*, July 13, 1926, 5.
12   "War Debts," July 14, 1926, *Complete Speeches*, 4:4039–40.

13   Garrard Winston to Benjamin Strong, July 16, 1926, Papers of
        Benjamin Strong, Jr.

14   "Coolidge Disowns Federal Reserve," *Baltimore Sun*, May 26, 1926,
        18; "Who's Who: Garrard B. Winston," *Bayonne Evening News* (NJ),
        November 11, 1926, 7.

15   "Who's Who in the Days News," *Morning Call* (Paterson, NJ),
        November 11, 1926, 4; "U.S. Puts Sentry at Anglo-French Debts
        Meeting," *Chicago Tribune*, May 17, 1926, 7; Frederick J. Haskin, "The
        Undersecretary of the Treasury," *Knoxville Journal* (TN), March 1, 1925, 24.

16   "Eloquent Appeal for Cancellation of War Debts Made to Coolidge,"
        St. Louis Post-Dispatch, July 4, 1926, 15; "Calls on Coolidge to Drop
        War Debts," *New York Times*, July 4, 1926, 1.

17   Calvin Coolidge, "Report of the Newspaper Conference," July 6,
        1926, in Calvin Coolidge, *Remarks by the President to Newspaper
        Correspondents*, vol. 7, Calvin Coolidge Presidential Foundation.

18   Garrard Winston to Benjamin Strong, July 16, 1926, Papers of
        Benjamin Strong, Jr.

19   Few newspapers ran the entire Peabody letter. For a complete text, see
        "Eloquent Appeal for Cancellation of War Debts Made to Coolidge,"
        St. Louis Post-Dispatch, July 4, 1926, 15.

20   "European War Debts: Mr. Mellon's Statement," *The Times* (London),
        July 19, 1926, 11.

21   "Movement of Liners," *Western Daily Press* (Bristol, England), July 21,
        1926, 3.

22   "French Debt Pact Attacked," *Liverpool Post and Mercury*, July 20,
        1926, 9.

23   "'Uncle Shylock' Pays Us a Visit," *Daily Mirror* (London), July 20,
        1926, 7.

24   "Unpopular Americans," *Daily Mirror* (London), July 20, 1926, 7.

25   "Britain Denies Try to Revise U.S. Debt Pact," *Tampa Times*, July 21,
        1926, 1–2; "Hate-Mongering," *Daily Herald* (London), July 20, 1926, 4.

26   "London Letter: Anti-American Feeling," *Gloucester Citizen*
        (England), July 21, 1926, 22.

27   "Parisians Attack U.S. Tourists as 'Sons of Shylock,'" *St. Louis Post-
        Dispatch*, July 20, 1926, 1; "Americans Getting Bad Time Abroad,"
        Vancouver Daily Province, July 20, 1926, 22.

28   "Manisfestation contre des etrangers," *Echo de Paris*, July 20, 1926, 3;
        "The Next Ministry," *The Guardian* (Manchester), July 22, 1926, 9;
        "Parisians Hoot at Yanks," *Chicago Tribune*, July 24, 1926, 1; "Parisians
        Attack U.S. Tourists as 'Sons of Shylock,'" *St. Louis Post-Dispatch*,

July 20, 1926, 1; "Americans Break Tourist Records," *Evening Star* (Washington, DC), July 17, 1926, 14.

29   "French Franc Falls to Below Two Cents," *New York Times*, July 21, 1926, 2; "Edge of the Abyss," *Daily Telegraph* (London), July 21, 1926, 9. See also L. O. Frossard, "Savoir ce qu'on veut," *Paris-Soir*, July 20, 1926, 1.

30   "Movement of Liners," *Liverpool Daily Post*, July 22, 1926, 12; "Mellon Declines Interview," *Hartford Courant*, 23 Jul 1926, 1.

31   "Mellon Refuses Reply to Churchill," *Huntington Herald* (IN), July 23, 1926, 1.

32   A. L. Bradford, "Poincaré Assembles New Slate," *Portland Evening Express* (ME), July 23, 1926, 24.

33   "T. D. Rousseau Dies in France," *Nashville Tennessean*, April 1, 1953, 27.

34   "Mellon in France, Parries All Issues," *New York Times*, July 24, 1926, 2.

35   P. Mellon, *Reflections*, 87–89.

36   Raymond de Nys, "M. Mellon Secrétaire Américain du Trésor a Débarqué a Cherbourg," *Le Petit Parisien*, July 24, 1926, 1. The speed of ninety kilometers an hour would equal fifty-six miles per hour.

37   A. G. Gardiner, "England Resenting Shylock Outbreak," *Commercial Appeal* (Memphis), July 25, 1926, 5; see also "Mellon-Churchill Row Stirs Feeling in England," *Atlanta Journal*, July 25, 1926, 4; and "British Irked with American View of Debts: Mellon-Churchill Dispute Stirs Ill-Feeling," *Charlotte Observer*, July 25, 1926, 25.

38   Edward Price Bell, "Churchill Prime Mover in Abuses," *Birmingham News* (AL), July 24, 1926, 2; "Cancellation of Debts Aim of Churchill," *Buffalo Evening News*, July 26, 1926, 3.

39   "The Churchill-Mellon Controversy," *Nottingham Evening Post*, July 24, 1926, 1; Pertinax [André Géraud], "La querelle anglo-américain," *Echo de Paris*, July 23, 1926, 3.

40   "London Papers Sound Warning: Churchill-Mellon Duel Held World Menace," *The State* (Columbia, SC), July 25, 1926, 1.

41   Ernest Marshall, "Outburst on Debt Disturbs Britain," *New York Times*, July 25, 1926, sec. 2, 1, 3.

42   "Mr. Mellon Arrives," *Evening Standard* (London), July 23, 1926, 8.

43   "Mellon Holds Aloof from Debt Tangle," *Miami Herald*, July 25, 1926, 8.

44   "Mellon in France," *Brooklyn Daily Eagle*, July 25, 1926, 4; "Mellon Maintains Silence in France," *Philadelphia Inquirer*, July 25, 1926, 3.

45   Allene Sumner, "Ailsa Mellon Sure She'll Be Happy on Hubby's $50 a Week," *Pittsburgh Press*, May 24, 1926, 6; Frederic William Wile, "Washington Observations," *Los Angeles Evening Express*," July 14,

1926, 32. The ship on which they crossed was the SS *President Harding*.

46 Burton Hersh, *The Mellon Family: A Fortune in History* (New York: William Morrow and Company, 1978), 193, 336, 410-11, 444.

47 Cannadine, *Mellon*, 353.

48 Benjamin Strong to Parker Gilbert, June 21, 1926; Parker Gilbert to Benjamin Strong, July 15, 1926, Papers of Benjamin Strong, Jr.

49 P. W. Wilson, "Criticism of America Grows in Europe," *New York Times*, July 25, 1926, sec. 8, 1.

50 J. L. Garvin, "The Devil and the Debts," *The Observer* (London), July 25, 1926, 12.

51 "President and Debts," *Daily Telegraph* (London), July 28, 1926, 10.

52 Calvin Coolidge, *Remarks by the President to Newspaper Correspondents*, vol. 3, "Report of the Newspaper Conference," Calvin Coolidge Presidential Foundation, July 30, 1926, 1–2.

53 "No 'Cap in Hand' Plea to U.S.A.," *Evening Standard* (London), August 4, 1926, 9.

54 Garrard Winston to Benjamin Strong, July 16, 1926, Papers of Benjamin Strong, Jr.; Benjamin Strong to Garrard Winston, August 3, 1926, Papers of Benjamin Strong, Jr.

55 "The Debt Controversy," *Economist*, July 31, 1926, 196.

56 "Foreign News: Churchill vs. Mellon," *Time*, August 2, 1926, 9.

57 "The American War Debt: Mr. Churchill Criticized," *The Times* (London), July 30, 1926, 11.

58 "Secretary Mellon Leaves Tours Today," *Boston Globe*, July 30, 1926, 8; "Mellon Is Enjoying Vacationing in France," *New Britain Herald* (CT), July 30, 1926, 16.

59 "Mellon Has Talk with Mussolini," *Hartford Courant*, August 6, 1926, 1; "Mussolini Thanks Mellon on Funding," *New York Times*, August 6, 1926, 4; John T. Burke, "Mellon Takes Luncheon with Italy's Chief," *Shreveport Times* (LA), August 7, 1926, 1.

60 "European Debt Issues Closed, Mellon States," *Dayton Daily News* (OH), August 5, 1926, 10.

61 "Mellon Visits Vatican Museum," *Wilkes-Barre Times Leader* (PA), August 7, 1926, 1.

62 "Mellon and Volpi Talk on Finances," *New York Times*, August 5, 1926, 5.

63 "Mellon Deplores Debt Settlement Discussion," *Boston Globe*, August 4, 1926, 9.

10: Dinner at the Ritz

1 George F. Authier, "British-America Debt Storm Ended; Danger Point Past," *Lansing State Journal* (MI), August 11, 1926, 16.

2   Viscount Rothermere, "Britain and the United States," *Sunday Pictorial* (London), August 8, 1926, 6.

3   "Text of Clemenceau's Appeal," *St. Louis Post-Dispatch*, August 9, 1926, 15.

4   "Newton D. Baker Urges Policy of Cancellation," *Boston Globe*, August 30, 1926, 2.

5   Lankford, *Bruce*, 81.

6   "In Love With Évian," *Washington Times*, September 8, 1926, 6.

7   "La Saison d'Évian a été cette année particulièrment réussie," *Excelsior* (Paris), August 22, 1926, 1.

8   Benjamin Strong to Andrew Mellon, August 1, 1926, Papers of Benjamin Strong, Jr.

9   Benjamin Strong to Andrew Mellon, August 10, 1926, Papers of Benjamin Strong, Jr.

10 "Mellon Talks over Europe's Money Puzzles," *Miami Daily News*, August 21, 1926, 15; "Financiers at Évian," *Evening Standard* (London), August 21, 1926, 8.

11 "Mellon Holds Conferences with Bankers," *Tampa Times*, August 23, 1926, 5.

12 "Secretary of Treasury Mellon in Conference with Benjamin Strong and Parker Gilbert, Jr.," *Commercial and Financial Chronicle*, August 28, 1926, 1041; "Financiers End Parley with Mellon," *Boston Globe*, August 23, 1926, 17; Gerville Réache, "Summer Vacation of Peace Drawing to Close in France," *Allentown Morning Call* (PA), August 29, 1926, 1, 31.

13 "Mellon Starts for Paris," *New York Times*, August 30, 1926, 6.

14 Henry Wales, "'Uncle Andy' in Paris; Shocked by Lunch Cost," *Chicago Tribune*, August 31, 1926, 3.

15 "Mellon Reaches Paris," *Cincinnati Post*, August 31, 1926, 16; "Mellon Denies Debt Brought Him to Paris," *Miami Herald*, August 31, 1926, 1; Duveen Brothers Paris to Joseph Duveen, August 30, 1926, Duveen Brothers Records; and Wales, "Uncle Andy."

16 Wales, "Uncle Andy."

17 "Mellon Visits French Premier," *New York Times*, September 1, 1926, 6.

18 "Mellon Visits."

19 "Debt Talk Omitted by Mellon," *Cincinnati Enquirer*, September 1, 1926, 4.

20 "Une Entrevue avec M. Mellon," *Excelsior* (Paris), September 1, 1926, 3.

21 Leffingwell memorandum, "First Principles," July 26, 1924, cited in Schuker, *End of French Dominance*, 305.

22 "Sees Cancellation an Issue," *New York Times*, September 1, 1926, 6.

23 A. H. Kirchhofer, "Coolidge Won't Change Stand on War Debts," *Buffalo Evening News*, August 31, 1926, 3.

24   David Lawrence, "Cancellation of War Debt May Become Future
      Issue," *Quad-City Times* (Davenport, IA), September 1, 1926, 1.

25   Irving Fisher, "Shall the Debts Be Cancelled?," *Charlotte Observer*,
      August 30, 1926, 7.

26   "France Encouraged by Mellon's Visit," *Philadelphia Inquirer*,
      September 2, 1926, 4; "Franc Is Boosted By Mellon Visit," *Philadelphia
      Inquirer*, September 3, 1926, 4.

27   "The General Strike," May 3, 1926, *Complete Speeches*, 4:3952–3.

28   "General Strike Off," *British Gazette* (London), May 13, 1926, 1.

29   Edwin L. James, "Victory in Strike Is Won by Public," *New York
      Times*, May 13, 1926, 4.

30   Hansard, July 7, 1926, 197, column 2218.

31   Jenkins, *Churchill*, 409.

32   Stelzer, *Dinner With Churchill*, 1; Lough, *Champagne*, 171–72.

33   "Mr. Mellon's Tour Ending," *Liverpool Daily Post*, September 4, 1926,
      6; "Mellon Makes Quiet Entry into London," *Philadelphia Inquirer*,
      September 5, 1926, 3.

34   "Mellon Refuses Scotland Yard's Bodyguard Offer," *Idaho Statesman*
      (Boise), September 5, 1926, 1.

35   "Our London Correspondence," *The Guardian* (Manchester),
      September 6, 1926, 5.

36   "Mellon in London," *Commercial Appeal* (Memphis), September 7,
      1926, 19.

37   "Mellon-Churchill Talk Taboos Debt," *Philadelphia Inquirer*,
      September 8, 1926, 4; "Churchill Calls on Mellon; Visit Merely
      Personal," *St. Petersburg Times* (FL), September 8, 1926, 1.

38   "A Sketch of Mr. Mellon," *Evening Standard* (London), September 8,
      1926, 4.

39   "Mellon Avoids Debt, Discusses Weather as Churchill Caller," *New
      York Herald Tribune*, September 8, 1926, 4.

40   "Churchill Calls on Mellon; Visit Merely Personal," *St. Petersburg
      Times* (FL), September 8, 1926, 1.

41   "Mellon-Churchill Talk Taboos Debt," *Philadelphia Inquirer*,
      September 8, 1926, 4.

42   "Mellon Sails Home Today," *New York Times*, September 10, 1926, 14.

43   "Churchill Dines Mellon," *New York Herald Tribune*, September 10,
      1926, 17.

44   The diaries of Montagu Norman, Bank of England, online access:
      https://www.bankofengland.co.uk/archive/montagu-norman-diaries.

45   "Londoner's Diary: Farewell to Mr. Mellon," *Evening Standard*
      (London), September 10, 1926, 6.

46   "Churchill Dines Mellon."; "Mellon Leaves Britain for U.S. on
       Berengaria," *Evening Courier* (Camden, NJ), September 11, 1926, 1.

47   John Maynard Keynes, "Keynes Says We Pay Dawes Reparations,"
       New York Times, September 11, 1926, 5.

11: A Cease-fire

1   "Mellon Coming on *Berengaria*," *Minneapolis Daily Star*, September 11,
       1926, 1. Like the *Majestic*, the *Berengaria* was a German reparation. It
       was awarded as a replacement for the sunken liner, the *Lusitania*.

2   "Treasury Opposes Madden Tax Plan," *New York Times*, August 27,
       1926, 5.

3   Calvin Coolidge, 1926 State of the Union Address, quoted in the
       Congressional Record, vol. 71, April 1926, 656.

4   Mellon's interest in establishing a national gallery of art in the United
       States began in 1910 as a founder of the American Federation of Arts,
       which had been organized for that purpose, in response to President
       Theodore Roosevelt's call for a national art museum. Over the next
       two decades, Mellon methodically acquired not only masterpiece
       paintings to form the nucleus of a national collection but also a site
       on the Washington Mall; the name, "national gallery of art," held
       by the Smithsonian Institution; approvals from three jurisdictional
       authorities, including the Commission of Fine Arts; as well as the
       presidential and congressional approvals required for his gift to be
       accepted by the US government. See, for example, Lois Marie Fink,
       A History of the Smithsonian Art Museum (Amherst: University of
       Massachusetts Press, 2007), 54–93.

5   See "Mellon Visits Art Gallery," *Miami Herald*, September 11, 1926,
       1; "A Sketch of Mr. Mellon," *Evening Standard* (London), September 8,
       1926, 4; "Mellon Convinced Paris that He Was Art Connoisseur,"
       Brooklyn Daily Eagle, September 12, 1926, 25.

6   Andrew Mellon to Joseph Duveen, September 16, 1926, Duveen
       Brothers Records.

7   "Democrats Demand $560,000,000 Tax Cut at Short Session," *New
       York Times*, September 12, 1926, 1.

8   Senate, *Refunding*, July 21, 1921, 113.

9   "Surplus to Exceed Mellon Estimate," *Baltimore Sun*, September 24,
       1926, 4.

10   Frank R. Kent, "Mellon Is Given Plain Facts," *Baltimore Sun*,
       September 8, 1926, 1.

11   "Mellon Is Cheered by Trip to Europe," *New York Times*, September 21,
       1926, 10.

12   "Declares Allies Are Recovering," *New York Times*, October 15, 1926, 35.

13   "Berlin Lays Genesis of Appeal to Norman Who Is Declared to Have Shown It to Mellon," *New York Times*, October 20, 1926, 1.

14   Mike Heffernan and Benjamin J. Thorpe, "The Map That Would Save Europe: Clive Morrison-Bell, the Tariff Walls Map, and the Politics of Cartographic Display," *Journal of Historical Geography* 60 (April 2018): 13; Ahamed, *Lords of Finance*, 6.

15   "Washington Revises View on Tariff Plan," *New York Times*, October 21, 1926, 8.

16   Warren B. Wells, "British Adopt Silence Policy on Debt Pact," *New York Herald Tribune*, September 12, 1926, B1.

17   "Appeal for Lowered Tariff Barriers Is Made by Bankers and Industrialists of Sixteen Nations, Including America," *New York Times*, October 20, 1926, 1, 2.

18   "Planning to Repudiate," *Washington Post*, October 21, 1926, 6.

19   "The Tariff and the Debts," *New York Times*, October 23, 1926, 16.

20   Most notably, the Fordney-McCumber Tariff of 1922. See Kennedy, *Over Here*, 313, 344–45, 367, 368; see also "Mellon Statement on Manifesto Soon," *Wall Street Journal*, October 22, 1926, 12.

21   "Truth for Export Only," *New York Times*, October 21, 1926, 24.

22   Andrew W. Mellon, Press Release, October 25, 1926, in *Press Releases of the United States Department of the Treasury*, Fraser, St. Louis Federal Reserve Archive, 4A: 108–17.

23   Albert W. Fox, "Mellon Formally Bans Free Trade Plan for America," *Washington Post*, October 25, 1926, 1.

24   "War Debt Settlements with U.S.," *The Guardian* (Manchester), December 20, 1926, 11; "War Debts: U.S. Professors' Plea," *The Times* (London), December 20, 1926, 12; see, for example, "Plan for Fairer U.S. Debt Terms," *Daily Mail* (London), December 20, 1926, 3; "The Way to World Peace," *Liverpool Post and Mercury*, December 20, 1926, 7; "Facing the Facts," *Lincolnshire Echo* (England), December 20, 1926, 2; "American Economists and War Debt Settlements," *Evening Chronicle* (Newcastle), December 20, 1926, 1.

25   Quoted in "French Back Call for Debt Parleys," *New York Times*, December 21, 1926, 4.

26   Calvin Coolidge, "Report of the Newspaper Conference," December 21, 1926, 1, Calvin Coolidge Presidential Foundation.

27   "Statement of the Faculty of Princeton University," *International Conciliation*, no. 230, (May 1927), 249–50.

28   FRUS, 1927, 2:732–38.

29 "Mellon Illogical on Debt, Says Hibben," *New York Times*, March 18, 1927, 1.

30 "City Notes: British Payments to America," *The Times* (London), March 19, 1927, 16.

31 "Our London Correspondence: Mr. Mellon's Arithmetic," *The Guardian* (Manchester), March 19, 1927, 12.

32 "Questions in the Commons: Our Debt to the U.S.," *The Guardian* (Manchester), March 23, 1927, 5.

33 FRUS, 1927, 2:739–745.

34 "Britain Disputes Mellon's Claims on Allied Debts," *Philadelphia Inquirer*, May 5, 1927, 1.

35 "England Defends War Debt Stand in New Note to U.S.," *Evening Star* (Washington, DC), May 4, 1927, 1.

36 See Benjamin D. Rhodes, "The Image of Britain in the United States, 1919–1929: A Contentious Relative and Rival," in McKercher, *Anglo-American Relations*, 202; the length of the note is given in "Britain Disputes Mellon's Claims on Allied Debts," *Philadelphia Inquirer*, May 5, 1927, 6.

37 Edwin L. James, "Britain Reproves Mellon for His War Debt Figures," *New York Times*, May 6, 1927, 1.

38 FRUS, 1927, 2:745.

39 Frank B. Kellogg, Memorandum of a conversation with Henry G. Chilton, May 5, 1927, General Records of the Department of State, File no. 800.51W89 Great Britain/212, RG 59, NARA.

40 "Washington and the Note," *The Times* (London) May 6, 1927, 14.

41 "House of Commons: Mr. Mellon's Statements," *The Times* (London), May 6, 1927, 8.

42 "Our London Correspondence: Mr. Mellon and Mr. Churchill," *The Guardian* (Manchester), May 6, 1927, 10.

43 "Says Mellon Retreats under Heavy Smoke Screen," *Baltimore Sun*, May 6, 1927, 15.

44 M. Farmer Murphy, "Another Move by Britain on Debt Unlikely," *Baltimore Sun*, May 6, 1927, 1.

45 "Mellon's Refusal to Answer Churchill Angers British Press," *St. Louis Globe-Democrat*, May 6, 1927, 1, 8.

46 Esme Howard to Austen Chamberlain, R. L. Craigie minute, November 17, 1927, FO, A6875/935/45; DCC, January 31, 1927, viii.

47 Winston S. Churchill, House of Commons, November 10, 1927. Hansard 210, column 357.

48 Self, *Debt Controversy*, 218–19.

49 Leith-Ross, *Money Talks*, 95.

12: Prince's Gate

1   "Elect Hoover and Insure Prosperity," *Pittsburgh Sun-Telegraph*,
      November 4, 1928, 97; "Landslide Vote Elects Hoover," *Los Angeles
      Times*, November 8, 1928, 1.

2   Will Rogers, *The Autobiography of Will Rogers* (Boston: Houghton
      Mifflin Company, 1949), 159.

3   Mellon's plan to give his art collection to the nation was known to
      Ailsa, Paul, and close associates, and first reported by the *Chicago
      Evening Post* in an article titled "U.S. May Get Gift of National
      Gallery," on December 18, 1926.

4   "Tory Cabinet Job Hunting," *New York Times*, June 7, 1929, 4; see
      Williamson, "Safety First," 408–9.

5   See Lough, *Champagne*, 181.

6   Leith-Ross, *Money Talks*, 118.

7   Winston to Clementine, August 12, 1929, and August 15, 1929, in
      Soames, *Letters*, 337, 339.

8   Tolppanen, *Churchill*, 124; "Churchill," *Daily Province* (Vancouver),
      September 4, 1929, 6.

9   Robert T. Elson, "Britain Must Guard All," *Daily Province*
      (Vancouver), September 4, 1929, 1; "Churchill," *Daily Province*
      (Vancouver), September 4, 1929, 6; "Churchill Expounds Empire
      Policies in Address Here," *Vancouver Sun*, September 4, 1929, 3; and
      Tolppanen, *Churchill*, 123–24.

10   Winston to Clementine, August 22, 1929, Soames, *Letters*, 340,
      343; David Coombs, ed., *Churchill: His Painting* (New York: World
      Publishing Company, 1967), 13; Tolppanen, *Churchill*, 107–17.

11   "Nature's Panorama in California," *Daily Telegraph* (London),
      December 23, 1929, 9; "Peter Pan Township in the Films," *Daily
      Telegraph* (London), December 30, 1929, 8.

12   Costigliola, *Awkward Dominion*, 210; William Klingaman, *1929: The
      Year of the Great Crash* (New York: Harper & Row, 1989), 252.

13   Tolppanen, *Churchill*, 9, 206–7.

14   Winston S. Churchill, "Fever of Speculation in America," *Daily
      Telegraph* (London), December 9, 1929, 10; Lough, *No More
      Champagne*, 183–95.

15   Tolppanen, *Churchill*, 208.

16   "Mr. Churchill Is Entertained on Stop Here: Visitor at White House
      and Luncheon Guest of Embassy Aid," *Washington Post*, October 19,
      1926, 7.

17   Tolppanen, *Churchill*, 210, 229; Lough, *No More Champagne*, 190–95.

18   Churchill, "Fever of Speculation in America," 10.

19   Russell C. Leffingwell, quoted in Costigliola, *Awkward Dominion*,
        198; "Reparations: The Coming Crisis," *The Guardian* (Manchester),
        July 15, 1927, 17.
20   Quoted in Leith-Ross, *Money Talks*, 135.
21   Alfred L. Castle, *Diplomatic Realism: William R. Castle, Jr., and
        American Foreign Policy, 1919–1953* (Honolulu: University of Hawai'i
        Press, 1998), 51–55; Edward M. Lamont, *The Ambassador from Wall
        Street: The Story of Thomas W. Lamont, J. P. Morgan's Chief Executive*
        (Lanham, MD: Madison Books, 1994), 294–96; and Leith-Ross,
        Money Talks, 136; see also Ahamed, *Lords of Finance*, 407.
22   Hoover, *Memoirs: Great Depression*, 3:68.
23   "Premier to Visit Berlin," *Daily Mirror* (London), June 19, 1931, 3.
24   FRUS, 1931, 1:24–5.
25   Hoover, *Memoirs*, 3:70–71.
26   "Mellon Expected at His Leased Villa," *Boston Globe*, July 2, 1931, 19.
27   "Mellon Starts Debt Parleys in Paris," *New York Times*, June 26, 1931, 1.
28   Quoted in Edward W. Bennett, *Germany and the Diplomacy of the
        Financial Crisis, 1931* (Cambridge, MA: Harvard University Press,
        1962), 169–70.
29   Quoted in Self, *Debt Controversy*, 74.
30   "Churchill Urges Price Revaluation," *New York Times*, February 9,
        1932, 44.
31   Cannadine, *Mellon*, 442.
32   "Mills Appointed Secretary of Treasury; Mellon to Take Post in
        London," *Sheboygan Press* (WI), February 4, 1932, 1, 10.
33   "How Britain and U.S. Can Aid Recovery," *Daily Telegraph* (London),
        April 15, 1932, 10; "Andrew Mellon, United States Ambassador,
        Drinks Toast," *Anaheim Bulletin*, April 14, 1932, 1.
34   "Morgan Offers Hyde Park Home to Government," *Evening News*
        (Harrisburg, PA), May 26, 1920, 3; "Woman's World," *Evening
        Standard* (London), May 7, 1927, 15; "Wild London Mob Perils
        Landing of Captain Lindbergh," *Tampa Morning Tribune*, May 30,
        1927, 2.
35   Cannadine, *Mellon*, 456; Mary Morton, *Intimate Impressionism from
        the National Gallery of Art* (Washington, DC, National Gallery of Art,
        2014), 14.
36   Finley, *A Standard of Excellence*, 35.
37   Kopper, *America's National Gallery of Art*, 1.
38   "To-Night's Court: Mr. Mellon's Daughter to be Presented," *Gloucester
        Citizen* (England), May 11, 1932, 4; "Amelia Earhart Guest of Mellon
        at U.S. Embassy," *Nashville Tennessean*, May 23, 1932, 2; "Miss Earhart

Goes Out Shopping," *Evening Chronicle* (London), May 23, 1932, 1; "London Day by Day," *Daily Telegraph* (London), July 5, 1932, 10.

39   "Mellon in London Denies Debt Mission," *New York Times*, April 9, 1932, 1, 3.

40   "The Lausanne Conference II," *Bulletin of International News* (London), 9, no. 2 (July 21, 1932): 7.

41   "Satisfaction in France," *The Times* (London), July 11, 1932, 11; "Prime Minister's Return: Warm Welcome at Victoria," *The Times* (London), July 11, 1932, 12.

42   Hansard, July 11, 1932, 268: 941, 946

43   "Mr. Churchill on Lausanne," *Daily Telegraph*, July 12, 1932, 11.

44   "Parliament and Economy Demand: Mr. Churchill on Lausanne," *Daily Telegraph* (London), July 12, 1932, 11; "Chancellor's Sharp Rebuke of Mr. Churchill," *The Guardian* (Manchester), July 12, 1932, 9; "Churchillian Mischief," *Liverpool Echo*, July 12, 1932, 6; "Premier to Answer Attack of Churchill Today, *Western Daily Press* (Bristol, England), July 12, 1932, 12.

45   "Premier and Lausanne," *The Guardian* (Manchester), July 13, 1932, 12; "Our London Letter," *Liverpool Daily Post*, July 13, 1932, 6.

46   Hansard, 1133.

47   "Our London Letter," *Liverpool Daily Post*, July 13, 1932, 6.

48   "Allies Treaty on Debts Will Be Published," *Winnipeg Tribune*, July 13, 1932, 5.

49   "George Washington Bicentenary," *The Times* (London), July 13, 1932, 8.

Epilogue

1   Garbade, *Birth of a Nation*, 221.

2   The first world war debts of Great Britain, France, Belgium, and Italy and those of seven other debtor nations, remain outstanding on the books of the US Treasury. Only Finland and Hungary repaid the United States in full. See US Department of the Treasury and Office of Management and Budget, "U.S. Government Foreign Credit Exposure as of December 31, 2009, Part I: Summary Analysis"; and Gill, *Long Shadow of Default*, 2–5, 225–34.

3   Board of Tax Appeals, Docket no. 76499, December 7, 1937, 1, 72, 78-79; Cannadine, *Mellon*, 566, 583–85; "Mellon Is Cleared of Fraud on Taxes by Board's Ruling," *New York Times*, December 8, 1937, 1. See also Hoover, *Memoirs*, 2: 59-60.

4   John F. Kennedy, Remarks on signing honorary citizenship for Sir Winston Churchill, February 9, 1963, Papers of John F.

Kennedy, John F. Kennedy Presidential Library and Museum, Boston, MA.

5   "U.S. Turns into Debtor Nation," *New York Times*, September 17, 1985, Section D, 1.

6   "Making a Franco-German War Impossible," *The Guardian* (London), May 10, 1950, 7.

7   The bust of Churchill was donated by the International Churchill Society. See "The Churchill Centre to Donate Bust of Winston Churchill to U.S. Capitol," *Churchill Society News*, September 27, 2013. See also Tracie Mauriello, "Love Affair in Bronze," *Pittsburgh Post-Gazette*, October 31, 2013, 1, 3.

8   International Monetary Fund, *Fiscal Monitor*, Washington, DC: International Monetary Fund, April 2024, xi, 3-7. See also The Budget and Economic Outlook, Congressional Budget Office, June 18, 2024; "Uncle Sam's Fiscal Folly," *Economist*, May 4, 2024; Hanna Ziady, "America's Debt Problem Is Storing up Trouble for the Rest of the World," CNN online, April 17, 2024; "Moody's Changes Outlook on United States' Ratings to Negative, Affirms Aaa Ratings," Moody's Investor Services, November 10, 2023; "Fitch Downgrades the United States' Long-Term Ratings to 'AA+' from 'AAA'; Outlook Stable," Fitch Ratings, August 1, 2023; "United States of America Long-Term Rating Lowered To 'AA+' On Political Risks And Rising Debt Burden; Outlook Negative," Standard & Poor's Ratings Direct, August 5, 2011; Fiscal Data, US Department of the Treasury, *Debt to the Penny*.

9   "The Room Where It Happens," *Hamilton, An American Musical*, music and lyrics by Lin-Manuel Miranda, 2015.

SELECTED BIBLIOGRAPHY

Adams, R. J. Q. *Bonar Law*. Stanford, CA: Stanford University Press, 1999.

Ahamed, Liaquat. *Lords of Finance: The Bankers Who Broke the World*. New York: Penguin, 2009.

Balfour, Arthur James. *Chapters of an Autobiography*. London: Cassell & Co., 1930.

Ball, Stuart. *Baldwin and the Conservative Party: The Crisis of 1929–1931*. New Haven, CT: Yale University Press, 1988.

Beebe, Lucius. *Mansion on Rails: The Folklore of the Private Railway Car*. Berkeley, CA: Howell-North, 1959.

Behrend, George. *Luxury Trains from the Orient Express to the TGV*. New York: Vendome Press, 1982.

Bonham Carter, Violet. *Winston Churchill: An Intimate Portrait*. New York: Harcourt, Brace & World, 1965.

Boyle, Andrew. *Montague Norman: A Biography*. London: Cassell & Co., 1967.

Burk, Kathleen. "The Diplomacy of Finance: British Missions to the United States, 1914–1918." *Historical Journal* 22, no. 2 (June 1979): 351–72.

Cannadine, David. *In Churchill's Shadow: Confronting the Past in Modern Britain*. Oxford: Oxford University Press, 2003.

———. *Mellon: An American Life*. New York: Alfred A. Knopf, 2006.

Cannadine, David, ed. *Churchill: The Statesman as Artist*. London: Bloomsbury Continuum, 2018.

———. *Westminster Abbey: A Church in History*. New Haven, CT: Yale University Press, 2019.

Chandler, Lester V. *Benjamin Strong: Central Banker*. Washington, DC: Brookings Institution, 1958.

Chernow, Ron. *Alexander Hamilton*. New York: Penguin, 2004.

Churchill, Winston S. *Painting as a Pastime*. New York: Whittlesey House, 1950.

———. *The World Crisis.* 5 vols. New York: Scribner's, 1923–29.

Clay, Sir Henry. *Lord Norman.* London: Macmillan, 1957.

Coombs, David, ed. *Churchill: His Painting.* New York: World Publishing Company, 1967.

Costigliola, Frank. *Awkward Dominion: American Political, Economic, and Cultural Relations with Europe.* Ithaca, NY: Cornell University Press, 1984.

Danelski, David J., and Joseph S. Tulchin, eds. *The Autobiographical Notes of Charles Evans Hughes.* Cambridge, MA: Harvard University Press, 1973.

Dayer, Roberta Allbert. "The British War Debts to the United States and the Anglo-Japanese Alliance, 1920–1923." *Pacific Historical Review* 45, no. 4, (November 1976): 569–95.

Essary, J. F. *Covering Washington Government: Government Reflected in the Public Press, 1822–1926.* Boston: Houghton Mifflin Company, 1927.

Finley, David Edward. *A Standard of Excellence: Andrew W. Mellon Founds the National Gallery of Art at Washington, D.C.* Washington, DC: Smithsonian Institution Press, 1975.

Fuess, Claude M. *Calvin Coolidge: The Man from Vermont.* Boston: Little, Brown and Company, 1940.

Galbraith, John Kenneth. *The Great Crash, 1929.* New York: Harper, 2009.

Garbade, Kenneth D. *Birth of a Market: The U.S. Treasury Securities Market from the Great War to the Great Depression.* Cambridge: MIT Press, 2012.

Gilbert, Clinton W. "The Paradox of Andrew Mellon," *Current History* 34, no. 4 (July 1931): 521–26.

Gilbert, Martin. *Churchill: A Life.* New York: Henry Holt and Company, 1991.

———. *The Churchill Documents.* 23 vols. Hillsdale, MI: Hillsdale College Press, 1981–2019. Volume 11: *The Exchequer Years, 1922–1929,* 1979.

———. Companion Volume to Winston S. Churchill. 17 vols. Boston: Houghton Mifflin Company, 1967–2019. Volume 4: Part III, 1978.

———. *Winston S. Churchill.* 8 vols. Boston: Houghton Mifflin Company, 1966–1988. Volume 4: *The Stricken World,* 1975.

Gill, David James. *The Long Shadow of Default: Britain's Unpaid War Debts to the United States, 1917–2020.* New Haven, CT: Yale University Press, 2022.

Grant, James. *The Forgotten Depression: 1921: The Crash That Cured Itself.* New York: Simon & Schuster, 2014.

Grigg, Percy J. *Prejudice and Judgment.* London: Jonathan Cape, 1948.

Hall, George J., and Thomas J. Sargent. "A History of the U.S. Debt Limits." Working Paper 21799, National Bureau of Economic Research, December 2015.

Halle, Kay, ed. *Winston Churchill on America and Britain.* New York: Walker and Company, 1970.

Harvey, George. *Henry Clay Frick: The Man.* Washington, DC: Beard Books, 1928.

Haynes, John Earl, ed. *Calvin Coolidge and the Coolidge Era*. Washington, DC: Library of Congress, 1998.

Hays, Will H. *Memoirs of Will H. Hays*. Garden City, NY: Doubleday & Company, 1955.

Heffernan, Mike, and Benjamin J. Thorpe. "The Map That Would Save Europe: Clive Morrison-Bell, the Tariff Walls Map, and the Politics of Cartographic Display." *Journal of Historical Geography* 69 (April 2018): 24–40.

Hilt, Eric, and Wendy M. Rahn. "Financial Asset Ownership and Political Partisanship: Liberty Bonds and Republican Electoral Success in the 1920s." Working Paper 24719, National Bureau of Economic Research, June 2018.

History of the George Washington Bicentennial Celebration. Washington, DC: United States George Washington Bicentennial Commission, 1932.

Hogan, Bill. "Losing It." *Washington History* (blog), February 1982. https ://www.billhogan.com/1982/02/losing-it/.

Hoover, Herbert. *The Memoirs of Herbert Hoover*. 3 vols. New York: Macmillan, 1951.

Houghton, David F. *Eight Years with Wilson's Cabinet*. 2 vols. Garden City, NY: Doubleday, Page & Company, 1926.

Hyde, Montgomery. *Baldwin: The Unexpected Prime Minister*. London: Hart-Davis, 1973.

James, Robert Rhodes. *Memoirs of a Conservative: J. C. C. Davidson's Memoirs and Papers, 1910–1937*. London: Weidenfeld & Nicolson, 1969.

James, Robert Rhodes, ed. *Winston S. Churchill: His Complete Speeches, 1897–1963*. 8 vols. New York: Chelsea House, 1974.

Jenkins, Roy. *Churchill: A Biography*. New York: Penguin, 2001.

Johnson, Elizabeth, ed. *The Collected Writings of John Maynard Keynes*. 30 vols. Cambridge: Cambridge University Press for the Royal Economic Society, 2013.

Kennedy, David M. *Over Here: The First World War and American Society*. New York: Oxford University Press, 1980.

Keynes, John Maynard. "The Economic Consequences of Mr. Churchill." In *Essays in Persuasion*. London: Macmillan, 1933.

———. *The Economic Consequences of the Peace*. New York: Harcourt, Brace and Howe, 1920.

Kopper, Philip. *America's National Gallery of Art: A Gift to the Nation*. New York: Harry N. Abrams, 1991.

Langworth, Richard M. *Winston Churchill, Myth and Reality: What He Actually Did and Said*. Jefferson, NC: McFarland & Company, 2017.

Lankford, Nelson D. *The Last American Aristocrat: The Biography of Ambassador David K. E. Bruce*. Boston: Little, Brown and Company, 1996.

Larson, Erik. *Dead Wake: The Last Crossing of the Lusitania*. New York: Random House, 2015.

———. *In the Garden of Beasts: Love, Terror and an American Family in Hitler's Berlin*. New York: Random House, 2011.

Leffingwell, R. C. "An Analysis of the International War Debt Situation." *Annals of the American Academy of Political and Social Science* 102 (July 1922): 108–15.

———. "Treasury Methods of Financing the War in Relation to Inflation." *Proceedings of the Academy of Political Science in the City of New York* 9, no. 1 (June 1920): 16–41.

———. "War Debts." *Yale Review* 12 (October 1922): 22–40.

Leffler, Melvyn P. *The Elusive Quest: America's Pursuit of European Stability and French Security, 1919–1933*. Chapel Hill: University of North Carolina Press, 1979.

Leith-Ross, Frederick. *Money Talks: Fifty Years of International Finance*. London: Hutchinson & Co., 1968.

Lloyd George, David. *The Truth about Reparations and War Debts*. New York: Howard Fertig, 1970.

———. *War Memoirs*. 6 vols. London: Ivor Nicholson & Watson, 1934.

Lough, David. *No More Champagne: Churchill and His Money*. New York: Picador, 2015.

MacMillan, Margaret. *Paris 1919: Six Months That Changed the World*. New York: Random House, 2001.

Mannock, James H. "Anglo-American Relations, 1921–1928." PhD diss., Princeton University, 1961.

McKercher, B. J. C., ed. *Anglo-American Relations in the 1920s: The Struggle for Supremacy*. London: Macmillan, 1991.

Mellon, Andrew. "Our Best Customer." *Saturday Evening Post* 198, no. 51 (June 19, 1926): 3-4, 82.

———. *Taxation: The People's Business*. New York: Macmillan, 1924.

———. "What I Am Trying To Do." *Worlds Work* 47, no. 1 (November 1923): 73-76.

Mellon, James R. *The Judge: A Life of Thomas Mellon, Founder of a Fortune*. New Haven, CT: Yale University Press, 2011.

Mellon, Paul. *Reflections in a Silver Spoon: A Memoir*. New York, William Morrow & Company, 1982.

Mellon, William Larimer. *Judge Mellon's Sons*. Pittsburgh: privately printed, 1948.

Memorial Service for Walter Hines Page. New York: Doubleday, Page & Co., 1923.

Merritt, Robert L. "Woodrow Wilson and the 'Great Solemn Referendum,' 1920." *Review of Politics* 27, no.1 (January 1965): 78–104.

Middlemas, Keith, and John Barnes. *Baldwin: A Biography*. London: Weidenfeld & Nicolson, 1969.

Montgomery-Massingberd, Hugh, and David Watkin. *The London Ritz: A Social and Architectural History*. London: Aurum Press, 1989.

Moreau, Émile. *Souvenirs d'un gouverneur de la Banque de France*. Paris: Éditions M.-T. Génin, 1954.

Morrison-Bell, Clive. *Tariff Walls: A European Crusade*. London: John Murray, 1930.

Morton, Mary. *Intimate Impressionism from the National Gallery of Art*. Washington, DC: National Gallery of Art, 2014.

Moulton, Harold Glenn, and Leo Pasvolsky. *War Debts and World Prosperity*. New York: Century Company for the Brookings Institution, 1932.

———. *World War Debt Settlements*. New York: Macmillan, 1926.

Murray, Lawrence III. "Andrew W. Mellon, Secretary of the Treasury, 1921–1932: A Study in Policy." PhD diss., Michigan State University, 1970.

———. "Andrew Mellon: The Reluctant Candidate." *Pennsylvania Magazine of History and Biography* 7, no. 4 (October 1973): 511–31.

Murray, Robert K. *The Harding Era: Warren G. Harding and His Administration*. Minneapolis: University of Minnesota Press, 1969.

Page, Walter Hines. *The United States and Great Britain*. London: Privately printed, 1927.

Raymond, John. *The Baldwin Age*. London: Eyre & Spottiswoode, 1960.

Reevy, Tony, and Dan Cupper. "Mixed Legacy." *Railroad History* 193 (Fall-Winter 2005): 28-39.

Rhodes, Benjamin D. "The United States and the War Debt Question." PhD diss., University of Colorado, 1965.

———. *United States Foreign Policy in the Interwar Period, 1918–1941: The Golden Age of American Diplomatic and Military Complacency*. Westport, CT: Praeger Studies of Foreign Policies of the Great Powers, 2001.

Riddell, George A. *Lord Riddell's Intimate Diary of the Peace Conference and After, 1918–1923*. New York: Reynal & Hitchcock, Inc., 1934.

Roberts, Andrew. *Churchill: Walking with Destiny*. New York: Viking, 2018.

———. "When Churchill Dissed America." *Smithsonian Magazine* 49 (November 2018): 10ff.

Rodwell, Warwick. *The Chapter House and Pyx Chamber, Westminster Abbey*. London: English Heritage, 2002.

Schuker, Stephen A. "American Foreign Policy: The European Dimension, 1921–1929." In *Calvin Coolidge and the Coolidge Era: Essays on the History of the 1920s*, edited by John Earl Haynes, 289–308.

———. *American "Reparations" to Germany, 1919–1933: Implications for the Third-World Debt Crisis*. Princeton NJ: Princeton University Press, 1988.

———. *The End of French Predominance in Europe: The Financial Crisis of 1924 and the Adoption of the Dawes Plan.* Chapel Hill: University of North Carolina Press, 1976.

———. "Origins of American Stabilization Policy in Europe: The Financial Dimension, 1918–1924." In *Confrontation and Cooperation: Germany and the United States in the Era of World War I, 1900–1924,* edited by Hans-Jürgen Schröder. Oxford: Berg, 1993.

Scott, Pamela. *Fortress of Finance: The United States Treasury Building.* Washington, DC: Treasury Historical Association, 201.

Self, Robert. *Britain, America and the Debt Controversy: The Economic Diplomacy of an Unspecial Relationship.* London: Routledge, 2006.

Shelden, Michael. *Young Titan: The Making of Winston Churchill.* New York: Simon & Schuster, 2013.

Shlaes, Amity. *Coolidge.* New York: HarperCollins, 2013.

———. *The Forgotten Man: A New History of the Great Depression.* New York: HarperCollins, 2007.

Skidelsky, Robert. *John Maynard Keynes 1883–1946: Economist, Philosopher, Statesman.* New York: Penguin Books, 2003.

Soames, Mary. *A Daughter's Tale.* London: Doubleday, 2011.

———. *Clementine Churchill: The Biography of a Marriage.* Boston: Houghton Mifflin, 1979.

———. *Winston Churchill: His Life as a Painter.* Boston: Houghton Mifflin, 1990.

Soames, Mary, ed. *Winston and Clementine: The Personal Letters of the Churchills.* Boston: Houghton Mifflin, 1999.

Stafford, David. *Oblivion or Glory: 1921 and the Making of Winston Churchill.* New Haven, CT: Yale University Press, 2019.

Stelzer, Cita. *Churchill's American Network: Churchill and the Forging of the Special Relationship.* New York: Pegasus Books, 2024.

———. *Dinner With Churchill: Policy-Making at the Dinner Table.* New York: Pegasus Books, 2012.

———. *Working With Winston: The Unsung Women Behind Britain's Greatest Statesman.* New York: Pegasus Books, 2019.

Stone, Ralph. *The Irreconcilables: The Fight Against the League of Nations.* Lexington: University Press of Kentucky, 1970.

Thompson, Walter Henry. *Assignment Churchill.* New York: Farrar, Straus and Giroux, 1955.

Tolppanen, Bradley P. *Churchill in North America, 1929.* Jefferson, NC: McFarland & Company, Inc., 2014.

US Government. *Annual Report of the Secretary of the Treasury.* Washington, DC: Government Printing Office, 1921–1932.

——. *Combined Annual Reports of the World War Foreign Debt Commission, 1922–1926*. Washington, DC: Government Printing Office, 1927.

——. *Minutes of the World War Foreign Dept Commission, 1922–1926*. Washington, DC: Government Printing Office, 1927.

——. *Papers Relating to the Foreign Relations of the United States*. Washington, DC: Government Printing Office, 1936.

——. *Public Papers of the Presidents of the United States: Herbert Hoover, 1931*. Washington, DC: Government Printing Office, 1976.

——. *Refunding of Obligations of Foreign Governments*. US Senate Committee on Finance, 67th Congress. Washington, DC: Government Printing Office, 1921.

——. *Treaty of Versailles*, June 28, 1919. In *Treaties and Other International Agreements of the United States of America, 1776–1949*. Washington, DC: US Department of State, Publication 8441, May 1969.

Wheeler-Bennett, John W. "The Lausanne Conference II." *Bulletin of International News* 9, no. 2 (Jul 21, 1932): 3–17.

Williamson, Philip. "'Safety First': Baldwin, the Conservative Party, and the 1929 General Election." *Historical Journal* 25, no. 2 (June 1982): 385–409.

Williamson, Philip, and Edward Baldwin. *Baldwin Papers: A Conservative Statesman 1908–1947*. Cambridge: Cambridge University Press. 2004.

Withers, Bob. *The President Travels By Train*. Brattleboro, VT: Echo Point Books. 2017.

INDEX